International Law, Human Rights and Public Opinion

This book explores situations in which public opinion presents itself as an obstacle to the protection and promotion of human rights. Taking an international law perspective, it primarily deals with two questions: first, whether international law requires States to take an independent stance on human rights issues; second, whether international law encourages States to inform and mobilise public opinion with regard to core human rights standards. The discussion is mainly organised within the framework of the UN system. The work is particularly relevant to situations in which public opinion appears as discriminatory attitudes based on race, gender, age, health, sexual orientation and other factors. It is also pertinent to circumstances in which public opinion is responsible for the existence of certain harmful customs and practices such as female genital mutilation and capital punishment. Noting that the death penalty is increasingly recognised as an infringement of human rights, this study further challenges States' argument that capital punishment cannot be abolished because of public opinion. The book also discusses the role that education bears under international law in moulding favourable attitudes towards human rights. Finally, the book challenges States' acceptance that public opinion cannot be confronted in this respect.

Heping Dang is a lecturer at the Chinese University of Hong Kong, Shenzhen. Her research and publications focus on international human rights law, criminal law and capital punishment.

We recognise public education as a fundamental right but do not insist enough on the duty of the State to ensure its progressive content. Heping Dang provides great insight into this dimension of modern human rights practice, answering governments who invoke public opinion as a pretext for their refusal to undertake important reforms.

William A. Schabas (OC MRIA), Professor of International Law

Calling public authorities to engage with their public opinions on non-discrimination and human rights is not only a timely issue but something which has been overlooked by the literature. Heping Dang offers a rich, well-researched and convincing perspective on States' duty to engage and mobilise their public opinion on human rights issues. A rewarding and timely read.

Jérémie Gilbert (PhD, LLM), Professor of International and Comparative Law

International Law, Human Rights and Public Opinion

The Role of the State in Educating on Human Rights Standards

Heping Dang

Routledge
Taylor & Francis Group
LONDON AND NEW YORK

First published 2017 by Routledge

2 Park Square, Milton Park, Abingdon, Oxfordshire OX14 4RN
52 Vanderbilt Avenue, New York, NY 10017

Routledge is an imprint of the Taylor & Francis Group, an informa business

First issued in paperback 2018

British Library Cataloguing-in-Publication Data
A catalogue record for this book is available from the British Library

Library of Congress Cataloging-in-Publication Data
Names: Dang, Heping, author.
Title: International law, human rights, and public opinion: the role of the state in educating on human rights standards / Heping Dang.
Description: Abingdon, Oxon [UK]; New York: Routledge, 2017. | Includes bibliographical references and index
Identifiers: LCCN 2016039426| ISBN 9781472481955 (hardback) | ISBN 9781317073574 (adobe reader) | ISBN 9781317073567 (epub) | ISBN 9781317073550 (mobipocket)
Subjects: LCSH: Human rights--Government policy. | International law and human rights.
Classification: LCC K3240 .D36 2017 | DDC 341.4/8--dc23
LC record available at https://lccn.loc.gov/2016039426

ISBN: 978-1-4724-8195-5 (hbk)
ISBN: 978-0-367-18969-3 (pbk)

Typeset in Galliard by
Servis Filmsetting Ltd, Stockport, Cheshire

Contents

Acknowledgements

During the years that it has taken to produce this book, I have incurred many debts and obligations. It is a pleasure to finally acknowledge them. My chief debt is to Professor William Schabas, who has been a constant guide in my research and life. I came across the idea of engaging in a study on capital punishment and public opinion in Professor Schabas' office while reading his books. It is he who suggested that I expand my study to include public opinion and human rights in general. I am truly privileged to receive many suggestions and much guidance from him, concerning both research and how to be a decent person. I am also indebted to Professor Jérémie Gilbert, Professor Michael O'Flaherty and two anonymous reviewers who have read my work and provided valuable comments. I would like to thank Penelope Soteriou and Rick O'Connor, who helped to improve the level of English in the work. Needless to say, none of the above can be held responsible for any mistakes this work may contain.

I owe a debt also to the European Commission, who has sponsored this research through the EU–China Human Rights Network based at the Irish Centre for Human Rights, National University of Ireland Galway. My colleagues at the EU–China Human Rights Network, Dr Nancie Prud'homme and Dr Annabel Egan, constantly encouraged me to finish this work. I am grateful to other colleagues and fellows at the Irish Centre for Human Rights, with whom I often had intellectual discussions. Those include Professor Ray Murphy, Dr Kathleen Cavanaugh, Professor Vinodh Jaichand and Dr Shane Darcy, Ms Kim Turcotte, Dr Michelle Farrell, Dr Bi Yingxi, Dr Yang Bochao, Ms Wang Jia, Dr Tara Smith, Ms Tanja Florath and Dr Aimé Muyoboke Karimunda. I especially thank Dr Helen McDermott and Ms Caroline Sweeney for commenting on part of my work. I have also to thank the British Library and UN Library at Geneva and New York for allowing me access to numerous UN archives. I would also like to offer my deepest thanks to colleagues at Routledge, including Alison Kirk, Lucy Loveluck, Ruth Noble and Helen Baxter. I am so impressed by their efficiency and kindness.

Finally, I wish to express my thanks to my family for their ever-lasting support. My parents are brave enough to encourage their daughter to make her own path. As to my husband, Wang Yu, he has been there for every joy and difficulty for more than twelve years. Thanks to him, I have become a better person.

Legal table

African Charter on Human and People's Rights 1981
Bill of Rights of the US Constitution 1791
Charter of the United Nations 1945
Constitution of the United Nations Educational, Scientific and Cultural Organization 1945
Constitution of the United States of America 1787
Convention (I) for the Amelioration of the Condition of the Wounded and Sick in Armed Forces in the Field 1949
Convention (II) for the Amelioration of the Condition of Wounded, Sick and Shipwrecked Members of Armed Forces at Sea 1949
Convention (III) relative to the Treatment of Prisoners of War 1949
Convention (IV) relative to the Protection of Civilian Persons in Time of War 1949
Convention on the Elimination of All Forms of Discrimination against Women 1979
Convention for the Protection of the Architectural Heritage of Europe 1985
Convention on Prohibitions or Restrictions on the Use of Certain Conventional Weapons which may be deemed to be Excessively Injurious or to have Indiscriminate Effects 1980
Convention on the Rights of Persons with Disabilities 2006
Convention against Torture and Other Cruel, Inhuman or Degrading Treatment or Punishment 1984
Council of Europe Convention on the Protection of Children against Sexual Exploitation and Sexual Abuse 2007
Declaration of the Inter-Parliamentary Union and the South African Parliament during the World Conference against Racism, Racial Discrimination, Xenophobia and Related Intolerance 2001
Durban Declaration and Programme of Action adopted by the World Conference against Racism, Racial Discrimination, Xenophobia and Related Intolerance 2001
European Convention on Offences Relating to Cultural Property 1985
European Convention for the Protection of Human Rights and Fundamental Freedoms (the European Convention on Human Rights) 1950

European Convention on Spectator Violence and Misbehaviour at Sports Events and in particular at Football Matches 1985
French Declaration of the Rights of Man and of the Citizen 1789
Hague Convention on the Laws and Customs of War on Land 1899
International Convention on the Elimination of All Forms of Racial Discrimination 1965
International Convention on the Protection of the Rights of All Migrant Workers and Members of Their Families 1990
International Covenant on Civil and Political Rights 1966
International Covenant on Economic, Social and Cultural Rights and the Convention on the Rights of the Child 1966
International Labour Organization Convention Concerning Discrimination in Respect of Employment and Occupation 1958
International Labour Organization Convention Concerning Equal Opportunities and Equal Treatment for Men and Women Workers: Workers with Family Responsibilities 1981
International Labour Organization Convention Concerning Indigenous and Tribal Peoples in Independent Countries 1989
International Labour Organization Declaration on Equality of Opportunities and Treatment of Women Workers 1975
Magna Carta 1215
Petition of Right 1628
Protocol Additional to the Geneva Conventions of 12 August 1949, and relating to the Protection of Victims of International Armed Conflicts (Protocol I) 1977
Protocol Additional to the Geneva Conventions of 12 August 1949, and relating to the Protection of Victims of Non-International Armed Conflicts (Protocol II) 1977
UNESCO Convention against Discrimination in Education 1960
UNESCO Convention for the Safeguarding of the Intangible Cultural Heritage 2003
UNESCO Declaration on Fundamental Principles concerning the Contribution of the Mass Media to Strengthening Peace and International Understanding, to the Promotion of Human Rights and to Countering Racialism, apartheid and incitement to war 1978
UNESCO Declaration of Principles on Tolerance 1995
UNESCO Declaration on Race and Racial Prejudice 1978
UNESCO Statement on Race and Racial Prejudice 1967
UNESCO Universal Declaration on Cultural Diversity 2001
United Nations Declaration on the Elimination of All Forms of Intolerance and of Discrimination Based on Religion or Belief 1981
United Nations Declaration on the Elimination of All Forms of Racial Discrimination 1963
United Nations Declaration on the Elimination of Discrimination against Women 1967

United States Declaration of Independence 1776
Universal Declaration of Human Rights 1948
United Nations Declaration of the Rights of Indigenous Peoples 2007
Vienna Convention on the Law of Treaties 1969
Vienna Declaration and Programme of Action adopted by the World Conference on Human Rights in Vienna 1993

1 Introduction

Issues and methods

It is without dispute that public opinion does not always coincide with the principles of human rights. Such opinion includes attitudes that discriminate against people based on race, gender, age, health, sexual orientation and other factors. It is closely associated with violence against people belonging to a particular group, including harmful customs and other practices that target women and children especially. If nothing is done to mobilise societal attitudes, this type of violence and its accompanying practices will never be eradicated and equality cannot be achieved. States typically cite public opinion as the reason to maintain certain practices that are increasingly being recognised as infringements on human rights, with the death penalty being at the vanguard. Confronting these situations, this book raises the question as to whether human rights should be confined to the development of public opinion, in the sense that human rights provisions are often bifurcated to the oversimplified statement that 'the public is in favour or not in favour of such provisions'.

The concept of public opinion has a long history, emerging during the Enlightenment and coming into widespread discourse in the eighteenth century.[1] Ideas about public opinion became dispersed throughout eighteenth-century philosophy, drawing also on Renaissance literature and the works of Plato and Aristotle.[2] Notable philosophers such as John Locke, Jean-Jacques Rousseau and Jeremy Bentham all embedded the idea of public opinion in their respective works of *Two Treatises of Government*,[3] *The Social Contract*[4] and *The Book of Fallacies*.[5]

1 Vincent Price, 'The Public and Public Opinion in Political Theories' in Wolfgang Donsbach and Michael W. Traugott (eds), *The SAGE Handbook of Public Opinion Research* (SAGE Publications 2008) 11–13; Vincent Price, *Public Opinion* (SAGE Publications 1992) 5.

2 Vincent Price, *Public Opinion* (SAGE Publications 1992) 1.

3 John Locke, *Two Treatises of Government* (first published 1690, Peter Laslett ed, 3rd edn, Cambridge University Press 1964).

4 Jean-Jacques Rousseau, *The Social Contract* (first published 1762, Maurice Cranston tr, Penguin Books 1968).

5 Jeremy Bentham, *The Book of Fallacies*, in vol. 2 of *The Works of Jeremy Bentham* (first published 1838, John Bowring ed, Russell & Russell 1962).

Public opinion has been studied and explored from the spectrum of social inquiry and it is present in the arguments of democratic theorists and social critics,[6] sociology and social psychology,[7] and empirical studies on the effects of mass media.[8]

The concept of human rights was also developed during the Enlightenment era, although its historic roots can be traced to the Cyrus Cylinder of 539 BC. The Cyrus Cylinder is recognised as the first charter of human rights, declaring that all people had the right to choose their own religion and establishing racial equality. The concept of human rights is not wholly, but to a considerable extent, *legal*.[9] Historically, it has been propagated through the Magna Carta (1215), the Petition of Right (1628), the United States Declaration of Independence (1776), the Constitution of the United States of America (1787), the French Declaration of the Rights of Man and of the Citizen (1789), the Bill of Rights of the US Constitution (1791), the First Geneva Convention (1864) and the Charter of the United Nations (1945). Human rights experienced a major advancement in the landscape of international law after World War II and the establishment of the United Nations in 1945. The starting point of this boom came from the adoption of the Universal Declaration of Human Rights in the United Nations General Assembly on 10 December 1948. The Universal Declaration of Human Rights represents the first global expression of the rights to which all human beings are inherently entitled.[10]

There has been a plethora of literature scrutinising how public opinion views human rights and how these opinions vary. Many studies have tried to describe public opinion concerning one or several human rights issues at a given time. Others intended to monitor the shift of public opinion over the course of relatively long periods of time, simultaneously exploring the factors that had contributed to the change. Based on their observations, these studies put forward strategies designed to mobilise public opinion toward the protection and promotion of human rights. The vast majority of research has been carried out to analyse public opinion. Its centre of mobilisation in regard to human rights has been around

6 Jean-Jacques Rousseau, *The Social Contract* (first published 1762, Maurice Cranston tr, Penguin Books 1968); Jeremy Bentham, *The Book of Fallacies*, in vol. 2 of *The Works of Jeremy Bentham* (first published 1838, John Bowring ed, Russell & Russell 1962); James Bryce, *The American Commonwealth* (first published 1888, Cosimo 2007); Abbott Lawrence Lowell, *Public Opinion and Popular Government* (first published 1913, Nabu Press 2012); Walter Lippmann, *Public Opinion* (first published 1922, Createspace Independent Publishing Platform 2016); Vincent Price, *Public Opinion* (SAGE Publications 1992).

7 Gabriel Tarde, *The Laws of Imitation* (first published 1890, Henry Holt & Company 1903); William McDougall, *The Group Mind* (Cambridge University Press 1920); Floyd Henry Allport, *Social Psychology* (Houghton Mifflin 1924).

8 Paul Felix Lazarsfeld, Bernard Berelson and Hazel Gaudet, *The People's Choice: How the Voter Makes Up His Mind in a Presidential Campaign* (Duell, Sloan & Pearce 1944); Carl I. Hovland, Arthur A. Lumsdaine and Fred D. Sheffield, *Experiments on Mass Communication: Studies in Social Psychology in World War II: Volume III* (Princeton University Press 1949).

9 Michael Freeman, *Human Rights: An Interdisciplinary Approach* (2nd edn, University of Michigan Press 2011) 3.

10 UNGA Res. 217 A (III); UN Doc. A/810.

issues such as racial discrimination,[11] immigration policies,[12] women's advancement,[13] the rights of persons with disabilities,[14] children's rights,[15] gay rights,[16] discrimination based on weight,[17] mental illness,[18] HIV and AIDS,[19] schizophrenia,[20] eating disorders[21] and alcohol or drug addiction,[22] abortion,[23] euthanasia,[24]

11 Taeku Lee, *Mobilizing Public Opinion: Black Insurgency and Racial Attitudes in the Civil Rights Era* (University of Chicago Press 2002); Scott H. Beck, Kenneth J. Mijeski and Meagan M. Stark, '¿Qué Es Racismo?: Awareness of Racism and Discrimination in Ecuador' (2011) 46 (1) *Latin American Research Review* 102; Margo J. Monteith, 'Contents and Correlates of Whites' and Blacks' Racial Attitudes' (2000) 36 (2) *Journal of Experimental Social Psychology* 125.

12 Peter Burns and James G. Gimpel, 'Economic Insecurity, Prejudicial Stereotypes, and Public Opinion on Immigration Policy' (2013) 115 (2) *Political Science Quarterly* 201.

13 Nayda Terkildsen and Frauke Schnell, 'How Media Frames Move Public Opinion: An Analysis of the Women's Movement' (1997) 50 (4) *Political Research Quarterly* 879.

14 Anthony J. Goreczny, Erin E. Bender, Guy Caruso and Celia S. Feinstein, 'Attitudes toward Individuals with Disabilities: Results of a Recent Survey and Implications of those Results' (2011) 32 (5) *Research in Developmental Disabilities* 1596.

15 Peggy O. Jessee, M. Christine Nagy and Cathy Gresham, 'Public Opinion concerning Group Involvement for Children with Aids' (2001) 166 (1) *Early Child Development and Care* 29; Ragnhild Hollekim, Hilde Slaatten and Norman Anderssen, 'A Nationwide Study of Norwegian Beliefs about Same-sex Marriage and Lesbian and Gay Parenthood' (2012) 9 (1) *Sexuality Research and Social Policy* 15.

16 Paul R. Brewer, 'The Shifting Foundations of Public Opinion about Gay Rights' (2003) 65 (4) *Journal of Politics* 1208; Jeffery R. Lax and Justin H. Phillips, 'Gay Rights in the States: Public Opinion and Policy Responsiveness' (2009) 103 (3) *American Political Science Review* 367.

17 Rebecca M. Puhl and Chelsea A. Heuer, 'Public Opinion about Laws to Prohibit Weight Discrimination in the United States' (2011) 19 (1) *Obesity* 77.

18 Patrick W. Corrigan (ed), *On the Stigma of Mental Illness: Practical Strategies for Research and Social Change* (American Psychological Association 2005); Arthur H. Crisp, Michael G. Gelder, Susannah Rix, Howard I. Meltzer and Olwen J. Rowlands, 'Stigmatisation of People with Mental Illnesses' (2000) 177 *British Journal of Psychiatry* 4.

19 Richard Parker and Peter Aggleton, 'HIV and AIDS-related Stigma and Discrimination: A Conceptual Framework and Implications for Action' (2003) 57 (1) *Social Science & Medicine* 13; Gregory M. Herek, John P. Capitanio and Keith F. Widaman, 'Stigma, Social Risk, and Health Policy: Public Attitudes toward HIV Surveillance Policies and the Social Construction of Illness' (2003) 22 (5) *Health Psychology* 533.

20 Matthias C. Angermeyer and Herbert Matschinger, 'The Stereotype of Schizophrenia and Its Impact on Discrimination against People with Schizophrenia: Results from a Representative Survey in Germany' (2004) 30 (4) *Schizophrenia Bulletin* 1049.

21 Arthur Crisp, 'Stigmatization of and Discrimination against People with Eating Disorders including a Report of Two Nationwide Surveys' (2005) 13 (3) *European Eating Disorders Review* 147.

22 Leoniekel C. van Boekel, Evelien P. M. Brouwers, Jaap van Weeghel and Henk F. L. Garretsen, 'Public Opinion on Imposing Restrictions to People with an Alcohol or Drug Addiction: A Cross-Sectional Survey' (2013) 48 (12) *Social Psychiatry and Psychiatric Epidemiology* 2007.

23 Stephanie M. McMurtrie, S. G. García, K. S. Wilson, C. Diaz-Olavarriet and G. M. Fawcett, 'Public Opinion about Abortion-Related Stigma among Mexican Catholics and Implications for Unsafe Abortion' (2012) 118 *International Journal of Gynaecology & Obstetrics* 160; Curtis P. Ogland and Ana Paula Verona, 'Religion and Attitudes toward Abortion and Abortion Policy in Brazil' (2011) 50 (4) *Journal for the Scientific Study of Religion* 812.

24 Nia Williams, Charlotte Dunford, Alice Knowles and James Warner, 'Public Attitudes to Life-Sustaining Treatments and Euthanasia in Dementia' (2007) 22 (12) *International Journal of Geriatric Psychiatry* 1229; O. D. Duncan and L. F. Parmelee, 'Trends in Public Approval of Euthanasia and Suicide in the US, 1947–2003' (2006) 32 (5) *Journal of Medical Ethics* 266;

and criminal justice and punishments,[25] particularly the retention of the death penalty.[26] Most of the research was carried out in the area of political science and sociology.

The language of human rights, if not human rights *per se*, is nearly universal.[27] Governments everywhere claim to believe in and respect the dignity and the basic rights of their peoples. For the majority of the world's States, as noted by Johannes Morsink, 'there is not a single nation, culture, or people that is not in one way or another enmeshed in human rights regimes', except small areas such as Taiwan, Northern Cyprus, Kosovo and Occupied Territories.[28] David Weissbrodt claimed that 'international human rights is the world's first universal ideology'.[29] Granted, a continuing debate exists regarding the universality of human rights.[30] For instance, Rhoda Howard has insisted that 'most known human societies did not and do not have conceptions of human rights'.[31] Regardless of this debate, international landscapes have been profoundly changed and scattered with human rights protocols, conventions, treaties and derivative declarations of all kinds following the adoption of the Universal Declaration of Human Rights in 1948.[32]

Considering this situation, this book questions how international human

Joachim Cohen, Isabelle Marcoux, Johan Bilsen, Patrick Deboosere, Gerrit van der Wal and Luc Deliens, 'Trends in Acceptance of Euthanasia among the General Public in 12 European Countries (1981–1999)' (2006) 16 (6) *European Journal of Public Health* 663.

25 Jacqueline M. Gray, 'What Shapes Public Opinion of the Criminal Justice System' in Jane L. Wood and Theresa A. Gannon (eds), *Public Opinion and Criminal Justice* (Willian Publishing 2009) 49–73; Julian V. Roberts and Mike Hough (eds), *Changing Attitudes to Punishment: Public Opinion, Crime and Justice* (Willian Publishing 2002).

26 Roger Hood and Surya Deva (eds), *Confronting Capital Punishment in Asia: Human Rights, Politics and Public Opinion* (Oxford University Press 2013); Roger Hood and Carolyn Hoyle, *The Death Penalty: A Worldwide Perspective* (4th edn, Oxford University Press 2008) 350–383; William Schabas, 'Public Opinion and the Death Penalty' in Peter Hodgkinson and William Schabas (eds), *Capital Punishment: Strategies for Abolition* (Cambridge University Press 2004) 309–331.

27 Austin Sarat and Thomas R. Kearns (eds), *Human Rights: Concepts, Contests, Contingencies* (University of Michigan Press 2001) 2.

28 Johannes Morsink, *The Universal Declaration of Human Rights: Origins, Drafting, and Intent* (University of Pennsylvania Press 1999) x.

29 David Weissbrodt, 'Human Rights: An Historical Perspective' in Peter Davies (ed), *Human Rights* (Routledge 1988) 2.

30 Jack Donnelly, *Universal Human Rights in Theory and Practice* (Cornell University Press 2013) 75–112; Yvonne Donders, 'Do Cultural Diversity and Human Rights Make a Good Match?' (2010) 6 (199) *International Social Science Journal* 15; Richard Mullender, 'Human Rights: Universalism and Cultural Relativism' (2003) 6 (3) *Critical Review of International Social and Political Philosophy* 5; Richard Wilson, *Human Rights, Culture and Context: Anthropological Perspectives* (Pluto Press 1997); Fernando R. Tesón, 'International Human Rights and Cultural Relativism' (1985) 25 *Virginia Journal of International Law* 869; Jack Donnelly, 'Cultural Relativism and Universal Human Rights' (1984) 6 *Human Rights Quarterly* 400.

31 Rhoda Howard, 'Dignity, Community, and Human Rights' in Abdullahi A. An-Na'im (ed), *Human Rights in Cross-Cultural Perspectives: A Quest for Consensus* (University of Pennsylvania Press 1992) 80.

32 Johannes Morsink, *The Universal Declaration of Human Rights: Origins, Drafting, and Intent* (University of Pennsylvania Press 1999) x.

rights law perceives public opinion and whether it demands that public opinion be mobilised in order to protect and promote core human rights. The book focuses on the duties of States in the mobilisation of public opinion, as they bear the primary responsibility to protect and promote human rights. States are parties with the ability to sign and accede to human rights treaties, and subsequently to implement these treaties and other relevant declarations and recommendations. However, often many States label public opinion as the reason why human rights are moving forward at such a slow pace or cannot move at all. This work challenges the legitimacy of State assertions that public opinion is immutable with regard to core human rights standards. It explores the issue of whether States should remain indifferent to public opinion on core human rights issues. Advancing from this debate, the book also examines to what extent States have a duty to mobilise public opinion in favour of fundamental human rights. It is conceded that the second question is certainly harder to answer in favour of human rights, but the examination of this issue is of particular relevance to human rights predicaments in the modern age.

To answer the two questions, this current work thoroughly examines UN mechanisms. It scrutinises the major treaties and related declarations, their *travaux préparatoires*, the material generated by these treaties such as periodic reports, concluding observations and general recommendations, other historical legal documents and the newly established mechanism – the Universal Periodic Review. Among these mechanisms, the Universal Periodic Review was relatively new, created by the United Nations General Assembly in 2006 and its first session started in 2008.[33] However, this mechanism is quite unique as every UN member State, whether big or small, bound by certain conventions or not, has to answer the question of how it fulfils its human rights obligations and commitments. In practice, States often answer questions that they are not bound to respond to by human rights treaties. For instance, China is not a party of the International Covenant on Civil and Political Rights, but it replies to questions regarding capital punishment in the process.[34]

Reservations exist regarding the role of the *travaux préparatoires* of human rights instruments in their interpretation. Addressing this issue, the Vienna Convention on the Law of Treaties lists preparatory work of a treaty as a supplementary means of interpretation only when other methods leave the interpreted meaning ambiguous or obscure, or lead to a result that is manifestly absurd or unreasonable.[35] In practice, the *travaux préparatoires* of international legal instruments are regularly consulted by courts without much insistence on the exhaustion of other techniques of interpretation. For instance, the International Court of Justice has often used the *travaux* to 'confirm its reading of the relevant texts'.[36] Of course, there exists inevitable objection to relying on the drafting

33 UN Doc. A/RES/60/251.
34 UN Doc. A/HRC/11/25; UN Doc. A/HRC/25/5.
35 The Vienna Convention on the Law of Treaties, article 32.
36 *Application of the International Convention on the Elimination of All Forms of Racial Discrimination*

history to interpret treaties. In this regard, Alejandro Alvarez submitted to the International Court of Justice that: 'a treaty or a text that has once been established acquires a life of its own. Consequently, in interpreting it, we must have regard to the exigencies of contemporary life rather than to the intentions of those who framed it.'[37] Nonetheless, the principle of dynamic or evolutive interpretation is especially significant with respect to instruments that protect human rights.[38] Therefore, consultation of the *travaux préparatoires* would be beneficial for exploring a subject that concerns fundamental human rights.

Concluding observations and general recommendations are made by international human rights bodies in the process of supervising human rights treaties. These observations and recommendations serve as authentic interpretations of treaty provisions. The United Nations and other organisations also adopt resolutions, decisions and recommendations, encouraging States to promote and protect human rights. These documents form an integral part of the system of international law.[39] The observations, recommendations and resolutions manifest the evolution of State obligations in international law. In fulfilling their human rights obligations, States submit periodic reports to international human rights bodies, stating how they realise their obligations. These reports are a good platform on which to display how States view their duties and carry out actions to inform and educate public opinion with regard to core human rights standards.

The topic of public opinion has aroused heated discussion in political science and sociology circles but it has not been thoroughly examined in the human rights law area thus far. In this area, States usually invoke public opinion to explain why they delay the protection and promotion of human rights. Research connecting human rights law and public opinion is mostly confined within the realm of human rights education, which in its content and objectives is directed to moulding beneficial attitudes to human rights. Occasionally, attention has been paid to the educational duties of States in various human rights instruments, for instance the International Convention on the Elimination of All Forms of Racial Discrimination.[40] As a matter of fact, such educational duties

(Georgia v. Russia), Preliminary Objections, 1 April 2011, para. 142; *Sovereignty over Pulau Ligitan and Pulau Sipadan (Indonesia/Malaysia)*, Judgment, [2002] ICJ Reports 653, para. 53; *Maritime Delimitation and Territorial Questions between Qatar and Bahrain (Qatar v. Bahrain)*, Jurisdiction and Admissibility, Judgment, [1995] ICJ Reports21, para. 40.

37 *Competence of the Assembly for the Admission of a State to the United Nations*, [1950] ICJ Reports 18.

38 *Vo c. France* [GC], no. 53924/00, ECHR 2004 VIII, para. 82. Also: *Zolotukhin v. Russia* [GC], no. 14939/03, 10 February 2009, para. 80; *Micallef v. Malta* [GC], no. 17056/06, 15 October 2009, para. 81; *Scoppola v. Italy (no. 2)* [GC], no. 10249/03, 17 September 2009, para. 104.

39 F. Blaine Sloan, 'The Binding Force of a "Recommendation" of the General Assembly of the United Nations' (1948) 25 (1) *British Yearbook of International Law* 1; D. H. N. Johnson, 'Effect of Resolutions of the General Assembly of the United Nations' (1955) 32 *British Yearbook of International Law* 97.

40 Stephanie Farrior, 'The Neglected Pillar: The "Teaching Tolerance" Provision of the International Convention on the Elimination of All Forms of Racial Discrimination' (1998–1999) 5 *ILSA Journal of International & Comparative Law* 291, 297.

are often neglected by States and commentators. Legal research on human rights has not scrutinised the educational duties of States to inform and mobilise public opinion in order to promote and advance core human rights standards. This book takes the first step in this area of significant importance of academic research and practice.

The book also confronts a controversial topic, which is that of the death penalty. It draws attention to the phenomenon that many States invoke public opinion to explain why capital punishment cannot be abolished, while they seldom use public opinion to affirm that racial discrimination or discrimination against women cannot be eradicated. It also asserts that a growing consensus confirms that the abolition of the death penalty is a requirement of the right to life and the prohibition of inhuman and degrading treatment. In this context, the study compiles international documents that recommend how States may lead public opinion on the death penalty. These documents may witness an evolving standard concerning the death penalty issue. This analysis helps to test boundaries of the State duty to inform public opinion on core human rights. Furthermore, the educational duty of States to inform and educate public opinion may inevitably be implied from the case of the death penalty. In doing so, this book broadcasts a clear message that States can no longer blame public opinion for their inaction in the field of advancing human rights. In addition, this book may inspire further studies concerning the rights of children, persons with disabilities, indigenous and tribal peoples, gays, lesbians, bisexuals and transsexuals and the rights of asylum seekers.

Measuring public opinion

Definition of public opinion

States easily invoke public opinion to explain their passive role in complicated human rights situations. What they fail to mention, either intentionally or unintentionally, is that the concept of public opinion is not only old but also complex at a fundamental level. Many scholars have posed the basic question of what the term 'public opinion' exactly means. In 1968, W. Phillips Davison declared that 'there is no generally accepted definition of the term'.[41] Three years earlier, Harwood Childs compiled four dozen different definitions of public opinion.[42] Philosophers, jurists, historians, political theorists and journalism scholars 'have torn their hair in the attempt to provide a clear definition' of the term.[43] The literature of the field is 'strewn with zealous attempts'.[44] In 1992, Vincent Price

41 W. Phillips Davison, 'Public Opinion' in David L. Sills (ed), *International Encyclopedia of the Social Sciences* (Volume 13, Free Press and Macmillan 1968) 189.

42 Harwood Childs, *Public Opinion* (Van Nostrand 1965) 12–28.

43 Elisabeth Noelle-Neumann, *The Spiral of Silence: Public Opinion, Our Social Skin* (University of Chicago Press 1984) 58.

44 Harwood Childs, *Public Opinion* (Van Nostrand 1965) 14.

concluded that '[a]ny search for a single, clear definition of the concept will [. . .] prove fruitless.'[45]

Nonetheless, scholars have succeeded in revealing different aspects of the meaning of public opinion. They approached the concept through different disciplines, noting that this concept was also a term of everyday language. Some took a historical approach aiming to lay down a broader foundation for understanding contemporaneous uses of the term. Vincent Price wrote that the separate words 'public' and 'opinion' held much longer histories than the combined term of 'public opinion', each with a range of meanings that informed the contemporary use of 'public opinion'.[46] 'Public' was mainly used as a concept held in contradistinction to the elite. Price identified that the term originally meant:

> both 'of the people' (when referring to common access) and 'for the people' (when referring to the common good). It only came to mean 'by the people' (that is, carried out by common people, the sense in which we often think of the term today) much later.[47]

Price also wrote that opinion can express an inferior way of knowing, as we often use in the expression: 'in my opinion'. This serves to distinguish a matter of judgment from a matter of fact, or something uncertain from something known to be true, either by demonstration or by faith.[48] Opinion can also be equated with reputation, esteem and general regard of others.[49] An example for this is the expression 'I have a high opinion of somebody/something.'

As to the combined term of public opinion, Hans Mathias Kepplinger believed that this term meant distribution of individual opinions within a population, while most empirical researchers used the term to identify the majority opinion in society.[50] Price, for instance, saw the majority view as the operational definition of public opinion in an unregulated 'marketplace of ideas'.[51] Roger Tourangeau and Mirta Galešić observed that public opinion is sometimes used as a synonym for mass political attitude.[52] Under this definition, public opinion

45 Vincent Price, *Public Opinion* (SAGE Publications 1992) 5.

46 Vincent Price, 'The Public and Public Opinion in Political Theories' in Wolfgang Donsbach and Michael W. Traugott (eds), *The SAGE Handbook of Public Opinion Research* (SAGE Publications 2008) 11.

47 Vincent Price, *Public Opinion* (SAGE Publications 1992) 8.

48 Vincent Price, 'The Public and Public Opinion in Political Theories' in Wolfgang Donsbach and Michael W. Traugott (eds), *The SAGE Handbook of Public Opinion Research* (SAGE Publications 2008) 11–12.

49 Hans Speier, 'Historical Development of Public Opinion' (1950) 55 (4) *American Journal of Sociology* 376.

50 Hans Mathias Kepplinger, 'Effects of the News Media on Public Opinion' in Wolfgang Donsbach and Michael W. Traugott (eds), *The SAGE Handbook of Public Opinion Research* (SAGE Publications 2008) 192–204.

51 Vincent Price, 'The Public and Public Opinion in Political Theories' in Wolfgang Donsbach and Michael W. Traugott (eds), *The SAGE Handbook of Public Opinion Research* (SAGE Publications 2008) 12.

52 Roger Tourangeau and Mirta Galešić, 'Conceptions of Attitudes and Opinions' in Wolfgang

is measured by representative opinion polls in the name of finding the 'popular will', although there is no consensus on whether the use of public opinion in political issues should be restricted.[53] Sir Robert Peel questioned whether public opinion connects with the finding of the popular will when he described 'that great compound of folly, weakness, prejudice, wrong feeling, right feeling, obstinacy and newspaper paragraphs which is called public opinion'.[54] His view was not commonly shared by others. Alternative perceptions believed the existence of settled aims that the public pursued and the existence of 'a collective soul, a national mind, a spirit of the age which imposes order upon random opinion'.[55] The existence of a collective soul helped to explain the acceptance of members of a group of statements that are so simple and crystalline, which, in other words, are statements of their public opinion.[56]

Instead of an 'over soul' material, others believed that public opinion only included well-informed and interested citizens' points of view, excluding thoughts 'off the top of one's head'. Wilhelm Hennis argued that only valuable opinions deriving from general values and detailed information about current affairs can take a stand for the public and lead the way in pursuing collective goods, and that they are qualified representative of public opinion.[57] Public opinion under this definition cannot be measured by opinion polls but has to be deduced from public statements, according to the research of Susan Herbst.[58] Well-informed opinions should not be equated with the elite's opinion. As Lippmann warned, the elite might not be able to recognise a reality independent of their individual preferences.[59]

Public opinion sometimes was viewed as a mechanism or platform on which topics were selected to be discussed in the public from unlimited potential issues in society. It was regarded as a mechanism that established and stabilised dominant opinions concerning controversial issues through different voices.[60] Those who did not agree with such a view considered public opinion as an 'analysis of

Donsbach and Michael W. Traugott (eds), *The SAGE Handbook of Public Opinion Research* (SAGE Publications 2008) 141.

53 Susan Herbst, Garrett J. O'Keefe, Robert Y. Shapiro, Mark Lindeman and Carroll J. Glynn, *Public Opinion* (2nd edn, Westview Press 2004).

54 Walter Lippmann, *Public Opinion* (first published 1922, Createspace Independent Publishing Platform 2016).

55 Walter Lippmann, *Public Opinion* (first published 1922, Createspace Independent Publishing Platform 2016).

56 Walter Lippmann, *Public Opinion* (first published 1922, Createspace Independent Publishing Platform 2016).

57 Wilhelm Hennis, *Meinungsforschung und representative Demokratie [Opinion polls and representative democracy]* (Mohr 1957).

58 Susan Herbst, *Reading Public Opinion: How Political Actors View the Democratic Process* (University of Chicago Press 1998).

59 Walter Lippmann, *Public Opinion* (first published 1922, Createspace Independent Publishing Platform 2016).

60 Hans Mathias Kepplinger, 'Effects of the News Media on Public Opinion' in Wolfgang Donsbach and Michael W. Traugott (eds), *The SAGE Handbook of Public Opinion Research* (SAGE Publications 2008) 192–204.

private opinions about public affairs',[61] or 'attitudes one can express without running the danger of isolating oneself; a tangible force that keeps people in line'.[62] These opinions and attitudes could be identified by public polls but this does not always constitute the majority opinion. Some research equated public opinion with majority rule. Writers such as Joseph Schumpeter argued that people behave primarily to satisfy their individual desires, with everyone intending on maximising their own interest.[63] In line with this argument, David W. Minar claimed that public opinion was best expressed as the 'agglomerate interests of the men of the community'.[64] The society needs one mechanism to resolve the separate and conflicting interest, which is majority rule.

International humanitarian law employs a concept which is close to public opinion – public conscience, in its principle of the Martens Clause. The Martens Clause was first formulated in the 1899 Hague Convention on the Laws and Customs of War on Land, which read:

> Until a more complete code of the laws of war is issued, the High Contracting Parties think it right to declare that in cases not included in the Regulations adopted by them, populations and belligerents remain under the protection and empire of the principles of international law, as they result from the usages established between civilized nations, from the laws of humanity, and the requirements of the *public conscience*.[65]

Since then, the dictates of public conscience has been reaffirmed by the 1949 Geneva Conventions for the Protection of Victims of War,[66] the 1977 Additional Protocols to those Conventions[67] and the Convention on Prohibitions or Restrictions on the Use of Certain Conventional Weapons, with slightly different wording.[68] It has been invoked by the Nuremberg Trial in the Altstötter case[69] and the International Court of Justice, in its Advisory Opinion on Nuclear Weapons.[70]

Dictates of public conscience can be understood as public opinion that shapes the conduct of State parties to international conventions and promotes the development of international law, including customary law. In the Sixth

61 James A. Stimson, *Public Opinion in America: Moods, Cycles, and Swings* (Westview Press 1999).
62 Elisabeth Noelle-Neumann, 'Public Opinion and the Classical Tradition: A Re-evaluation' (1979) 43 (2) *Public Opinion Quarterly* 143, 150.
63 Joseph Schumpeter, *History of Economic Analysis* (Oxford University Press 1996).
64 David W. Minar, 'Public Opinion in the Perspective of Political Theory' (1960) 13 (1) *Western Political Quarterly* 31.
65 The 1899 Hague Convention on the Laws and Customs of War on Land, preamble (emphasis added).
66 The 1949 Geneva Conventions for the Protection of Victims of War, article 62.
67 Protocol I additional to the Geneva Conventions, article 1; Protocol II additional to the Geneva Conventions, preamble.
68 The Convention on Prohibitions or Restrictions on the Use of Certain Conventional Weapons, preamble.
69 The Altstötter case, 6 Law Reports of Trials of War Criminals 40, 58–59 (United Nations War Crimes Commission1948).
70 Legality of the Threat or Use of Nuclear Weapons, Advisory Opinion, 1996 ICJ REP. 226, 406 (July 8) (Shahabuddeen, J., dissenting).

Committee of the UN General Assembly in 1973, the Italian representative understood the Martens Clause as the recognition of the demands of world opinion as 'the sources of principles of international law applicable when written rules proved to be inadequate'.[71] However, Christopher Greenwood entertained serious doubts that 'public conscience' is too vague a term to serve as a basis for a separate rule of law.[72] Australia cast doubts on the reliability of the 'dictates of public conscience' since they are not static. Australia submitted to the International Court of Justice that conduct which may be considered acceptable earlier in the twentieth century might be condemned as inhuman by the international community at the end of the century.[73] Examples can be found in the State-enforced doctrine of anti-Semitism in pre-war Nazi Germany and the anti-Kosovar policies of Miloševič's Serbia.[74] Rupert Ticehurst further contended that 'there is no accepted interpretation of the Martens Clause' and that the Clause is subject to a variety of interpretations.[75]

Conceptualisation of public opinion

Not every issue engages people's attention: it is unrealistic to expect that every member of the community engages in a debate over public affairs. James Bryce and Walter Lippmann expressed such suspicions long ago.[76] Survey research conducted over 50 years confirmed that the bulk of the general population is both uninterested in and uninformed on most matters that could be constructed as public affairs.[77] Due to subjective and objective reasons, participants of public discussions do not shape public opinion to the same extent. Reasons for this include that each participant possesses a different extent of willingness to be involved, a different ability of access to information and varied degrees of influence in society. In this context 'public' as in 'public opinion' cannot refer to the whole population, even though the distribution of citizens who take part in public discussion do cross various classes and backgrounds.

Herbert Blumer established a model to denote the conceptualisation of public opinion. He said that 'the term public is used to refer to a group of people

71 UN Doc. A/C.6/SR.1452.

72 Christopher Greenwood, 'Historical Development and Legal Basis', in Dieter Fleck (ed), *Hand Book of Humanitarian Law in Armed Conflicts* (Oxford University Press, 1995) 129.

73 Australian Oral Statement before the ICJ, reprinted in *Aust YB Int'l L* 685 (1996) at 704; see also ICJ Verbatim Records, CR/95/22, 30 October 1995, p. 39, para. 9.

74 Theodor Meron, 'The Martens Clause, Principles of Humanity, and Dictates of Public Conscience' (2000) 94 (1) *American Journal of International Law* 78, 85.

75 Rupert Ticehurst, 'The Martens Clause and the Laws of Armed Conflict' (1997) 37 (317) *International Review – Red Cross* 125, 126.

76 James Bryce, *The American Commonwealth* (Cosimo 2007); Walter Lippmann, *Public Opinion* (first published 1922, Createspace Independent Publishing Platform 2016).

77 Hazel Gaudet Erskine, 'The Polls: The Informed Public' (1962) 26 (4) *Public Opinion Quarterly* 669; Hazel Gaudet Erskine, 'The Polls: Exposure to International Information' (1963) 27 (4) *Public Opinion Quarterly* 658; Times Mirror Center for the People and the Press, 'The Age of Indifference: A Study of Young Americans and How They View the News', 28 June 1990, 3.

(a) who are confronted by an issue, (b) who are divided in their ideas as to how to meet the issue, and (c) who engage in discussion over the issue'.[78] According to Blumer, disagreement and discussion give birth to public opinion and argument and counterargument are means by which public opinion is shaped.[79] He further contended that public opinion is issue oriented, the size and composition of which changes throughout the conceptualisation of public opinion.[80] In the discussion of public issues, it is unavoidable that some people are more active and dedicate more energy in defining the problems, proposing solutions and trying to persuade others to follow their solutions. These people are identified as actors. Others are less and less active until they become part of a group defined as spectators who comprise an audience for the actors by following their actions with varying degrees of interest and activity. In other words, they simply follow the scene as it unfolds.[81]

Indicators of public opinion

Measuring public opinion is closely linked with how the definition of public opinion is perceived. If it consists of the opinion of a nation's citizenry, or a country's whole population, representative opinion polls and survey research would be an operational method to detect public opinion. Polls and surveys are among the tools best known for accessing public opinion. According to this definition, David A. Green commented that the public is 'a problematic, collective term for disparate groups of people, historically excluded from positions of power, and it connotes levels of social and political equality that are artificial'.[82] Following on from the long-existing suspicions that not all the members of society will think together over most public issues, research estimates that 33 per cent of the opinions gathered in general population surveys were 'top of the head' responses, offered without previous thought or discussion.[83] John Zaller established a model describing how respondents of survey questions store inconsistent information in their minds and use information that is immediately accessible to make choices that are offered to them. Zaller claimed that 'survey responses are a function of immediately accessible

78 Herbert Blumer, 'Collective Behavior' in Alfred McClung Lee (ed), *New Outline of the Principles of Sociology* (Barnes & Noble, 1946) 167–222.

79 Herbert Blumer, 'Collective Behavior' in Alfred McClung Lee (ed), *New Outline of the Principles of Sociology* (Barnes & Noble, 1946) 191.

80 Herbert Blumer, 'Public Opinion and Public Opinion Polling' (1948) 13 *American Sociological Review* 542–554.

81 John Dewey, *The Public and Its Problems* (Holt, Allen & Unwin 1927).

82 David A. Green, 'Public Opinion Versus Public Judgment: Correcting the "Comedy of Errors"' (2006) 46 *British Journal of Criminology* 131, 131.

83 George F. Bishop, Robert W. Oldendick, Alfred J. Tuchfarber and Stephen E. Bennett, 'Pseudo-Opinions on Public Affairs' (1980) 44 (2) *Public Opinion Quarterly* 198; Doris A. Graber, 'The Impact of Media Research on Public Opinion Studies' (1982) 3 *Mass Communication Review Yearbook* 555; W. R. Neuman, *The Paradox of Mass Politics: Knowledge and Opinion in the American Electorate* (Harvard University Press 1986).

consideration'.[84] Test-retest reliability tests showed that only about half of the response variance is true.[85]

Opinion polls and surveys also have technological issues. For instance, complex opinions and progressive opinions are hard to be discovered if questions are not designed accordingly.[86] Researchers attempted to search for measures of opinion that are of higher quality, in line with the understanding that public opinion should only include well-informed opinions.[87] Susan Herbst suggested that well-informed opinions can be deduced from public statements.[88] A number of other researchers developed various polling and survey techniques to gather informed public opinion, including information questionnaires,[89] educational surveys,[90] citizen planning cells,[91] deliberative polls[92] and choice questionnaire.[93] The main point of these techniques is to inform respondents with background information before asking them to make choices.

Election outcomes can indicate people's collective and conclusive attitude toward public affairs according to representative democratic theory. The electorate is one of the most common operational definitions of the public. Voting is also a good way to reveal people's conclusive attitude toward a range of public issues. For instance, constituents may be unhappy with governmental decisions such as tax increases, but they may still vote for the government in question despite its unpopular decision. A controversial example lies in the French abolition of the death penalty in 1981 when opinion polls indicated that the French public supported the punishment. The 'unpopular' decision was made during the presidency of François Mitterrand who identified his

84 John Zaller (ed), *The Nature and Origins of Mass Opinion* (Cambridge University Press 1992), 35–36.

85 Duane F. Alwin and Jacqueline Scott, 'Attitude Change: Its Measurement and Interpretation Using Longitudinal Surveys' (1996) *Understanding Change in Social Attitudes* 75.

86 Francis T. Cullen, Bonnie S. Fisher and Brandon K . Applegate, 'Public Opinion about Punishment and Corrections' (2000) 27 *Crime and Justice* 1, 7.

87 Vincent Price and Peter Neijens, 'Deliberative Polls: Toward Improved Measures of "Informed" Public Opinion?' (1998) 10 (2) *International Journal of Public Opinion Research* 145.

88 Susan Herbst, *Reading Public Opinion: How Political Actors View the Democratic Process* (University of Chicago Press 1998).

89 Willem E. Saris, Peter C. Neijens and Jan A. de Ridder, *Kernenergie: Ja of Nee?* (SSO 1984).

90 A. F. Kay, H. Henderson, F. Steeper and C. Lake, *Interviews with the Public Guide U.S.: On the Road to Consensus* (Americans Talk Issues Foundation 1994); A. F. Kay, H. Henderson, F. Steeper, C. Lake, S. B. Greenberg and C. Blunt, *Steps for Democracy: The Many Versus the Few* (Americans Talk Issues Foundation 1994).

91 Peter C. Dienel, *Die Planungszelle: Eine Alternative zur Establishment-Demokratie. Der Bürger plant seine Umwelt* (Westdeutscher Verlag 1978); Peter C. Dienel, 'Contributing to Social Decision Methodology: Citizen Reports on Technological Projects' in Charles Vlek and George Cvetkovich (eds), *Social Decision Methodology for Technological Projects* (Kluwer Academic Publishers 1989).

92 James S. Fishkin, *The Voice of the People: Public Opinion and Democracy* (Yale University Press, 1997).

93 Peter Neijens, 'Coping with the Nonattitutdes Phenomenon: A Survey Research Approach', in Willem E. Saris and Paul M. Sniderman (eds) *Studies in Public Opinion: Attitudes, Nonattitudes, Measurement Error, and Change* (Princeton University Press 2004) 295.

commitment to abolition during his presidential campaign in 1981. This case illustrated that voting revealed the French people's conclusive or ultimate attitude: although they may not favour the abolition decision, they still support their government as a whole. By the same token, voting as a representation of public opinion has its shortcomings, its first being low voter turnout. Many respondents to opinion polls and social surveys are unlikely to vote.[94] The second issue is that voting does not change the fact that many voters go to the polls without sufficient information to guide their selections. As Neuman put it, '[t]he picture of uninformed voters in the election booth staring vainly at their shoes in search of cues to help them in their vote decision is in all likelihood not a hyperbole.'[95]

There exist other ways to collect public opinion. For instance, Zambia appointed a constitutional review commission to discern public attitude toward capital punishment in law in 2002.[96] The Zambian government considered the result of the review as a representation of the majority view of Zambians.[97] Saint Lucia relied on a constitutional review in order to find out public opinion on the same topic in 2011, after discussions by different sectors of its population.[98] In 2010, Kenya concluded that its public had demonstrated an 'overwhelming rejection' of the abolition of the death penalty according to a constitutional review.[99] Sierra Leone also addressed questions relating to the abolition of the death penalty in a review process in 2007.[100] Some countries have used nationwide referendum to reveal their population's attitude over important issues. For example, Ireland put the death penalty issue to referendum in June 2001 and found that there was clear public support for the removal of all references to the death penalty in law (62 per cent in favour and 38 per cent against).[101] The Belarusian government repeatedly invoked the results of its 1996 referendum to state that more than 80 per cent of Belarusians were in favour of retaining the death penalty.[102] Kazakhstan adopted a constitutional amendment in 2007 to abolish the death penalty, which, according to its constitution, could only be introduced by an all-nation referendum.[103] Moreover, public opinion may be reflected in news media, national legislation, juries' opinions, courts' findings, as well as the development of international law and treaties.[104]

94 Vincent Price, *Public Opinion* (SAGE Publications 1992) 37.
95 W. R. Neuman, *The Paradox of Mass Politics: Knowledge and Opinion in the American Electorate* (Harvard University Press 1986) 173.
96 UN Doc. A/HRC/8/43, para. 5; UN Doc. A/HRC/8/43/Add.1, p. 2.
97 UN Doc. A/HRC/8/43, para. 5.
98 UN Doc. A/HRC/17/6, para. 66.
99 UN Doc. A/HRC/15/8, para. 49.
100 UN Doc. A/HRC/18/10, para. 7.
101 Twenty-First Amendment of the Constitution Act 2001 [Prohibition of death penalty and removal of references to death penalty].
102 UN Doc. A/65/280, para. 31.
103 2007 Amendment to the Constitution of Kazakhstan.
104 William Schabas, 'Public Opinion and the Death Penalty' in Peter Hodgkinson and William Schabas (eds), *Capital Punishment: Strategies for Abolition* (Cambridge University Press 2004).

Reconciliation with other fundamental rights and freedoms

Defining and quantifying public opinion are complicated issues. Different measurements reveal different aspects of public opinion but carry their own flaws. Political and sociological studies suggested that it may not be practical to access a real and accurate opinion of the public. These findings make governments' oversimplified statements, that they cannot promote or progress human rights due to public opinion, less convincing. The Human Rights Committee, the supervisory body of the International Covenant on Civil and Political Rights, repeated in 1998 and 2008 that the protection of human rights and human rights standards should not be determined by public opinion or opinions derived from popularity polls.[105] The Human Rights Committee warned that the repeated use of popularity statistics to justify governments' passive attitudes toward human rights may violate obligations under the International Covenant on Civil and Political Rights.[106]

Confronting their sounding doubts whether public opinion represented by statistics should guide human rights law and policies, this book examines whether States bear a duty to inform and educate the public on core human rights standards. One may wonder whether such a duty could lead to the abuse and infringement of other fundamental rights and freedoms, such as the rights to freedom of thought and freedom of opinion and expression. According to the Universal Declaration of Human Rights and the International Covenant on Civil and Political Rights, the right to freedom of thought includes freedom to adopt a belief of one's choice and freedom to change and manifest it; no coercion is permitted.[107]

As stated in the Universal Declaration of Human Rights and the International Covenant on Civil and Political Rights, the right to freedom of opinion, which means freedom to hold opinions without interference, does not permit any exception or restriction.[108] The Human Rights Committee deemed that a State reservation to freedom of opinion would be incompatible with the object and purpose of the Covenant.[109] According to the Committee, any form of effort to coerce the holding or not holding of any opinion is prohibited, not to mention the action of criminalising it.[110] Freedom of opinion, nonetheless, extends to the right to change an opinion whenever and for whatever reason a person so freely chooses.[111]

105 UN Doc. A/HRC/WG.6/2/JPN/2, para. 35; UN Doc. CCPR/C/79/Add.102, para. 7.

106 UN Doc. A/HRC/WG.6/2/JPN/2, para. 35; UN Doc. CCPR/C/79/Add.102, para. 7.

107 Universal Declaration of Human Rights, article 18; International Covenant on Civil and Political Rights, article 18.

108 International Covenant on Civil and Political Rights, article 19.

109 UN Doc. CCPR/C/GC/34, para. 5.

110 See Human Rights Committee communication No. 878/1999, *Kang v. Republic of Korea*, Views adopted on 15 July 2003; communication No. 550/93, *Faurisson v. France*, Views adopted on 8 November 1996.

111 UN Doc. CCPR/C/GC/34, para. 9.

The right to freedom of expression includes freedom to seek, receive and impart information and ideas regardless of frontiers.[112] This right includes the expression and receipt of communications of every form of idea and opinion capable of transmission to others, the scope of which embraces those that may be regarded as deeply offensive.[113] According to the Human Rights Committee, a general reservation to the right to freedom of expression would be incompatible with the object and purpose of the Covenant.[114] The Committee further denotes that the right to freedom of expression embraces a right of access to information held by public bodies.[115] To give effect to the right of access to information, States should proactively put in the public domain government information of public interest.[116] Limitations on freedom to manifest one's beliefs or freedom of expression must be prescribed by law and are necessary to protect public safety, order, health, or morals or the fundamental rights, reputations and freedoms of others.[117]

To answer the question of whether States taking an active role in shaping public opinion would damage freedoms of thought, opinion and expression, the content of such State actions should be clarified. It does not mean that States coerce their people into believing or not believing in something. It is mainly concerned with an expectation for States to provide thorough information with regard to complex human rights issues and to create an open space for public debate. Taking a step forward, this work argues that States should have an independent stance on human rights issues, not blindly being led by the so-called 'public opinion' gathered by opinion polls. This volume also urges that States have a duty to explain relevant human rights standards to their citizens. By doing these, States play an active role in leading public opinion with regard to core human rights standards. The public have the opportunity to be fully informed and enlightened on fundamental human rights issues but retain the freedom to be (or not to be) 'led' by State actions.

To some extent, the provision of information and the creation of an open space for public debate may still allow States to retain their 'neutral' place. Analysts have pointed out that information or knowledge is not in and of itself motivational, and that there is no reason why it should *motivate* people to engage in any specific behaviour.[118] George Y. Bizer and others commented that '[p]eople who

112 Universal Declaration of Human Rights, article 19; International Covenant on Civil and Political Rights, article 19.

113 See Human Rights Committee communications Nos. 359/1989 and 385/1989, *Ballantyne, Davidson and McIntyre v. Canada*, Views adopted on 18 October 1990; communication No. 736/97, *Ross v. Canada*, Views adopted on 18 October 2000.

114 Human Rights Committee general comment No. 24.

115 UN Doc. CCPR/C/GC/34.

116 UN Doc. CCPR/C/GC/34.

117 Universal Declaration of Human Rights, article 19; International Covenant on Civil and Political Rights, articles 18 and 19.

118 George Y. Bizer, Penny S. Visser, Matthew K. Berent and Jon A. Krosnick, 'Importance, Knowledge, and Accessibility: Exploring the Dimensionality of Strength-Related Attitude

simply happen to know a great deal about the issue may not be especially likely to use the issue as a criterion for deciding with whom to affiliate.'[119] But for people who do not have structured beliefs about the issue that it is being discussed, the providing of information may have the effect of helping them in the formulation of an informed opinion.

As far as democracy is concerned, providing space for conflicting arguments to be heard in falls in line with the very meaning of democracy. After all, '[p]olitics, at its core, is about arguments, about the justification advanced for a policy, about criticism leveled against it.'[120] Democratic politics is about the full and open exchange of arguments within an open space. Thus, the definite stability of individual opinions is never the pursuit of democratic politics. 'Ideally, under democratic principles people are expected to have an open mind, ready to change their views on the basis of the arguments exchanged in the public debate.'[121] The change implies not only rational opinion change, but also the formation of opinions among those who had not held any prior opinion on the matter.

From the point of view of human rights law, providing information and initiating public debate does not violate freedom of expression and thought, rather it promotes it. States are not allowed to squeeze space for other opinions to be heard in, provided that other opinions are tolerated by law and respect others' rights and freedoms. States' further actions of voicing an independent standpoint and explaining human rights standards will be in a similar situation. If diverse arguments can be fully expressed, States' active participation in public debate does not violate individuals' freedom of expression and thought. However, when elements of public opinion are responsible for human rights violations such as discriminatory attitudes based on race, gender and disability, States' active involvement would be necessary and will facilitate the realisation of individual rights, particularly in the long run. Notably, it is States that are primarily responsible for the protection and promotion of human rights and for the elimination of human rights violations such as discrimination.

It is not suggested here that States should intervene in each public debate, but only when aspects of public opinion are not consistent with core human rights standards. States' information and explanation for their stance on human rights should be centred around human rights principles. Regarding the appropriate

Properties' in Willem E. Saris and Paul M. Sniderman (eds) *Studies in Public Opinion: Attitudes, Nonattitudes, Measurement Error, and Change* (Princeton University Press 2004) 220.

119 George Y. Bizer, Penny S. Visser, Matthew K. Berent and Jon A. Krosnick, 'Importance, Knowledge, and Accessibility: Exploring the Dimensionality of Strength-Related Attitude Properties' in Willem E. Saris and Paul M. Sniderman (eds) *Studies in Public Opinion: Attitudes, Nonattitudes, Measurement Error, and Change* (Princeton University Press 2004) 220.

120 Paul M. Sniderman and Edward G. Carmines, *Reaching beyond Race* (Harvard University Press 1997) 154.

121 Hanspeter Kriesi, 'Stability and Change of Opinion: The Case of Swiss Policy against Pollution Caused by Cars' in Willem E. Saris and Paul M. Sniderman (eds) *Studies in Public Opinion: Attitudes, Nonattitudes, Measurement Error, and Change* (Princeton University Press 2004) 262.

resources and channels for States to inform and educate the public on human rights, the current work proposes the use of education (whether formal or non-formal), the mass media, public awareness-raising campaigns and the personal impact of political figures. These measures are all recommended by different human rights bodies. More detailed and technical issues regarding these measures may require further research and practice. Nonetheless, our main point here is to assert that public opinion should not constitute an easy excuse for States to use to avoid their human rights obligations.

Layout of the book

Chapter 1 introduces the main thesis of the book as well as its outline, methodology and significance. It describes the complex concept of public opinion and its conceptualisation and quantification. It also explains the possible findings of the study, i.e. the extent of the State duty to inform and educate public opinion on core human rights standards, and how this can be reconciled with individuals' fundamental rights and freedoms.

Chapter 2 explores whether States have a duty to inform and educate public opinion with regard to ethnic equality. It describes historic documents in international law that recommend States to enlighten, guide and educate public opinion concerning issues relating to racial discrimination, discrimination in education and in the matters of political and religious rights. In doing so, this section analyses the two main approaches that international law prescribes for States to promote ethnic equality, which are legal and educational measures. They both play a role in informing and educating public opinion: legal measures warn the public of what is not tolerated by States and educational measures persuade them to embrace the principle of ethnic equality. This chapter also finds that States have an educational duty to mobilise public opinion on issues relating to ethnic equality, such as the matters of religious rights and the rights of migrants, indigenous and tribal peoples. The chapter further evidences considerable State compliance to enact such a duty.

Chapter 3 describes the shift of international law from the expectation that States play a subsidiary role in educating public opinion with respect to women's equality toward a full obligation. Earlier United Nations resolutions urged States to collaborate with the UN in educating public opinion on women's rights and introduced means with which to influence public opinion. Article 3 of the Declaration on the Elimination of Discrimination against Women states that '[a]ll appropriate measures shall be taken to educate public opinion'. Since then, international law expects States to bear a full obligation in this regard. In developing the Declaration, the Convention on the Elimination of All Forms of Discrimination against Women requires States to eliminate gender role stereotypes and prejudice. To achieve this, States are expected to modify tradition, culture and customs, and to actively deploy educational measures to promote harmony with human rights. International human rights bodies have further developed this State obligation, having specified three concrete situations and encouraging States to undertake positive actions with a view to influencing public opinion and promoting women's status. States found that they abided by such a duty, treating it as a duty derived from treaty law and customary law.

Chapter 4 raises the question of whether States have a general duty to mould public opinion in favour of fundamental human rights. Discussion on this topic begins with provisions concerning the function of education and the right to education in the Constitution of the United Nations Educational, Scientific and Cultural Organization and the Universal Declaration of Human Rights. These provisions recommend that States disseminate understanding, tolerance, friendship and knowledge of each other's ways and lives, and strive to promote respect for human rights and freedoms through teaching and education. Education bears the aim of raising awareness and moulding attitudes toward human rights. This principle was inherited by international and regional human rights treaties and other documents. Human rights education, aimed at moulding amicable attitudes toward human rights, is becoming increasingly recognised as an integral part in the right to education and is even viewed as a human right in itself in some areas. At the national level, many States have taken actions to mobilise public opinion and have tasked national institutions, including national human rights institutions, to lead the mission. Recipients of States' educational measures include not just their citizens but also those of territories under their jurisdiction.

Chapter 5 discusses whether States have a duty to inform and change public opinion regarding an issue that is gradually being recognised as a violation of fundamental human rights, i.e. the death penalty. There is growing consensus that the abolition of the death penalty is a requirement for the right to life and the prohibition of inhuman and degrading treatment. In this context, this chapter questions the abilities of States to use public opinion as a justification or excuse to retain the death penalty. The chapter also discusses the educational duty of States to promote and advance human rights and whether this duty can be extended to the issue of the death penalty. In doing so, the chapter captures recent developments in international law in which States are urged to lead public opinion on capital punishment.

Chapter 6 summarises the main conclusions of the study and identifies areas for further research. It concludes that States have an educational duty to inform public opinion with regard to core human rights standards, although the degree of duty in different issues may vary. It suggests that further study can provide exploration on the applicability of affirmative education duties to issues such as the rights of gays, lesbians, bisexuals and transsexuals and the rights of asylum seekers. How States should implement such a duty is presented as another potential topic for research.

2 Public opinion and racial discrimination

Public opinion can be quite a negative force within society, manifesting itself as racial discrimination and prejudice, which serve to create stereotypes as well as xenophobic and hostile attitudes toward others based on their ethnic background. In the name of respecting public opinion, can States remain indifferent or silent in these situations? Apparently, they cannot. International law requires States not only to condemn racist opinion, organisations and propaganda, but also urges States to encourage, respect and observe human rights and fundamental freedoms. These principles are stated in the United Nations Declaration on the Elimination of All Forms of Racial Discrimination which was adopted by the General Assembly of the United Nations in 1963 (articles 1, 2, 8, 9 and 11). The preamble of the Declaration highlights the importance of the stance that any doctrine of racial differentiation or superiority is morally condemnable by anybody, including States, and that governmental policies, if based on racial prejudice or hatred, tend to jeopardise international peace and security.

These principles were supplemented by the International Convention on the Elimination of All Forms of Racial Discrimination which was adopted by the General Assembly of the United Nations in 1965. The Convention requires States to 'promote understanding among all races' (article 2, introductory paragraph) and 'encourage, where appropriate, integrationist multiracial organizations and movements and other means of eliminating barriers between races, and to discourage anything which tends to strengthen racial division' (article 2 (1) (e)). It urges States to 'condemn all propaganda and all organizations which are based on ideas or theories of superiority of one race or group of persons of one colour or ethnic origin, or which attempt to justify or promote racial hatred and discrimination in any form' (article 4). At the same time, States are required to be proactive in the fields of teaching, education, culture and information, with a view to combating racial prejudice and to promoting understanding, tolerance and friendship among nations and racial or ethnical groups, as well as to propagating core human rights principles (article 7).

These are strong indications that States cannot take a neutral position on public opinion with regard to ethnic equality, but rather must use their moral influence to encourage certain ideas in society and condemn some others. These provisions are not without question however. For instance, Natán Lérner asked what 'integrationist' movements are and which movements can actually 'strengthen racial division'.[1] On this point, he criticised article 2 (1) (e) of the Convention as 'broadly and vaguely worded'.[2] Yet the question was more to the degree of explicitness in wording than the principle of urging States to be independent and to try to lead public opinion in this regard. C. Wilfred Jenks categorised these provisions of articles 2, 4 and 7 as 'promotional' elements of a convention, a type of obligation with the purpose of promoting a defined objective rather than maintaining a defined standard.[3]

The principle of educating public opinion

'All appropriate means' to combat racial discrimination

International law often prescribes 'all appropriate means' for States to battle against racial discrimination. This term is significant as it creates space for States to lead public opinion on related issues. For instance, according to article 2 (1)(d) of the International Convention on the Elimination of All Forms of Racial Discrimination, '[e]ach State Party shall prohibit and bring to an end, by all appropriate means, including legislation as required by circumstances, racial discrimination by any persons, group or organization.' Egon Schwelb viewed this ideal as the most important and far-reaching provision among all the articles of the Convention, playing a decisive role in the fight against racial discrimination.[4]

During the drafting of the Convention, the United Kingdom proposed changing the wording of the text from 'to prohibit' to 'adopt all necessary measures . . . for the purpose of bringing to an end'.[5] The motive behind this alteration was that actions to target discrimination would inevitably require time.[6] This revision was controversial in the discussion of the Commission on Human Rights. The representative of the Soviet Union said that the text 'would prolong the struggle against discrimination indefinitely and would provide a number of loopholes by means of which compliance with various provision of the Convention could be evaded'.[7] The British text was adopted after revision, appearing as the current article 2 (1) (d).

1 Natán Lérner, *The UN Convention on the Elimination of All Forms of Racial Discrimination* (Sijthoff & Noordhoff 1980) 38–39.

2 Natán Lérner, *The UN Convention on the Elimination of All Forms of Racial Discrimination* (Sijthoff & Noordhoff 1980) 38–39.

3 Clarence Wilfred Jenks, 'The Application of International Labour Conventions by Means of Collective Agreements' (1958) 19 *Zeitschrift für ausländisches öffentliches Recht und Völkerrecht* 197, 203.

4 Egon Schwelb, 'The International Convention on the Elimination of All Forms of Racial Discrimination' (1966) 15 *International and Comparative Law Quarterly* 996, 1017.

5 Egon Schwelb, 'The International Convention on the Elimination of All Forms of Racial Discrimination' (1966) 15 *International and Comparative Law Quarterly* 996, 1017.

6 Egon Schwelb, 'The International Convention on the Elimination of All Forms of Racial Discrimination' (1966) 15 *International and Comparative Law Quarterly* 996, 1017.

7 UN Doc. E/CN.4/SR.787.

Essentially, the content of 'all appropriate means' as prescribed by international law contains two vehicles: legislation to prohibit and educational measures to persuade, both of which have an impact on people's ideology of ethnic equality. Does international law explicitly call on States to educate public opinion in this regard? Such a principle was shaped in the early 1950s as the discussion on how to fight racial discrimination deepened in the United Nations. The spirit of leading public opinion on ethnic equality was later absorbed in international instruments and has been increasingly highlighted ever since, particularly in recent years.

To guide and educate public opinion in order to tackle racial discrimination

The United Nations has dealt with the issue of discrimination since its beginnings in 1946, demanding States 'put an immediate end' to racial and religious discrimination.[8] The Committee on Information from Non-Self-Governing Territories of the United Nations, which later merged into the Special Committee on Decolonization in 1963, stated at its 12th session in 1961 that 'it was the duty of the Governments concerned to guide public opinion' since prejudice was one of the most important contributing factors promoting racial discrimination.[9] Prior to this, the Commission on Human Rights encouraged States' sustained efforts to educate public opinion in order to achieve ethnic equality in 1960.

Established in 1947 and concluding its activities in 2006, the Sub-Commission on Prevention of Discrimination and Protection of Minorities was the main subsidiary body and the 'think tank' of the Commission on Human Rights.[10] At its 16th session in 1960, the Commission on Human Rights received a proposal from the Sub-Commission inviting public authorities to initiate or intensify educational programmes designed to eradicate racist views and prejudices.[11] Concerning this proposal, the Commission on Human Rights concurred with India's suggestion that it is not enough merely to mention education designed to eradicate racist views and prejudices but that provisions should be clear that public opinion is a subject of education.[12] This opinion was adopted despite the fact that some members of the Commission contemplated that such an amendment served to weaken the original text which had been unanimously adopted by the Sub-Commission.[13] In resolution 6 (XVI) of 16 March 1960, the Commission called on 'public authorities [. . .] to make sustained efforts to educate public opinion with a view to the eradication of the racial prejudice and religious intolerance'.[14]

8 UN Doc. A/RES/103(I).
9 UN Doc. E/CN.4/Sub.2/213/Rev.1, p. 71.
10 UN Human Rights Council resolution 5/1.
11 UN Doc. E/3335, para. 176, point 3.
12 The text proposed by India: Calls upon public authorities [. . .] to make sustained efforts to educate public opinion with a view to eradicating the racial and religious prejudices reflected in such manifestations and for the elimination of all undesirable influences promoting such prejudices. UN Doc. E/3335, para. 183.
13 UN Doc. E/3335, para. 184.
14 UN Doc. E/3335, para. 200.

The Sub-Commission continued to discuss measures on tackling racial discrimination at its 13th session in 1961. During the discussion, it was stated that 'while punitive measures might be necessary in some cases, they should not be allowed to stand in the way of educational activities designed to transform the attitudes of people' toward racial and national hatred.[15] Some members expected UNESCO encouragement of governments to mobilise global public opinion by drawing the attention of their people to the dangers and evils of racial, national and religious hatred.[16] In this way, 'the weight of world public opinion would fall upon those who instigated such manifestations and would compel them to desist from their activities'.[17] The Sub-Commission did not directly call on States to mobilise public opinion.

Moving to the discussion in the Commission on Human Rights at its 17th session in 1961, India reinforced the view that governments of all States should make sustained efforts to educate public opinion with a view to eradicate racial, national and religious intolerance, hatred and prejudice.[18] It recommended to them to 'take ... legislative or other appropriate measures to combat such prejudices' and to 'discourage in every possible way the creation, propagation and dissemination, in whatever form, of such prejudices'.[19] Afghanistan, India and Pakistan submitted a joint proposal, highlighting the need for urgent and universal educational measures to educate public opinion in order to eliminate such prejudices and discrimination.[20] Regret was expressed in the Commission that the Sub-Commission 'should have placed greater emphasis upon the need to enlighten the public and to combat prejudice among young people'.[21]

The aforementioned proposals were largely endorsed by the Commission on Human Rights (Commission resolution 5 (XVII)), the Economic and Social Council (ECOSOC resolution 826 B (XXXII)) and the General Assembly of the United Nations (A/RES/1779 (XVII)) between 1961 and 1962. All these UN bodies confirmed that States should be persistent in their efforts to educate public opinion with a view to eliminating racial prejudice and national and religious intolerance.[22] They commended the concrete measures undertaken by States to achieve this aim, including legislation, education and the use of the media.[23] The Commission on Human Rights fully agreed that 'urgent and universal

15 UN Doc. E/CN.4/815, para. 176.
16 UN Doc. E/CN.4/815, para. 174.
17 UN Doc. E/CN.4/815, para. 174.
18 UN Doc. E/CN.4/L.593, recommendation 1.
19 UN Doc. E/CN.4/L.593, recommendations 2 and 3.
20 UN Doc. E/CN.4/L.592/Rev.1.
21 UN Doc. E/3456, para. 111.
22 UN Doc. E/3456, para. 124, and Chapter XIII, draft resolution II, recommendation 1; ECOSOC Res 826 B (XXXII) (27 July 1961) UN Doc. E/3555, recommendation 1; UN Doc. A/RES/1779(XVII), recommendation 1.
23 UN Doc. E/3456, para. 124, and Chapter XIII, draft resolution II, recommendations 2 and 3; ECOSOC Res 826 B (XXXII) (27 July 1961) UN Doc. E/3555, recommendations 2 and 3; UN Doc. A/RES/1779 (XVII), recommendations 2 and 3; ECOSOC Res 826 B (XXXII) (27 July 1961).

educational measures are necessary to educate public opinion in this regard to eliminate such prejudice and discrimination'.[24]

To enlighten public opinion for equality in education

The Sub-Commission on Prevention of Discrimination and Protection of Minorities carried out a series of studies on discrimination in education on the grounds of race, colour, sex, language, religion, political or other opinion, national or social origin, property, birth, or other status in the 1950s.

One purpose of the reports was to educate world opinion.[25] In 1956 the Special Rapporteur, Charles D. Ammoun, submitted concrete recommendations for practical actions to be taken. One national measure suggested was to educate public opinion in order to eliminate discrimination in this area.[26] The full study of Charles D. Ammoun was released in 1957, further announcing that public authorities 'should make a concerted effort to enlighten the public through the use of all modern media of information'.[27] The study found that the United States at that time was pursuing the education of public opinion with a view to achieving equality in education.[28] The study recommended that States carry out national campaigns to enlighten the public and to incorporate the use of the mass media in these campaigns, including the press, radio, television and the cinema.[29] In the study, legislation was deemed as serving a purpose of educating public opinion since it developed the belief that discrimination was wrong and tended to create a social climate that would assist the law in setting the necessary collective forces in motion.[30]

The Sub-Commission on Prevention of Discrimination and Protection of Minorities considered these recommendations at its eighth and ninth sessions in 1956 and 1957 respectively.[31] There was a general agreement in 1956 that governments should treat the education of public opinion as a national measure.[32] In 1957 the Sub-Commission recommended to governments at the national and local level that '[e]ffort should be made to enlighten public opinion concerning discrimination in education' and '[t]o this end use should be made of all modern means of mass communication, including the press, radio, television and the cinema'.[33] Interestingly, in 1956 there was also a discussion on how to prompt States to carry out these recommendations – namely whether the weight of UN recommendations would be sufficient or an international convention was needed

24 UN Doc. E/3456, para. 139, and Chapter XIII, draft resolution III.
25 UN Doc. E/CN.4/703, para. 97, II, (v).
26 UN Doc. E/CN.4/721, para. 88.
27 UN Doc. E/CN.4/Sub.2/181/Rev.1, p. 141.
28 UN Doc. E/CN.4/Sub.2/181/Rev.1, p. 11.
29 UN Doc. E/CN.4/Sub.2/181/Rev.1, p. 159.
30 UN Doc. E/CN.4/Sub.2/181/Rev.1, p. 133.
31 UN Doc. E/CN.4/721, para. 35; UN Doc. E/CN.4/740, p. 52.
32 UN Doc. E/CN.4/721, para. 91.
33 UN Doc. E/CN.4/740, p. 52.

to create binding obligations.[34] A year later, these recommendations were made to States in the form of UN resolutions.

To educate public opinion in order to achieve equality in the matters of political and religious rights

Political and religious equality cannot be conflated with the issue of ethnic equality, although discrimination in the former often manifests itself through racial discrimination. Regarding discrimination within the framework of political rights, the Sub-Commission on Prevention of Discrimination and Protection of Minorities expressed a conviction at its 10th session in 1958 that 'constant care should be taken . . . to make a constructive contribution . . . towards the educating of world public opinion.'[35] This notion was reaffirmed in a 1960 report prepared by Special Rapporteur, Hernán Santa Cruz. In Cruz's report, the customary notion for written constitutions to include provisions prohibiting discrimination and ensuring equality before the law was found to have contributed to 'the moulding of public opinion in a sense adverse to discrimination'.[36] The Sub-Commission, at its 13th session in 1961, highlighted the importance of national measures aimed at combating discrimination on the basis of political rights.[37] In particular, educational measures were called on to be accorded greater prominence.[38]

Regarding discrimination in the matter of religious rights and practices, the Sub-Commission on Prevention of Discrimination and Protection of Minorities also endorsed a study carried out between 1957 and 1960, with the purpose of educating world opinion.[39] The study was led by Arcot Krishnaswami, ultimately pointing out that '[p]ublic authorities should not follow blindly the view prevailing in the society, but must assume leadership in order to achieve the goal of non-discrimination.'[40] Calling on '[f]orces within a society' to consider ways and means of educating public opinion,[41] Krishnaswami's report particularly urged States to strive, through 'educational measures which may be expected to transform the social climate', toward non-discrimination.[42] Legal techniques were also analysed as having an educational function, as '[i]ndividuals are inclined to consider wrong what the law prohibits, and right what it enjoins them to do.'[43]

Furthermore, the study proposed a set of rules to facilitate States' efforts to realise religious equality and clarify the principles of the Universal Declaration

34 UN Doc. E/CN.4/721, para. 91.
35 UN Doc. E/CN.4/Sub.2/213/Rev.1, p. 102.
36 UN Doc. E/CN.4/Sub.2/L.217, para. 166.
37 UN Doc. E/CN.4/Sub.2/L.217.
38 UN Doc. E/CN.4/815, para. 76.
39 UN Doc. E/CN.4/Sub.2/200/Rev. 1, p. 77; UN. Doc. E/CN.4/800, para. 36.
40 UN Doc. E/CN.4/778, para. 60; UN Doc. E/CN.4/Sub.2/L.123, para. 233.
41 UN Doc. E/CN.4/778, para. 60; UN Doc. E/CN.4/Sub.2/L.123, para. 233.
42 UN Doc. E/CN.4/778, para. 60; UN Doc. E/CN.4/Sub.2/L.123, para. 233.
43 UN Doc. E/CN.4/Sub.2/200/Rev. 1, p. 63.

of Human Rights.[44] The first rule was that '[e]very effort should be exerted by public authorities to educate public opinion and to create proper leadership for this purpose.'[45] The rationale behind this guideline was the realisation that public opinion may oppose the repeal of discriminatory legislation or the implementation of preventive measures and penalties for violating religious rights, practices or beliefs.[46] 'Even if the basic rules cannot be followed immediately to a full extent, they may nevertheless be useful since one of the main purposes of this study is to educate world opinion.'[47]

When these rules were presented to the Sub-Commission on Prevention of Discrimination and Protection of Minorities, some members preferred language that created an obligation on the part of the State, as '[p]ublic authorities *must* educate public opinion regarding the wrongfulness of discrimination.'[48] Some pointed out that leadership in educating public opinion by unofficial organisations and individuals on a voluntary basis was also desirable and even essential.[49] Provoked by the discussion, the Special Rapporteur, Arcot Krishnaswami, amended the rule to read: '[p]ublic authorities should make every effort to educate public opinion to an acceptance of the principle of non-discrimination in respect of the right to freedom of thought, conscience and religion and to create proper leadership for this purpose.'[50] He also added a new preambular paragraph, which stated that:

> [i]t is therefore the duty of Governments, organizations and private persons to promote through all means, including education, respect for the dignity of man and a spirit of understanding, tolerance and friendship among all religious and so-called racial groups, as well as among all nations.[51]

After the amended rule was revealed, some members suggested a full stop be added after the word 'religion' and that the text be altered slightly:

> To create proper leadership for this purpose, it should be the duty of the public authorities to encourage, through education, respect for the dignity of man, and to promote a spirit of understanding, tolerance and friendship among all nations and all racial and religious groups.[52]

The modified provision included the approach of education and the promotion of understanding, tolerance and friendship in the proposed rule for States to

44 UN Doc. E/CN.4/Sub.2/L.123/Add.1, paras 335–336.
45 UN Doc. E/CN.4/778, para. 61; UN Doc. E/CN.4/Sub.2/L.123/Add.1, para. 339.
46 UN Doc. E/CN.4/Sub.2/L.123/Add.1, para. 233.
47 UN Doc. E/CN.4/Sub.2/L.123/Add.1, para. 337.
48 UN Doc. E/CN.4/778, para. 62 (emphasis added).
49 UN Doc. E/CN.4/778, para. 62.
50 UN Doc. E/CN.4/Sub.2/200/Rev. 1, pp. 54 and 66; UN. Doc. E/CN.4/800, para. 124, rule 3.
51 UN Doc. E/CN.4/800, para. 151.
52 UN Doc. E/CN.4/800, para. 134.

educate public opinion. After this discussion, the Sub-Commission on Prevention of Discrimination and Protection of Minorities issued a resolution in the hope that national governments could be guided by this principle.[53] It also hoped that superior bodies of the United Nations would consider this rule (as well as the discussion surrounding it) when preparing article 18 of the draft Covenant on Civil and Political Rights on freedom of thought, conscience and religion.[54] It also adopted the newly drafted preambular paragraph with minor grammatical changes.[55]

It is worth noting that the study on discrimination based on religious rights and practices also enclosed an action plan. Commenting on this plan, Pierre Juvigny of the Sub-Commission agreed with 'the importance of establishing a favourable atmosphere which would lead to world-wide acceptance of measures designed to eradicate discrimination' in this regard.[56] Juvigny supported the idea of establishing 'standards in education which would instil in youth a sense of tolerance and brotherhood, and to create conditions which would bring the force of aroused public opinion to bear against acts of discrimination'.[57] He further noted that private individuals and groups were also effective in the mobilisation of public opinion, especially when discrimination was a result of action or inertia on the part of the State.[58] Juvigny's views found favour with other members of the Sub-Commission.[59] The Sub-Commission on Prevention of Discrimination and Protection of Minorities emphasised that the most effective way to combat discrimination was through sustained educational efforts,[60] urging States to continue to 'accentuate their programmes of education designed to eradicate discrimination based on religion or belief'.[61]

Legal measures with an effect to transform social attitudes

Provisions

In 1957 and 1960 research carried out by the Sub-Commission on Prevention of Discrimination and Protection of Minorities repeatedly found that legislative measures played a large role in leading public opinion through signalling what is perceived as right or wrong.[62] Consistent with this research, the United Nations Declaration on the Elimination of All Forms of Racial Discrimination, which was adopted by the General Assembly of the United Nations in 1963,

53 UN Doc. E/CN.4/800, para. 160, resolution 1 (XII), A, point 4, B, point 2 (a) and B, point 3.
54 UN Doc. E/CN.4/778, para. 111; UN Doc. E/CN.4/800, para. 160, resolution 1 (XII), B, point 3.
55 UN Doc. E/CN.4/800, para. 153.
56 UN Doc. E/CN.4/800, para. 50.
57 UN Doc. E/CN.4/800, para. 50.
58 UN Doc. E/CN.4/800, para. 50.
59 UN Doc. E/CN.4/800, para. 50.
60 UN Doc. E/CN.4/800, para. 160, resolution 1 (XII), B.
61 UN Doc. E/CN.4/800, para. 160.
62 UN Doc. E/CN.4/Sub.2/200/Rev. 1, p. 63; UN Doc. E/CN.4/Sub.2/181/Rev.1, p. 133.

condemns propaganda and organisations based on racist ideas, incitement of ethnic violence and organisations that promote or incite racial discrimination (article 9).[63] Adopted by the General Assembly of the United Nations in 1965, the International Convention on the Elimination of All Forms of Racial Discrimination requires States to amend, rescind or nullify any laws and regulations that have the effect of creating or perpetuating racial discrimination (article 2); to punish the dissemination of racist ideas, incitement to racial discrimination or ethnic violence (article 4 (a)); and to prohibit organisations and other propaganda activities, which promote and incite racial discrimination, and punish participation in such organisations or activities (article 4 (b)).

The UNESCO Statement on Race and Racial Prejudice, which was adopted in 1967, recognised law as being among the most important means of ensuring ethnic equality and outlawing propaganda and acts based on racial discrimination (para. 17). UNESCO envisaged that legislation can in the long run transform social attitude toward racial discrimination:

> It is not claimed that legislation can immediately eliminate prejudice. Nevertheless, by being a means of protecting the victims of acts based upon prejudice, and by setting a moral example backed by the dignity of the courts, it can, in the long run, even change attitudes.[64]

In the following year, UNESCO adopted the Declaration on Race and Racial Prejudice, which urges States to enact legislation intended to prohibit and eradicate racism, racist propaganda and organisations, as well as actions to justify or incite racial hatred and discrimination (articles 6 and 7).

Breakthroughs

The International Convention on the Elimination of All Forms of Racial Discrimination confers a binding obligation for States to undertake legal measures in order to tackle racial discrimination. The Convention appropriates strong wording in article 2 (1) calling for States to 'amend, rescind or nullify' laws and regulations that create or perpetuate racial discrimination. The word 'nullify' was added after 'rescind' to firmly drive the point that such legislation should be suppressed entirely.[65] Further examples of what law must prohibit and punish are outlined in article 4, which makes it one of the most (if not the most) controversial provisions in the Convention. The first paragraph of it alone, as described by the Ghanaian representative to the General Assembly of the United Nations in 1965, was an 'outcome of a difficult compromise after hours, and even days, of discussion, drafting and redrafting'.[66]

63 UN Doc. A/RES/1904 (XVIII).

64 The UNESCO Statement on Race and Racial Prejudice, para. 17.

65 Natán Lérner, *The UN Convention on the Elimination of All Forms of Racial Discrimination* (Sijthoff & Noordhoff 1980) 37.

66 UN Doc. A/PV/1406, para. 9.

Legal approaches to the issue of racial discrimination were particularly opposed by States with common law traditions. They claimed that their jurisdictions did not allow for the criminalisation of racial discrimination, instead placing it under the protection of equality before the law without distinction.[67] These States were concerned that the use of legislation would jeopardise freedom of thought and expression and be an invasion of individuals' private life. The debate was primarily focused on article 4 (a) on the state duty to penalise the dissemination of ideas based on racial superiority or hatred and article 4 (b), which outlaws organisations and propaganda activities that promote and incite racial discrimination.

First, the International Convention on the Elimination of All Forms of Racial Discrimination imposes on States an obligation to target racial hatred, by condemning all propaganda and organisations that justify or promote racial hatred, and by punishing through law all dissemination of ideas based on racial hatred. It should be pointed out that hatred, according to the Oxford Dictionary, means a strong feeling of dislike for something or somebody, constituting a form of emotion deeply associated with racial discrimination and ethnic violence.[68] Prior to the drafting of the Convention, the UN Declaration on racial discrimination in its preamble expressed a conviction that governmental policies, if based on racial hatred, constitute a violation of fundamental human rights and tend to jeopardise international peace and security.[69] The Declaration does not mention hatred in its substantive articles, although the Convention does in article 4. This breakthrough confronted the question that hatred, as a *state of mind* and not an *act*, should not be subject to law.[70]

Second, the UN Convention on racial discrimination requires States to penalise the dissemination of racist ideas and incitement of racial discrimination, regardless of whether it results in physical acts of violence (article 4 (a)), removing the proviso that incitement to racial hatred and discrimination should 'result in or is likely to cause acts of violence', from earlier drafts of the Convention.[71] This stipulation is more progressive than the prior Declaration, which only condemns incitement to violence (article 9). Consulting the *travaux préparatoires*, this progression was raised in the Sub-Commission on Prevention of Discrimination and Protection of Minorities. In regard to incitement to racial discrimination and racist propaganda, which do not involve acts of violence, 'educational measures and the creation by governments of a climate of public opinion favourable to

67 Natán Lérner, *The UN Convention on the Elimination of All Forms of Racial Discrimination* (Sijthoff & Noordhoff 1980) 38.

68 For a discussion concerning the difference between hatred and ethnic violence, please see Roger D. Petersen, *Understanding Ethnic Violence: Fear, Hatred, and Resentment in Twentieth-century Eastern Europe* (Cambridge University Press 2002).

69 The United Nations Declaration on the Elimination of All Forms of Racial Discrimination, preamble.

70 UN Doc. E/CN.4/Sub.2/SR. 418, p. 9.

71 UN Doc. E/CN.4/Sub.2/L.308/Add.1; UN Doc. E/CN.4/Sub.2/L.308/Add.1/Rev.1; UN Doc. E/CN.4/Sub.2/L.330.

racial equality' would best enable them, not legislative measures.[72] In view of the debate, the Commission on Human Rights tried only penalising acts of violence and incitement to violence, since the language of 'likely to cause acts of violence' may have given space to subjective judgment and lead to an abuse of power.[73] It was not until the draft Convention reached the Third Committee of the General Assembly when Czechoslovakia filed the submission that bound States to penalise the dissemination of racist ideas regardless of the physical result or likelihood of violence, a submission that was subsequently adopted.[74]

Finally, the UN Convention obliges States to prohibit racist organisations' propaganda activities as well as the participation there in pursuant to article 4 (b). This provision, together with article 4 (a) on the penalisation of all dissemination of racist ideas, aroused major debate concerning the infringement of legislative measures on freedom of expression and association. Opinions in the *travaux préparatoires* were truly divided. To reach a consensus, a few countries proposed various clauses for the opening paragraph of article 4, including 'within the framework of the principles set forth in the Universal Declaration on Human Rights', 'with due regard to the rights expressly set forth in Article V', 'with due regard for the fundamental right of freedom of expression' and to preserve 'the right to freedom of expression and association'.[75] The reference to the Universal Declaration was subsequently adopted, omitting specific articles on freedom of expression and association in order to facilitate greater acceptance from States.[76] The reference to article 5 of this Convention was also adopted.

Reconciliation with freedom of expression and association

During the drafting of the International Convention on the Elimination of All Forms of Racial Discrimination, one side believed that legislative measures would not limit the right to freedom of expression and association. In support of this argument, it was first argued that freedoms are not unlimited, such as in the cases of blasphemous utterances, defamatory and libellous statements, national security, obscenity and pornography. The Universal Declaration of Human Rights was invoked to state that freedoms are not and *cannot* be allowed to be implemented in a way that threatens international peace and security:

> Article 29 (2)
> In the exercise of his rights and freedoms, everyone shall be subject only to such limitations as are determined by law solely for the purpose of securing

72 UN Doc. E/CN.4/Sub.2/SR. 418, p. 7.

73 Natán Lérner, *The UN Convention on the Elimination of All Forms of Racial Discrimination* (Sijthoff & Noordhoff 1980) 44–45.

74 Natán Lérner, *The UN Convention on the Elimination of All Forms of Racial Discrimination* (Sijthoff & Noordhoff 1980) 46.

75 Natán Lérner, *The UN Convention on the Elimination of All Forms of Racial Discrimination* (Sijthoff & Noordhoff 1980) 45–46.

76 UN Doc. A/C.3/SR.1315, paras 19, 26 and 29.

due recognition and respect for the rights and freedoms of others and of meeting the just requirements of morality, public order and the general welfare in a democratic society.

Article 30
Nothing in the Declaration may be interpreted as implying for any State, group or person any right to engage in any activity or to perform any act aimed at the destruction of any of the rights and freedoms set forth.

Second, precedents were found in international treaties where freedom of association was subject to limitation. The peace treaty between Italy and a number of other states after World War II forbade Italy to permit the resurgence of fascist organisations after taking measures to dissolve them.[77] Similar agreements existed between Austria and Finland in their peace treaties.[78] These stipulations can hardly be interpreted as an infringement of freedom of expression or assembly. Third, it was logically pointed out that freedom of the press, expression and association will only be impinged when fascist organisations and racist propaganda are permitted. If fascist organisations are allowed to engage in hateful propaganda, individual rights and freedoms would be jeopardised because the ultimate aim of such propaganda is to deprive individuals of their rights and freedoms.[79] It was observed that limitations on freedoms are imposed for these reasons, but such limitations remain consistent with the development of society, public morality and international public morality.[80] Public morality, as noted, 'varied considerably according to the times, and the debates to which it had given rise had made possible the gradual building-up of a body of law'.[81] International public morality was suggested as a lowest common denominator, a standard to guide States regardless of their structural differences.[82]

Finally, it was believed that the United Nations had set up a principle that racial discrimination *per se* is a punishable offence if it disturbs law and order and jeopardises peaceful coexistence among nations. Therefore, incitement to racial discrimination should be comparable to other types of incitement, such as incitement to armed revolt against a legally constituted government, irrespective of violent results.[83] These constitute the main arguments in support of the reconciliation between legislation to tackle racial discrimination and the preservation of freedom of expression and association.

Alongside these supporting arguments there lay serious concerns. For one, there was a worry that the prohibition and disbanding of racist organisations might open doors for totalitarian measures,[84] destroying something more

77 UN Doc. E/CN.4/Sub.2/SR. 418, p. 5.
78 UN Doc. E/CN.4/Sub.2/SR. 418, p. 5.
79 UN Doc. E/CN.4/Sub.2/SR. 418, p. 5.
80 UN Doc. E/CN.4/Sub.2/SR. 418, p. 12.
81 UN Doc. E/CN.4/Sub.2/SR. 418, p. 12.
82 UN Doc. E/CN.4/Sub.2/SR. 418, p. 12.
83 UN Doc. E/CN.4/Sub.2/SR. 418, pp. 7 and 11.
84 UN Doc. E/CN.4/Sub.2/SR. 418, p. 4.

important such as freedom of speech, thought, expression and association.[85] Additionally, it was said that legal sanctions were not the best approach to racial discrimination. Moral condemnation may be more suitable, as suggested by the first paragraph of article 9 of the Declaration on racial discrimination.[86] For example, France did not believe that the mere expression of an opinion should be declared an offence punishable by law and that an international convention should prescribe penal sanctions.[87] The representative warned that France would not subscribe to any systematic restriction on freedom of expression even in connection with racial discrimination.[88] A third concern was that the 'promotion' of racial hatred and discrimination carries a lower degree of motivation than incitement, which is a conscious and inchoate act. In contrast, promotion may occur even without intention or an endeavour to incite.[89] Colombia further stated that penal law should not prescribe penalties for subjective offences.[90]

Out of these concerns, Colombia[91] and the United Kingdom[92] opposed the ban on racist organisations, deeming it an infringement on freedom of speech and thought. A few Latin American States, namely Argentina, Colombia, Ecuador, Panama and Peru, proposed to decriminalise the dissemination of racist ideas.[93] Argentina explained its view that the mere expression of the notion of superiority of one race over another is not the same as incitement of racial discrimination or hatred and so cannot be treated in the same manner. Condemning such expressions, Argentina suggested, would limit freedom of expression.[94] Costa Rica tried to add a proviso 'as appropriate' after 'declare illegal and prohibit organizations', which was not adopted, based on the argument that freedom of expression and association are not unlimited.[95] Ultimately, the Latin American amendment was defeated in the General Assembly of the United Nations.[96]

Outlook

Many States that entertained doubts about legislative measures to battle racial discrimination turned to support article 4, after reference to the Universal

85 UN Doc. E/CN.4/Sub.2/SR. 418, p. 8.
86 UN Doc. E/CN.4/Sub.2/SR. 418, p. 10.
87 UN Doc. A/C.3/SR.1318, para. 54.
88 UN Doc. A/C.3/SR.1318, para. 54.
89 Natán Lérner, *The UN Convention on the Elimination of All Forms of Racial Discrimination* (Sijthoff & Noordhoff 1980) 52.
90 UN Doc. A/PV.1406, para. 72.
91 UN Doc. A/PV.1406, paras 70–71.
92 UN Doc. A/C.3/SR.1315, para. 2.
93 Natán Lérner, *The UN Convention on the Elimination of All Forms of Racial Discrimination* (Sijthoff & Noordhoff 1980) 46.
94 UN Doc. A/PV/1406, paras 47–49.
95 Natán Lérner, *The UN Convention on the Elimination of All Forms of Racial Discrimination* (Sijthoff & Noordhoff 1980)45.
96 Natán Lérner, *The UN Convention on the Elimination of All Forms of Racial Discrimination* (Sijthoff & Noordhoff 1980) 46.

Declaration and article 5 of the Convention was added. But the added reference did not fully answer the question of how to balance the State duty to eradicate racial discrimination and its duty to preserve fundamental freedoms. Instead, it left the interpretation of the provision to States. There were more questions and comments raised in the General Assembly of the United Nations and the Committee on the Elimination of Racial Discrimination, the supervisory body of the Racial Discrimination Convention, with regard to the nature of obligations contained in article 4 after the Convention was implemented.

In its final text, article 4 of the Racial Discrimination Convention envisions legal condemnation of all dissemination of ideas based on racial discrimination and hatred, with no further conditions attached. It prohibits organisations and propaganda activities which promote and incite racial discrimination. Even the participation in such organisations and activities is required to be punishable by law. These standards are more progressive than principles from the United Nations Declaration on the Elimination of All Forms of Racial Discrimination of 1963. Adopted in 1966, the International Covenant on Civil and Political Rights, in article 20 (2), declares that any advocacy of racial hatred 'that constitutes incitement to discrimination, hostility or violence shall be prohibited by law'. In the same year, the Council of Europe Model Law required States to penalise the acts of publicly calling for or inciting hatred, intolerance and discrimination based on race in article 1.[97] The two instruments of 1966 do not prohibit the dissemination of racist ideas under the proviso that such actions do not constitute incitement to racial discrimination or hatred. They do not specify whether racist organisations should be treated the same as individuals; neither do they ask States to condemn organisations that are based on racist ideas.

It may be argued that the design of the International Covenant on Civil and Political Rights and the Council of Europe Model Law was intended to avoid further controversy on this issue. When it comes to implementation, these remain to be vital tools from which to choose. In terms of defining the authoritative body on such matter, the doctrine of *lex specialis* specifies that a law governing a specific subject matter (*lex specialis*) overrides a law that governs general matters (*lex generalis*). In conformity with this principle, it would appear that article 4 of the UN Racial Discrimination Convention deals with the specific subject matter (*lex specialis*) over the more general nature of article 20 (2) of the International Covenant on Civil and Political Rights and thus should prevail here.

Educational measures to persuade

It has been long urged that international law, alongside combating acts of racial discrimination, should actively seek to remove the sources from which such acts

97 The full text of the Model Law can be found in Measures to Be Taken against Incitement to Racial, National and Religious Hatred, Council of Europe, Strasbourg 1966.

might spring, namely subjective prejudices and intolerance.[98] The role of education in this process has been strongly highlighted since the 1940s.[99] Compared to legislative measures, education was deemed to be a better approach to racial prejudice and discrimination. By way of illustration, when preparing the UN declaration and convention on the elimination of racial discrimination and of religious intolerance in 1962, New Zealand's delegation expressed the opinion in the General Assembly that 'the problem of removing prejudices could be solved by education, information and example, rather than by legislation.'[100]

UN declaration and convention: 'teaching, education, culture and information'

The UN declaration and convention on racial discrimination do not just direct legislative measures to combat racial hatred, but also deploy educational measures to root out racial prejudice. Adopted in 1963, the United Nations Declaration on the Elimination of All Forms of Racial Discrimination affirms in its preamble that national measures, including teaching, education and information, are needed to secure ethnic equality.[101] It repeats in its operative articles that among 'all appropriate measures' to fight prejudices that lead to racial discrimination (article 4), States shall take effective steps in the fields of 'teaching, education and information' with a view to eliminating racial discrimination and prejudice, as well as promoting understanding, tolerance and friendship among nations and racial groups (article 8).

When discussing article 7 of the UN Convention on Racial Discrimination, States did not find the notion of taking 'immediate effective measures, particularly in the fields of teaching, education, culture and information' controversial.[102] As a result, article 7 of the UN Convention on racial discrimination binds States to take educational measures in order to tackle racial prejudice, promote understanding, tolerance and friendship, and propagate core human rights principles as provided in the Charter of the United Nations, the Universal Declaration of Human Rights and the UN Declaration on racial discrimination. The objective purpose of article 7 of the UN Convention on Racial Discrimination is to destroy the root causes of racism. The representative of the United Kingdom commended the

98 UN Doc. A/33/18, p. 109; UN Doc. E/3456, para. 124, and Chapter XIII, draft resolution II, recommendation 2; ECOSOC Res 826 B (XXXII) (27 July 1961) UN Doc. E/3555, recommendation 2; UNGA Res 1779 (XVII), recommendation 2.

99 UN Doc. E/3456, paras. 124 and 139, and Chapter XIII, draft resolutions II, recommendation 3 and III; ECOSOC Res 826 B (XXXII) (27 July 1961) UN Doc. E/3555, recommendation 3; UNGA Res 1779 (XVII), recommendation 3; UN Doc. E/CN.4/L.592/Rev.1; UN Doc. E/CN.4/815, para. 174; UN Doc. E/CN.4/815, para. 171; UN Doc. E/CN.4/815, paras. 162 and 176; UN Doc. E/3456, paras. 116 and 124, and Chapter XIII, draft resolution II; UN Doc. E/CN.4/Sub.2/1994/12, para. 17; UN Doc. E/CN.4/52, pp. 17–18, Section VII.

100 UN Doc. A/C.3/SR.1171, p. 191.

101 UN Doc. A/RES/1904 (XVIII).

102 Natán Lérner, *The UN Convention on the Elimination of All Forms of Racial Discrimination* (Sijthoff & Noordhoff 1980) 166–167.

importance of article 7 by comparing it to article 4 on legal measures intended to suppress racial prejudices. The delegate addressed the General Assembly, highlighting that '[u]sing legislation by itself was like cutting down a noxious weed above the ground and leaving the roots intact.'[103] It would appear that article 7 met much less controversy than article 4 in the drafting process.

Educational measures were undoubtedly the emphasis of article 7. In the *travaux préparatoires*, the provisions adopted by the Sub-Commission on Prevention of Discrimination and Protection of Minorities were 'immediate and effective measures, particularly in the fields of teaching, education and information, with a view to promoting understanding, tolerance and friendship'.[104] During the discussion in the Commission on Human Rights, the United Kingdom suggested that an aim should be included to direct these educational measures, which prompted the inclusion of 'combating prejudices which lead to racial discrimination'.[105] When the draft Convention reached the Third Committee of the General Assembly of the United Nations, Bulgaria proposed a fourth area for States to act in: that of 'culture', in addition to the prescription of 'teaching, education and information'.[106] This proposal was similarly adopted. The inclusion of culture demonstrated an 'understanding of the impact on attitudes of such activities as theater performances, shows, concerts, cultural events, sports competitions, films and the like'.[107]

UNESCO statement and declaration: 'education, culture, communication' and to encourage research and disseminate knowledge

The UNESCO Statement on Race and Racial Prejudice, adopted in 1967, recognised in paragraph 13 that 'the basically important changes in the social structure that may lead to the elimination of racial prejudice may require decisions of a political nature'. However, it also recognised 'that certain agencies of enlightenment, such as education and other means of social and economic advancement, mass media, and law can be immediately and effectively mobilised for the elimination of racial prejudice'.[108] It goes on to state in paragraph 14 that schools are among the most effective agents for the achievement of broadened understanding.

103 Michael Banton, *International Action against Racial Discrimination* (Oxford University Press 1996) 59.
104 UN Doc. E/CN.4/Sub.2/241, paras 101–102; UNCHR (Sub-Commission) Res I (XVI) Annex, UN Doc. E/CN.4/Sub.2/241, para. 119.
105 Natán Lérner, *The UN Convention on the Elimination of All Forms of Racial Discrimination* (Sijthoff & Noordhoff 1980) 63.
106 Natán Lérner, *The UN Convention on the Elimination of All Forms of Racial Discrimination* (Sijthoff & Noordhoff 1980) 63.
107 Stephanie Farrior, 'The Neglected Pillar: The "Teaching Tolerance" Provision of the International Convention on the Elimination of All Forms of Racial Discrimination' (1998–1999) 5 *ILSA Journal of International & Comparative Law* 291, 297.
108 The UNESCO Statement on Race and Racial Prejudice, para. 13.

A decade later, the UNESCO Declaration on Race and Racial Prejudice was adopted by the General Conference of the United Nations Educational, Scientific and Cultural Organization in 1978. Similar to the UN declaration and convention on this topic, it encourages States to 'take all appropriate steps', 'particularly in the spheres of education, culture and communication, to prevent', prohibit and eradicate racism and racist propaganda.[109] Additionally, the Declaration expects States to encourage specialists in natural and social sciences and cultural studies, as well as scientific organisations and associations to undertake objective research on a wide interdisciplinary basis in the fields of racial prejudice and racist attitudes.[110] It further calls on States to 'encourage the dissemination of knowledge and the findings of appropriate research in natural and social sciences on the causes and prevention of racial prejudice and racist attitudes', with due regard to the principles of the Universal Declaration of Human Rights and the International Covenant on Civil and Political Rights.[111]

The UNESCO Declaration concedes that 'laws prescribing racial discrimination are not in themselves sufficient' and therefore that:

> [I]t is also incumbent on States to supplement them . . . by broadly based education and research programmes designed to combat racial prejudice and racial discrimination and by programmes of positive political, social, educational and cultural measures calculated to promote genuine mutual respect among groups.[112]

The Declaration declares in article 5, paragraph 1, that culture and education, in their broadest sense, offer men and women increasingly effective means of adaptation and that it rests with each group to decide on the maintenance and the adaptation or enrichment of the values that it regards as essential to its identity. This appeal indicates that culture and values, as a product of human beings, are subject to change, if the consent of the groups that possess them is present. In article 5, paragraph 2, the UNESCO Declaration provides States with a 'a responsibility to see that the educational resources of all countries are used to combat racism', especially 'by ensuring that curricula and textbooks include scientific and ethical considerations concerning human unity and diversity' and 'by training teachers to achieve these ends'.

Other UN documents

The General Assembly of the United Nations in resolution 48/134 of 1994 expressed a conviction that national institutions can play a significant role in enhancing public awareness of human rights and freedoms.[113] In 2002 it called

109 The UNESCO Declaration on Race and Racial Prejudice, article 6, para. 2.
110 The UNESCO Declaration on Race and Racial Prejudice, article 8, para. 2.
111 The UNESCO Declaration on Race and Racial Prejudice, article 6, para. 2.
112 The UNESCO Declaration on Race and Racial Prejudice, article 6, para. 3.
113 UN Doc. A/RES/48/134.

on States to instil human rights values among the youth. Specifically, the General Assembly encouraged States to:

> undertake and facilitate activities aimed at educating young people in human rights and democratic citizenship and instilling values of solidarity, respect and appreciation of diversity, including respect for different groups, and affirms that a special effort to inform and sensitize young people with regard to democratic values and human rights should be undertaken or developed to fight against ideologies based on the fallacious theory of racial superiority.[114]

The United Nations has up to now organised four world conferences against racism (Geneva in 1978, 1983 and 2009 and Durban in 2001). These conferences have encouraged States to deploy educational measures in order to pursue a change of public attitude. For instance, the Second World Conference to Combat Racism and Racial Discrimination held in Geneva in 1983 adopted plans in education, teaching and training, encouraging States to 'create an atmosphere for the eradication of racism and racial discrimination'.[115] Educational measures were intended to expose the myths and fallacies of theories, philosophies, ideas and attitudes that are inherent in the acts of racial discrimination.[116] To this end, textbooks, teachers and law enforcement agents were instructed to avoid racial prejudice.[117] National institutions were called on to 'inform the general public of the nature of their human rights' and to 'mobilise public opinion in their countries against violations of human rights, especially gross and massive violations, and in particular against the practice of apartheid, racism and genocide'.[118]

In 1997 the General Assembly decided to hold the World Conference against Racism, Racial Discrimination, Xenophobia and Related Intolerance in Durban in 2001.[119] The Conference was a landmark in the struggle against racism as it established a follow-up mechanism to examine whether States have delivered on their promises, according to Mary Robinson, the then High Commissioner for Human Rights.[120] In a preparatory report written by the Secretary-General of the United Nations, ombudspersons and national human rights institutions were listed as best practices for tackling the intersectional subordination of women based on race and gender, given that they were efficient in sensitising public opinion and have important educational functions.[121] It urged national institutions to undertake educational programmes to raise public awareness of racism

114 UN Doc. A/RES/56/268.
115 UN Doc. UN Doc. A/CONF.119/26, p. 19.
116 UN Doc. UN Doc. A/CONF.119/26, p. 19.
117 UN Doc. UN Doc. A/CONF.119/26, p. 19.
118 UN Doc. UN Doc. A/CONF.119/26, p. 20.
119 UN Doc. A/RES/52/111.
120 UN Doc. A/CONF.189/12, pp. 158–163.
121 UN Doc. A/CONF.189/PC.3/5, para. 180; UN Doc. A/CONF.189/PC.1/8, para. 82.

and disseminate information on available remedies.[122] It also called for the provision of training for judges and law enforcement officers regarding international human rights instruments, noting that the opinion of judges and law enforcement officers can be quite influential to the shape of public opinion.[123]

The 2001 World Conference against Racism, Racial Discrimination, Xenophobia and Related Intolerance adopted the Durban Declaration and Programme of Action. The Durban Declaration and Programme of Action emphasises the importance of politicians in the fight against racial discrimination. The Declaration states in its preamble that failure to combat racial discrimination and related intolerance by politicians is a factor that encourages its perpetuation.[124] The Programme of Action recommends the development of 'voluntary codes of conduct which include internal disciplinary measures for violations thereof, so their members refrain from public statements and actions that encourage or incite racism, racial discrimination, xenophobia and related intolerance' among political parties.[125] During the World Conference in 2001, the Inter-Parliamentary Union and the South African Parliament initiated a parliamentary meeting, subsequently adopting a declaration that placed personal responsibility on members of parliament to 'use their influence on public opinion to promote the values of diversity and tolerance'.[126]

The Programme of Action adopted by the World Conference against Racism, Racial Discrimination, Xenophobia and Related Intolerance in Durban in 2001 emphasises the use of education, including human rights education, in promoting the values of acceptance, tolerance, diversity and respect for culture of indigenous peoples.[127] It urges States to make a commitment to anti-racism education and media campaigns designed for the general public, particularly for children and young people, with a view to eliminating the elements that might promote racism and racial discrimination, concurrently targeting racial stereotypes and prejudice.[128] It insists on the vital importance of informing and sensitising young people to respect human rights in order to win the battle against ideologies based on the fallacious theory of racial superiority.[129]

To evaluate progress toward the goals set by the World Conference against Racism, Racial Discrimination, Xenophobia and Related Intolerance in Durban

122 UN Doc. A/CONF.189/PC.3/5, para. 183.
123 UN Doc. A/CONF.189/PC.3/5, para. 183.
124 The Declaration adopted by the World Conference against Racism, Racial Discrimination, Xenophobia and Related Intolerance, preamble.
125 The Programme of Action adopted by the World Conference against Racism, Racial Discrimination, Xenophobia and Related Intolerance, para. 115.
126 UN Doc. A/CONF.189/12, Annex V, para. 8
127 The Programme of Action adopted by the World Conference against Racism, Racial Discrimination, Xenophobia and Related Intolerance, para. 117.
128 The Programme of Action adopted by the World Conference against Racism, Racial Discrimination, Xenophobia and Related Intolerance, paras 117, 126, 127, 128,129, 131 and 132.
129 The Programme of Action adopted by the World Conference against Racism, Racial Discrimination, Xenophobia and Related Intolerance, para. 130.

in 2001, the Durban Review Conference took place in 2009 in Geneva. The Outcome Document of the Durban Review Conference recognises steps taken at the national level to promote human rights education with a view to sensitising the public at large and fostering respect for cultural diversity.[130] It continues to encourage States to develop national capacity for human rights education, training activities and public information in order to combat racism, racial discrimination, xenophobia and related intolerance.[131] It also urges measures from politicians, law enforcement and immigration officials to combat xenophobic attitudes and negative stereotyping toward non-citizens.[132]

Mass media

A number of studies have recorded racial stereotypical portrayals in the media. Psychologists have not established the link that those portrayals were directly accepted by audiences and become part of their racial prejudice.[133] Nonetheless, most studies assume that information provided by the media plays an important role in the process for citizens to form an opinion on racial discrimination.[134] The UN declaration and convention on the elimination of racial discrimination omits the mention of the role of the mass media, although some provisions may still be relevant. First, the media are forbidden to disseminate ideas based on racial superiority and hatred or to promote and incite racial discrimination.[135] Additionally, the media can be an effective way for States to promote human rights values and principles, in the fields of 'teaching, education, culture and information'.[136] The media certainly fall into the 'all appropriate means' proviso that States should employ to fight against racial discrimination.[137]

The UNESCO Statement on Race and Racial Prejudice of 1967 points out that '[t]he media of mass communication are increasingly important in promoting knowledge and understanding, but their exact potentiality is not fully known'

130 The Outcome Document of the Durban Review Conference, para. 22.

131 The Outcome Document of the Durban Review Conference, para. 107.

132 The Outcome Document of the Durban Review Conference, para. 76.

133 Lincoln Quillian, 'New Approaches to Understanding Racial Prejudice and Discrimination' (2006) 32 *Annual Review of Sociology* 299; David Domke, Kelley McCoy and Marcos Torres, 'News Media, Racial Perceptions, and Political Cognition' (1999) 26 (5) *Communication Research* 570, 571–572.

134 David Domke, Kelley McCoy and Marcos Torres, 'News Media, Racial Perceptions, and Political Cognition' (1999) 26 (5) *Communication Research* 570, 571–572.

135 The United Nations Declaration on the Elimination of All Forms of Racial Discrimination, preamble; The International Convention on the Elimination of All Forms of Racial Discrimination, article 4.

136 The United Nations Declaration on the Elimination of All Forms of Racial Discrimination, article 8; The International Convention on the Elimination of All Forms of Racial Discrimination, article 7.

137 The United Nations Declaration on the Elimination of All Forms of Racial Discrimination, article 4; The International Convention on the Elimination of All Forms of Racial Discrimination, article 2.

and that '[b]ecause the mass media reach vast numbers of people at different educational and social levels, their role in encouraging or combating race prejudice can be crucial.'[138] In 1978 the UNESCO Declaration on Race and Racial Prejudice urges the mass media and those who may control or serve them to contribute to the promotion of human rights principles and the eradication of racial discrimination in article 5 (3):

> The mass media and those who control or serve them, as well as all organized groups within national communities, are urged, with due regard to the principles embodied in the Universal Declaration of Human Rights, particularly the principle of freedom of expression to promote understanding, tolerance and friendship among individuals and groups and to contribute to the eradication of racism, racial discrimination and racial prejudice, in particular by refraining from presenting a stereotyped, partial, unilateral or tendentious picture of individuals and of various human groups.

Alongside its Declaration on Race and Racial Prejudice, UNESCO adopted the Declaration on Fundamental Principles concerning the Contribution of the Mass Media to Strengthening Peace and International Understanding, to the Promotion of Human Rights and to Countering Racialism, apartheid and incitement to war in 1978. This Declaration affirms the fundamental contribution that the mass media can make to the advancing of understanding and the countering of racialism and propaganda.[139] In article IV, it states that '[t]he mass media have an essential part to play in the education of young people in a spirit of peace, justice, freedom, mutual respect and understanding, in order to promote human rights, equality of rights as between all human beings and all nations.'

The four World Conferences on Racism have all emphasised the vital role that the mass media can play in the dissemination of information and the combating of racism and racial discrimination. The Second World Conference against Racism (1983) called on the mass media 'to contribute to eliminating ignorance and misunderstanding between peoples' and 'to ensur[e] respect for the rights and dignity of all nations, all peoples and individuals without distinction . . . and in that way to contribute to protecting them against any influence of propaganda supporting racism and racist regimes'.[140] To this end, detailed suggestions were offered, including:

1 to raise awareness of the close link between the struggle against racism and racial discrimination and the struggle for international peace and security
2 to raise public consciousness about the positive roles and achievements of racial and ethnic groups from all walks of life throughout history

138 The UNESCO Statement on Race and Racial Prejudice, para. 16.
139 The UNESCO Declaration on Fundamental Principles concerning the Contribution of the Mass Media to Strengthening Peace and International Understanding, to the Promotion of Human Rights and to Countering Racialism, apartheid and incitement to war, preamble.
140 UN Doc. A/CONF.119/26, p. 21.

3 to refrain from publicising any form of racial stereotyping, instead providing broad coverage for anti-racist events and activities
4 to depict the evils of racial discrimination and to provide an opportunity for victims of racial discrimination to express their views.[141]

Nowadays the internet is a new platform on which racial discrimination can be spread easily.[142] Given this situation, the Durban Conference in 2001 further drew attention to the use of new information and communications technologies, including the internet.[143] The Conference recommended that States promote the development through the media, including the internet and advertising, of a voluntary ethical code of conduct and policies aimed at: combating the proliferation of racist ideas; promoting respect, tolerance and understanding, for example through assistance in public awareness-raising campaigns; and avoiding stereotyping, particularly the promotion of inaccurate social constructions of migrants, namely migrant workers and refugees.[144] It further called on States to encourage internet service providers to establish specific voluntary codes of conduct and self-regulatory measures against the dissemination of racist messages and to that end set up mediating bodies at national and international levels.[145] Furthermore, States were urged to prosecute incitement to racial hatred through new information and communications technologies, including the internet.[146]

The General Assembly of the United Nations further suggested in the Revised Programme of Action for the Third Decade to Combat Racism and Racial Discrimination (1993–2003) that member States should:

> encourage the participation of journalist and human rights advocates from minority groups and communities in the mass media. Radio and television programmes should increase the number of broadcasts produced by and in cooperation with racial and cultural minority groups. Multicultural activities of the media should also be encouraged where they can contribute to the suppression of racism and xenophobia.[147]

141 UN Doc. A/CONF.119/26, pp. 21–22.
142 Brendesha Tynes, Michael Giang, David Williams and Geneene Thompson, 'Online Racial Discrimination and Psychological Adjustment among Adolescents' (2008) 43 *Journal of Adolescent Health* 565; Brendesha Tynes and Suzanne Markoe, 'The Role of Color-Blind Racial Attitude in Reactions to Racial Discrimination on Social Network Sites' (2010) 3 (1) *Journal of Diversity in Higher Education* 1.
143 The Programme of Action of the World Conference against Racism, Racial Discrimination, Xenophobia and Related Intolerance, paras 140–147.
144 The Programme of Action of the World Conference against Racism, Racial Discrimination, Xenophobia and Related Intolerance, para. 144.
145 The Programme of Action of the World Conference against Racism, Racial Discrimination, Xenophobia and Related Intolerance, para. 147.
146 The Programme of Action of the World Conference against Racism, Racial Discrimination, Xenophobia and Related Intolerance, para. 147.
147 UN Doc. A/RES/49/146, Annex.

Further interpretation

Legal and educational approaches to the issue of racial discrimination both confronted questions when they were brought into implementation. Many States made reservations to article 4 of the International Convention on the Elimination of All Forms of Racial Discrimination, primarily due to its binding nature. As for article 7 of the Convention with regard to States' educational duties, there was less controversy around the text *per se*. The main problem existed in the fact that educational duties are often neglected by States and commentators.[148] In confronting these issues, the Committee on the Elimination of Racial Discrimination, the supervisory body of the International Convention on the Elimination of All Forms of Racial Discrimination, reiterated the binding nature of articles 4 and 7, regarding them as the pillars on which the Convention rests.[149] The Committee found the two articles to be non-self-executing and requested that States take follow-up measures, including express legislation to penalise certain acts (article 4) and mandatory actions in the fields of teaching, education, culture and information (article 7).[150] The Committee disagreed with the misconception that no further action from the State was needed if the Constitution of a State condemns racial discrimination, or that the Convention becomes part of the supreme law of a State.[151] This stance was seconded by other human rights bodies including the Committee on Economic, Social and Cultural Rights, the Committee on the Rights of the Child, UNESCO, the General Assembly of the United Nations and regional human rights bodies, for example the Council of Europe Commissioner for Human Rights.

Legal measures

Reservations and declarations

As stated, article 4 of the International Convention on the Elimination of All Forms of Racial Discrimination is a highly controversial provision. Many States made reservations and declarations on signing and ratifying the Convention, including Antigua and Barbuda, Australia, Austria, the Bahamas, Barbados, Belgium, Fiji, France, Ireland, Italy, Japan, Malta, Monaco, Nepal, Papua New Guinea, Switzerland, Thailand, Tonga, the United Kingdom and the United States. These States argued that the nature of article 4 was not mandatory, given the context in which article 4 was developed, provided for its opening paragraph, 'with due regard to the principles embodied in the Universal

148 An earlier discussion on how this obligation is virtually ignored by commentators and States can be found in: Stephanie Farrior, 'The Neglected Pillar: The "Teaching Tolerance" Provision of the International Convention on the Elimination of All Forms of Racial Discrimination' (1998–1999) 5 *ILSA Journal of International & Comparative Law* 291, 294–95.

149 UN Doc. CERD/2.

150 UN Doc. A/CONF.92/8, para. 94.

151 UN Doc. A/CONF.92/8, paras 94–95.

Declaration of Human Rights and the rights expressly set forth in article 5 of this Convention'.

Specifically, France viewed the nature of article 4 as being non-mandatory. The United States insisted that article 4 imposes no obligation that is not fully consistent with freedom of speech and association.[152] On signing the Convention, the United States announced:

> The Constitution of the United States contains provisions for the protection of individual rights, such as the right of free speech, and nothing in the Convention shall be deemed to require or to authorize legislation or other action by the United States of America incompatible with the provisions of the Constitution of the United States of America.

The US government made it clear when ratifying the International Convention on the Elimination of All Forms of Racial Discrimination that it did not accept the obligation of article 4, or article 7, establishing that:

> The Constitution and laws of the United States contain extensive protections of individual freedom of speech, expression and association. Accordingly, the United States does not accept any obligation under this Convention, in particular under articles 4 and 7, to restrict those rights, through the adoption of legislation or any other measures, to the extent that they are protected by the Constitution and laws of the States.

The United Kingdom lodged a reservation and interpretative statement, claiming that these legislative actions are optional, stressing that the State:

> interprets article 4 as requiring a party to the Convention to adopt further legislative measures in the fields covered by sub-paragraphs (a), (b) and (c) of that article only in so far as it may consider with due regard to the principles embodied in the Universal Declaration of Human Rights and the rights expressly set forth in article 5 of the Convention (in particular the right to freedom of opinion and expression and the right to freedom of peaceful assembly and association) that some legislative addition to or variation of existing law and practice in those fields is necessary for the attainment of the end specified in the earlier part of article 4.

On similar grounds, Antigua and Barbuda, Australia, Austria, the Bahamas, Barbados, Belgium, Fiji, France, Ireland, Italy, Japan, Malta, Monaco, Nepal, Papua New Guinea, Switzerland, Thailand and Tonga all made reservations on article 4. These reservations were supported by some academic research on the basis that the provision may compromise the fundamental human value of free

152 UN Doc. A/PV.1406, para. 99; UN Doc. A/C.3/SR.1373, paras 41–42.

expression.[153] Such reservations were considered to play a role in shaping international obligations.[154]

Clarifying the nature of the legal duty to tackle racial discrimination

Given this situation, the Committee on the Elimination of Racial Discrimination came up with three general recommendations and one decision to reiterate the mandatory character of article 4. They are general recommendations No. 1 (1972), 7 (1985), 15 (1993), and Decision 3 of 4 May 1973, which serve as commentaries on the provisions of article 4. In general recommendation No. 15, the Committee reaffirmed that citizens' exercise of rights carries special duties and responsibilities pursuant to article 29 (2) of the Universal Declaration of Human Rights. One such duty is the obligation not to disseminate racist ideas. Both the Committee on the Elimination of Racial Discrimination and the General Assembly of the United Nations deemed the prohibition of the dissemination of racial ideas compatible with freedom of opinion and expression.[155]

The Committee on the Elimination of Racial Discrimination further communicated with certain States, prompting them to respect the provisions of article 4. This was carried out through concluding observations to States' periodic reports under the International Convention on the Elimination of All Forms of Racial Discrimination. In these observations, the Committee urged States that made reservations to article 4 such as Australia,[156] Canada,[157] Egypt,[158] Finland,[159] the United Kingdom[160] and the United States[161] to reconsider their interpretation and understanding. It called on Greece,[162] Italy,[163] Luxembourg,[164] New Zealand[165] and Uruguay[166] to bring their legislation into full compliance with article 4. In 2005 the Committee suggested to Luxembourg that racial motives

153 Michael A. G. Korengold, 'Lessons in Confronting Racist Speech: Good Intentions, Bad Results, and Article 4 (a) of the Convention on the Elimination of All Forms of Racial Discrimination' (1993) 77 *Minnesota Law Review* 719.

154 Massimo Coccia, 'Reservations to Multilateral Treaties on Human Rights' (1985) 15 *California Western International Law Journal* 1, 47.

155 The Committee on the Elimination of Racial Discrimination general recommendation No. 15 and UN Doc. A/Res/56/267.

156 UN Doc. CERD/C/AUS/CO/15–17, para. 17; UN Doc. CERD/C/AUS/CO/14, para. 12.

157 UN Doc. CERD/C/CAN/CO/19–20, para. 13; UN Doc. CERD/C/CAN/CO/18, para. 16.

158 UN Doc. A/56/18, para. 287.

159 UN Doc. CERD/C/304/Add.107, para. 9.

160 UN Doc. A/48/18, paras 382–425; UN Doc. CERD/C/63/CO/11, para. 12; UN Doc. CERD/C/GBR/CO/18–20, para. 11.

161 UN Doc. CERD/C/USA/CO/6, para. 18.

162 UN Doc. A/35/18, para. 247.

163 UN Doc. A/32/18, paras 286 and 291.

164 UN Doc. A/HRC/WG.6/3/LUX/2, para. 18; UN Doc. CERD/C/LUX/CO/13, paras 15–16.

165 UN Doc. A/36/18, para. 359.

166 UN Doc. CERD/C/URY/CO/16–20, para. 13.

should be defined as a general aggravating circumstance for offences.[167] Such a stance was concurred to by regional human rights institutions such as the Council of Europe Commissioner for Human Rights, who urged Germany to provide a penal law provision explicitly referring to racist motivation as an aggravating factor in the determination of sentences in 2007.[168] Moreover, the Committee on the Elimination of Racial Discrimination further developed its position that article 4 is applicable to racist expressions in the media and internet in its concluding observations to Argentina and Finland in 2003, 2004 and 2012 respectively.[169]

State compliance

In response to these measures, a number of States have reported their progress in adapting their legislation to article 4. These States include Argentina,[170] Australia,[171] Denmark,[172] Finland,[173] Greece,[174] Iran,[175] Italy,[176] New Zealand,[177] Pakistan,[178] Peru,[179] the Philippines[180] and Poland.[181] Some States have changed their position within a few years toward support for the stance of the Committee and other UN mechanisms. When voting for the operative paragraphs (a) and (b) of article 4, Canada abstained, claiming that these clauses went beyond the existing provisions of Canadian criminal law. Nevertheless, shortly thereafter in 1970 the Canadian Criminal Code was amended to penalise incitement to hatred and contempt against any 'identifiable group', including a group distinguished by colour, race, religion or ethnic origin.[182] New Zealand in 1979 passed sentence under its Race Relations Act for two leaders of the New Zealand National Socialist Party who had engaged in the dissemination of ideas based on racial superiority or hatred.[183] Other States such as Uruguay revealed an intention to implement article 4; however, it has since failed to carry it out.[184]

167 UN Doc. CERD/C/LUX/CO/13, para. 15.
168 CommDH (2007) 14, part 9, para. 19.
169 UN Doc. CERD/C/65/CO/1, para. 15; UN Doc. CERD/C/FIN/20–22, para. 94; UN Doc. CERD/C/63/CO/5, para. 14.
170 UN Doc. A/33/18, para. 248.
171 Racial Discrimination Act 1975 of Australia took part of article 4 into consideration.
172 UN Doc. A/9018, paras 303–07. It also reported to the Committee that it prepared guidelines for crimes based on racial discrimination. UN Doc. CERD/C/DNK/CO/18-19, para. 9.
173 UN Doc. CERD/C/FIN/20–22, paras 100–102.
174 UN Doc. A/35/18, paras 246–247.
175 UN Doc. A/33/18, paras 172 and 174.
176 UN Doc. A/32/18, paras 285–286.
177 UN Doc. CERD/C/NZL/17, paras 176 and 178.
178 UN Doc. A/32/18, para. 97; UN Doc. A/35/18, para. 338.
179 UN Doc. A/33/18, para. 86; UN Doc. A/35/18, para. 96.
180 UN Doc. A/34/18, para. 59.
181 UN Doc. A/33/18, para. 279; UN Doc. A/35/18, para. 438.
182 Natán Lérner, *The UN Convention on the Elimination of All Forms of Racial Discrimination* (Sijthoff & Noordhoff 1980) 52.
183 UN Doc. A/34/18, para. 120.
184 UN Doc. A/32/18, para. 121; UN Doc. A/33/18, para. 214; UN Doc. A/36/18, para. 289.

States report compliance on the legal and educational duties to tackle racial discrimination not only to the Committee on the Elimination of Racial Discrimination, but also to the newly established mechanism of the Universal Periodic Review. The Universal Periodic Review was established by the General Assembly of the United Nations in 2006 for the purpose of examining States' compliance with human rights obligations. It complements the work of human rights treaty bodies such as the Committee on the Elimination of Racial Discrimination.[185] For instance, through the process of the Universal Periodic Review in 2010, Bolivia accepted suggestions on the criminalisation of all forms of racial discrimination in keeping with recommendations of the Committee on the Elimination of Racial Discrimination and other international institutions.[186]

Persuasive measures

Clarifying the nature of educational duty

As mentioned, States do not find their duty to propagate human rights principles hard to accept. Fewer reservations have been made to article 7 of the International Convention on the Elimination of All Forms of Racial Discrimination, compared with article 4 of the Convention. A few have nevertheless been made, such as the United States' reservations on the basis of freedom of speech, expression and association. In practice, provisions of article 7 were often overlooked by both States and commentators.[187]

Occasionally the binding nature of article 7 has come under question. Italy and Norway, for example, claimed that they could not impose any restrictions on the press and other information media, as envisioned in article 7.[188] These statements were made in the UN General Assembly and through the periodic review process established under the International Convention on the Elimination of All Forms of Racial Discrimination.

The Committee on the Elimination of Racial Discrimination on the contrary attached great importance to provisions of article 7 in respect to the State duty in combating racial prejudice and promoting human rights values and core principles thereof. The Committee deemed that legal and educational measures remain the most important mechanisms with which States may tackle racial discrimination; therefore, accentuating the buttress nature of articles 4 and 7 for the Convention.[189] The Committee further contended that '[a]lthough

185 UN Doc. A/RES/60/251.

186 UN Doc. A/HRC/14/7, para. 98, recommendation 4.

187 An earlier discussion on how this obligation is virtually ignored by commentators and States can be found in: Stephanie Farrior, 'The Neglected Pillar: The "Teaching Tolerance" Provision of the International Convention on the Elimination of All Forms of Racial Discrimination' (1998–1999) 5 *ILSA Journal of International & Comparative Law* 291, 294–295.

188 UN Doc. A/C.3/33/SR.21, p. 11; UN Doc. A/33/18, para. 186.

189 UN Doc. A/35/18, para. 264.

legislation was important, it was even more important to eliminate the root causes of discrimination and the way to do so was through emphasis on cultural and educational means.'[190] UNESCO, in line with the view of the Committee, noted the lack of recognition concerning the importance of article 7 and pointed out that the implementation of the provision should be accompanied by specific suggestions.[191]

In 1977 the Committee on the Elimination of Racial Discrimination issued general comment No. 5, reiterating the binding nature of article 7 and urging State parties to give effect to the provisions therein.[192] The Committee, working with UNESCO, provided detailed guidelines on the implementation of article 7.[193] It also filed specific recommendations to States such as Austria,[194] Brazil,[195] Croatia,[196] Finland,[197] Haiti,[198] the Philippines,[199] Mongolia,[200] the Netherlands,[201] Nigeria,[202] Peru,[203] Tanzania,[204] Tonga[205] and the United Arab Emirates.[206]

Notably the Committee linked the implementation of article 7 to the work of educating public opinion. In the framework of the article, the Committee inquired how States educated their population on racial equality. It expressed satisfactions with the Indian government's efforts to 'enlighten public opinion on measures taken with a view to combating racial discrimination',[207] noted Pakistan's actions to inform public opinion regarding the struggle against racism,[208] requested Norway to provide information on steps taken to 'encourage the public to show a friendly attitude toward foreigners' and recommended to the Netherlands to enact a more comprehensive programme of action to educate public opinion.[209] With regard to negative attitudes, stereotypes or prejudices against Roma, gypsies, black people, Muslims and asylum seekers, the Committee recommended

190 UN Doc. A/35/18, para. 215.
191 UN Doc. CERD/C/69, para. 4.
192 UN Doc. HRI/GEN/1/Rev.1, pp. 62–63.
193 UN Doc. HRI/GEN/2/Rev.6, pp. 62–64; UN Doc. CERD/C/70/Rev.3, pp. 6–7; UN Doc. CERD/C/69; Draft Guidelines Proposed by UNESCO, UN Doc. CERD/C/69/Add.1, adopted by the Committee in 1982, UN Doc. CERD/C/SR.570, para. 201.
194 UN Doc. A/33/18, para. 123.
195 UN Doc. A/35/18, para. 172.
196 UN Doc. CERD/C/HRV/CO/8, para. 21.
197 UN Doc. A/35/18, para. 197.
198 UN Doc. A/31/18, para. 247.
199 UN Doc. A/35/18, para. 365.
200 UN Doc. A/35/18, para. 186.
201 UN Doc. A/HRC/WG.6/1/NDL/2, para. 9; UN Doc. CERD/C/64/CO/7, para. 10.
202 UN Doc. A/35/18, para. 183.
203 UN Doc. A/33/18, para. 87.
204 UN Doc. A/35/18, para. 317.
205 UN Doc. A/33/18, para. 277.
206 UN Doc. A/33/18, para. 234.
207 UN Doc. A/34/18, para. 371.
208 UN Doc. A/32/18, para. 98.
209 UN Doc. A/36/18, para. 480.

that the governments of Finland,[210] Mozambique,[211] Norway,[212] Sweden[213] and Switzerland[214] must modify the attitude of their population. It stressed the necessity to provide preventive programmes to remove subjective prejudices.[215]

Academic analysis has pointed out the difficulty in measuring the implementation of article 7. Academics have summarised the provisions of article 7 as educational measures[216] and conceptualised them as promotional elements, concluding that the purpose of the provisions would be the promotion of an objective rather than the maintenance of a given standard.[217] Another provision categorised as a promotional element is article 2, requiring States to 'promote understanding among all races' in its introductory paragraph and 'to encourage, where appropriate, integrationist multi-racial organizations and movements and other means of eliminating barriers between races, and to discourage anything which tends to strengthen racial division' in article 2 (1) (e). Given the promotional nature of this issue, the Committee on the Elimination of Racial Discrimination has repeatedly urged States to provide more information and to devote more effort toward reaching this goal.[218] Nonetheless, academics commended the insertion of 'culture' in article 7 as a demonstration of understanding of the impact of cultural activities on attitudes.[219]

210 The Committee encouraged Finland to combat negative attitudes and prevailing stereotypes concerning Roma, in particular among employers. UN Doc. A/HRC/WG.6/13/FIN/2, para. 15.

211 In 2007 the Committee was concerned about cases of hate speech, as well as racist and xenophobic attitudes and recommended that Mozambique strengthen measures to prevent and combat xenophobia and racial prejudice. UN Doc. A/HRC/WG.6/10/MOZ/2, para. 26; UN Doc. CERD/C/MOZ/CO/12, para. 22.

212 In 1980, the Committee requested Norway to provide information on the steps taken to encourage the public to show a friendly attitude towards foreigners. UN Doc. A/35/18, para. 229.

213 In 1981, the Committee hoped Sweden would initiate an information programme aiming at 'modifying the attitude of the population towards the gypsies'. UN Doc. A/36/18, para. 207.

214 In 2002, the Committee recommended that Switzerland continue its efforts to prevent and combat hostile attitudes towards black people, Muslims and asylum seekers, including through information campaigns and education of the general public. UN Doc. A/HRC/WG.6/2/CHE/2, para. 12; UN Doc. CERD/C/60/CO/14, para. 9.

215 UN Doc. A/33/18, p. 109.

216 Theodor Meron, 'The Meaning and Reach of the International Convention on the Elimination of All Forms of Racial Discrimination' (1985) 79 *American Journal of International Law* 283, 297.

217 Egon Schwelb, 'The International Convention on the Elimination of All Forms of Racial Discrimination' (1966) 15 *International and Comparative Law Quarterly* 996, 1016; C. Wilfred Jenks, 'The Application of International Labour Conventions by Means of Collective Agreements' (1958) 19 *Zeitschrift für ausländisches öffentliches Recht und Völkerrecht* 197, 203.

218 UN Doc. A/36/18, paras 48, 72, 84, 91, 99, 110, 118, 130, 145, 153, 162, 198, 220, 225, 241, 254, 277, 285, 292, 310, 351, 371, 412, 424, 432, 441 and 466; UN Doc. A/32/18, para. 74; UN Doc. A/35/18, paras 81, 98, 107, 123, 135, 144, 153, 161, 195, 215, 225, 229, 235, 287, 305, 308 and 341; UN Doc. A/34/18, paras 98, 111, 138, 182, 196, 205, 300, 391, 431 and 447; UN Doc. A/33/18, para. 106, 115, 129, 137, 147, 160, 216, 241, 323, 327, 329 and 361; UN Doc. A/31/18, paras 34, 168 and 211.

219 Stephanie Farrior, 'The Neglected Pillar: The "Teaching Tolerance" Provision of the International Convention on the Elimination of All Forms of Racial Discrimination' (1998–1999) 5 *ILSA Journal of International & Comparative Law* 291, 297.

On a national level, many States have reported their progress in implementing the provisions of article 7. Such States include Argentina, Australia, Belgium, Belarus, Canada, Cuba, Cyprus, Czechoslovakia, Egypt, Finland, Germany, Greece, Hungary, Iceland, India, Italy, Jamaica, Jordan, Madagascar, Malta, Mauritius, Mexico, New Zealand, Niger, Pakistan, the Philippines, Qatar, Senegal, the Soviet Union, Sweden, Ukraine, Upper Volta, Uruguay and Yugoslavia.[220] Among these States, Finland reported in 2011 that an integral part of their fight against racism on the internet involves educating the public on observed crimes through a system of hints via the internet.[221] In 2003 Italy established the National Office for the Promotion of Equal Treatment and the Removal of Discrimination Based on Race or Ethnic Origin (UNAR), tasked with addressing public opinion through awareness-raising campaigns in the mass media, as well as through education and information campaigns in schools and work places for the purpose of instilling the principle of equal treatment as part of each individual's cultural and educational 'baggage'.[222] Italy's actions may suggest a changing attitude within the Italian authority. In 1979 Italy's representative stated in the Third Committee of the General Assembly that it was 'unlikely to impose any restriction on the press', a restriction that may be recommended through the general guidelines for the implementation of article 7.[223] Since 2003, however, it has been working with the mass media toward altering public attitudes regarding ethnic equality.

Guidelines on 'teaching, education, culture and information'

The Committee on the Elimination of Racial Discrimination and the Sub-Commission on Prevention of Discrimination and Protection of Minorities provide further guidelines promoting the proactive duties of the State in teaching, education, culture and information. First and foremost, it is highlighted that teaching should not be confined to schools. Rather, it should target a variety of audiences, encompassing persons influential or integral to the conceptualisation of public opinion, such as law enforcement officials, magistrates, prosecutors, public figures, out-of-school individuals,[224] particularly the youth outside the classroom,[225] and 'teachers and other opinion leaders on eliminating prejudice

220 UN Doc. A/36/18, paras 134, 318, 355 and 389; UN Doc. A/35/18, paras 98, 113, 123, 170, 238, 263, 268–270, 275, 276, 281, 288, 297, 318, 325 and 365; UN Doc. A/34/18, paras 83, 122, 131, 147, 179, 210, 229, 275, 290, 313 and 371; UN Doc. A/33/18, paras 90, 102, 123, 160, 166, 207, 222, 227, 249, 293 and 351; UN Doc. A/32/18, paras 114 and 119; UN Doc. A/31/18, paras 134 and 193; CERD/C/ISL/CO/19–20, para. 14; UN Doc. CERD/C/304/Add.119, para. 13; UN Doc. CERD/C/FIN/20–22, para. 95.

221 UN Doc. CERD/C/FIN/20–22, para. 95.

222 UN Doc. CERD/C/ITA/15, para. 315.

223 UN Doc. A/C.3/33/SR.21, p. 11.

224 UN Doc. E/CN.4/Sub.2/1998/4, para. 46.

225 The Committee inquired of Germany if any effort was made to re-educate young adults or adolescents imprisoned for having committed racist acts. UN Doc. A/48/18, para. 435.

and fostering tolerance'.[226] In this regard, general recommendation No. 13 issued by the Committee on the Elimination of Racial Discrimination features the education of law enforcement officials or persons that assert power over individuals. In a working paper of the Sub-Commission on Prevention of Discrimination and Protection of Minorities, States are recommended to establish a national focal point for human rights education and to put into effect an action-oriented national plan for education with a particular emphasis on the provisions of article 7.[227]

The working paper of the Sub-Commission further requests States to develop and implement specific programmes as well as long-term strategies that incorporate different channels of culture and information to give effect to article 7. In order to achieve this, direct and active involvement of governmental departments was strongly encouraged in the working paper.[228] The Committee also urged States parties to contribute to the positive development of culture and tradition,[229] including measures such as the organisation of public awareness campaigns for the public,[230] as well as human rights training for officials.[231] This illustrates that the invocation of culture and tradition as a means to resist human rights reforms in many areas is not a static phenomenon, but rather one that is capable of progression toward an encompassing of human rights.

Such a view has been backed by anthropologists and human rights scholars.[232] Morten Kjærum found that '[i]nstead of being something well-defined and demarcated, culture becomes a network of perspectives which is developed in an ongoing dialogue.'[233] Human rights can be viewed as a new culture to be introduced into society, although there might be disagreement and conflict in the debate that is not necessarily unpleasant but rather constitutive.[234] Ann-Belinda S. Preis described the process of human rights being introduced in society as follows:

226 The General Assembly requested so in the Revised Programme of Action to the Decade. UN Doc. E/CN.4/Sub.2/1998/4, para. 32.
227 UN Doc. E/CN.4/Sub.2/1998/4, para. 171.
228 UN Doc. E/CN.4/Sub.2/1998/4, para. 176.
229 UN Doc. CERD/C/70/Rev.3, pp. 6–7.
230 UN Doc. A/HRC/WG.6/1/FIN/2, para. 10; UN Doc. CCPR/CO/82/FIN, para. 16; UN Doc. A/HRC/WG.6/7/BIH/2, para. 21; UN Doc. CCPR/C/BIH/CO/1, para. 24.
231 UN Doc. A/HRC/WG.6/3/LUX/2, para. 18; UN Doc. CERD/C/LUX/CO/13, para. 19.
232 Ann-Belinda S. Preis, 'Human Rights as Cultural Practice: An Anthropological Critique' (1996) 18 *Human Rights Quarterly* 286, 289; Morten Kjærum, 'Universal Human Rights: Between the Local and the Global', in Kirsten Hastrup (ed), *Human Rights on Common Grounds: The Quest for Universality* (Kluwer 2001) 77; Michael K. Addo, 'Practice of United Nations Human Rights Treaty Bodies in the Reconciliation of Cultural Diversity with Universal Respect for Human Rights' (2010) 32 *Human Rights Quarterly* 601, 608.
233 Morten Kjærum, 'Universal Human Rights: Between the Local and the Global', in Kirsten Hastrup (ed), *Human Rights on Common Grounds: The Quest for Universality* (Kluwer 2001) 77.
234 Ann-Belinda S. Preis, 'Human Rights as Cultural Practice: An Anthropological Critique' (1996) 18 *Human Rights Quarterly* 286, 305.

> [H]uman rights now form part of the multiple cultural flows between centers and peripheries in a world where 'cultures have lost their moorings in particular places' and 'the rapidly expanding and quickening mobility of people combines with the refusal of cultural products and practices, to "stay put"'.[235]

The remaining arena in which States should make efforts to progress is in 'information', often interpreted as the duty to encourage public and private information services, in particular the mass media, to take account of article 7 in their operations.[236] The reason given for this emphasis is that freedom of expression and freedom of the press are neither absolute nor unlimited. Certain statements in the media are not tolerated by the International Convention on the Elimination of All Forms of Racial Discrimination, including expressions of racial prejudices, stigmatisation, stereotypes and virulent attacks or negative portrayal based on race. The Committee on the Elimination of Racial Discrimination has expressed concerns about racist media coverage in Australia,[237] Canada[238] and the United Kingdom in 2002, 2005 and 2011 respectively when these States presented their periodic reports.[239] The Committee noted the existence and negative impact of such expressions toward ethnic minorities, immigrants, asylum seekers, refugees, foreigners and people of a particular genealogical descent. As such, the Committee held the belief that the media may have perpetrated organised violence based on ethnic origin, according to articles 2, 4 and 6.[240]

In confronting this issue, the Committee suggested that the States concerned should, in conformity with articles 4 and 7, closely monitor the media with a view to combating prejudices, hatred and xenophobic stereotypes, as well as countering any tendency to target, stigmatise, stereotype or profile any group based on race.[241] These suggestions were made to Iceland, Luxembourg, the Netherlands, Nicaragua and the United Kingdom. The Committee stressed in 2002 that article 4 (b) is applicable to the media as regards the prohibition of racist propaganda and

235 Ann-Belinda S. Preis, 'Human Rights as Cultural Practice: An Anthropological Critique' (1996) 18 *Human Rights Quarterly* 286, 309–10; Akhil Gupta and James Ferguson, 'Beyond "Culture": Space, Identity, and the Politics of Difference' (1992) 7 (1) *Cultural Anthropology* 6, 7 and 9.

236 UN Doc. CERD/C/ISL/CO/19–20, para. 177; UN Doc. A/36/18, paras 80 and 162; Stephanie Farrior, 'The Neglected Pillar: The "Teaching Tolerance" Provision of the International Convention on the Elimination of All Forms of Racial Discrimination' (1998–1999) 5 *ILSA Journal of International & Comparative Law* 291, 298.

237 UN Doc. CERD/C/AUS/CO/14, para. 14.

238 UN Doc. A/57/18, para. 335.

239 UN Doc. CERD/C/GBR/CO/18–20, para. 11.

240 UN Doc. CERD/C/GBR/CO/18–20, para. 11.

241 UN Doc. CERD/C/GBR/CO/18–20, para. 11; UN Doc. CERD/C/AUS/CO/14, para. 14; UN Doc. CERD/C/ISL/CO/19–20, para. 14; UN Doc. A/HRC/WG.6/3/LUX/2, para. 18; UN Doc. CERD/C/LUX/CO/13, para. 13; UN Doc. A/HRC/WG.6/7/NIC/2, para. 16; UN Doc. CERD/C/NIC/CO/14, para. 27; UN Doc. A/HRC/WG.6/13/GBR/2, para. 14; UN Doc. CERD/C/GBR/CO/18–20, para. 11; UN Doc. A/HRC/WG.6/1/NDL/2, para. 9; UN Doc. E/CN.4/Sub.2/2005/27, para. 19.

activities as well as the ban on racist organisations.[242] Such a statement was made when Canada presented its 13th and 14th periodic reports. The Committee also noted in 2010 that article 4 is applicable to organisations on the internet when Iceland presented its combined 19th and 20th periodic reports. It commended the Icelandic authority for closing down the website of the 'Society against Polish People in Iceland' which had nearly 700 registered members.[243]

Endorsement under other treaty bodies

In addition to article 7 of the International Convention on the Elimination of All Forms of Racial Discrimination, States' educational duties to battle racial discrimination, prejudice and stereotypes have been developed under other human rights mechanisms. The Human Rights Committee, the Committee on Economic, Social and Cultural Rights and the Committee on the Rights of the Child have urged States to introduce measures that fight against negative attitudes targeted at people from different ethnic backgrounds. These recommendations were made when States presented their periodic reports under the International Covenant on Civil and Political Rights, the International Covenant on Economic, Social and Cultural Rights and the Convention on the Rights of the Child. Through the publication of concluding observations, these treaty bodies serve to interpret the various human rights obligations enshrined in international treaties.

For instance, the Human Rights Committee was concerned about negative attitudes against immigrants in certain strata of the Finnish population in 2004. It recommended that Finland step up its efforts to promote tolerance and combat prejudice, particularly through public awareness campaigns.[244] In 2009 the Human Rights Committee recommended to Croatia that it should carry out intensified public information campaigns to overcome prejudices against the Serb population as well as other ethnic minorities in order to combat racial discrimination and ethnic attacks.[245]

In 2004 the Committee on Economic, Social and Cultural Rights expressed concern over the increasingly negative and hostile attitudes towards foreigners in Denmark, especially among the immigrant and refugee populations.[246] The Committee advised Denmark to combat racism and xenophobia and to continue to promote intercultural understanding and tolerance among all groups in society.[247] In regard to Roma children as well as children belonging to other minority groups, including refugee and internally displaced minors, the Committee on Economic, Social and Cultural Rights in 2005 urged Serbia and Montenegro to eradicate ethnically discriminatory attitudes and to take effective

242 UN Doc. A/57/18, para. 335.
243 UN Doc. CERD/C/ISL/CO/19–20, para. 14.
244 UN Doc. CCPR/CO/82/FIN, para. 16.
245 UN Doc. CCPR/C/HRV/CO/2, para. 5.
246 UN Doc. A/HRC/WG.6/11/DNK/2, para. 26; UN Doc. E/C.12/1/Add.102, para. 13.
247 UN Doc. E/C.12/1/Add.102, para. 24.

measures in the fields of teaching, education, culture and information with a view to promoting understanding, tolerance and mutual respect among all ethnic groups living in its territory.[248]

The Committee on the Rights of the Child in 2004 joined the Committee on the Elimination of Racial Discrimination in its concern about the lack of legal provisions prohibiting incitement to racial discrimination in Croatia, and about the adequacy of the State's efforts to prosecute persons responsible for fomenting ethnic hatred.[249] This concern was brought about through the *de facto* discrimination levelled against ethnic and national minorities, including Roma and foreign children, alongside incidents and expressions of hatred. The Committee stated that Croatia should take measures to develop a culture of tolerance in the society at large through all possible channels, including schools, the media and the law.[250] In 2005 the Committee urged Finland to educate young people with respect to discriminatory attitudes toward children, including those belonging to the Roma and foreign communities.[251] In 2008 the Committee on the Rights of the Child further suggested that Bulgaria initiate campaigns to address the negative attitudes toward the Roma community in society as a whole.[252] In addition, Roma history and culture was actively encouraged as an addition in school curricula in order to promote understanding, tolerance and respect for the rights of Roma in Bulgarian society.[253]

In the same year, the Committee on the Rights of the Child recommended that Bhutan undertake public education campaigns to prevent and combat negative societal attitudes toward different ethnic groups following Bhutan's presentation of its second periodic report.[254] Responding to Pakistan's submission of its third and fourth periodic reviews in 2009, the Committee on the Rights of the Child encouraged the State to conduct comprehensive public education programmes to tackle negative societal attitudes and mobilise political, religious and community leaders in the process of addressing traditional attitudes that discriminated against children belonging to religious or other minority groups, those with disabilities, as well as minors living in poverty and in remote and rural areas.[255]

Related issues

As stated in the Declaration of Principles on Tolerance, adopted by UNESCO in 1995, education is the most effective means of preventing intolerance.[256] The

248 UN Doc. E/C.12/1/Add.108, para. 64; UN Doc. A/HRC/WG.6/3/MNE/2, para. 25; UN Doc. A/HRC/WG.6/3/SRB/2, para. 38.
249 UN Doc. CRC/C/15/Add.243, para. 21.
250 UN Doc. CRC/C/15/Add.243, para. 22.
251 UN Doc. A/HRC/WG.6/1/FIN/2, para. 10; UN Doc. CRC/C/15/Add.272, para. 18.
252 UN Doc. A/HRC/WG.6/9/BGR/2, para. 21; UN Doc. CRC/C/BGR/CO/2, para. 72.
253 UN Doc. A/HRC/WG.6/9/BGR/2, para. 21; UN Doc. CRC/C/BGR/CO/2, para. 72.
254 UN Doc. A/HRC/WG.6/6/BTN/2, para. 15; CRC/C/BTN/CO/2, para. 26.
255 UN Doc. A/HRC/WG.6/14/PAK/2, para. 14; UN Doc. CRC/C/PAK/CO/3–4, para. 31.
256 The UNESCO Declaration of Principles on Tolerance, article 4 (1).

series of World Conferences against Racism, which took place in 1978, 1983, 2001 and 2009, also held that education is a determining factor in creating an atmosphere of tolerance and promoting equity.[257] The Declaration of Principles on Tolerance propagates the idea of tolerance education, aimed at supporting the promotion of the will to protect those of other cultures and creeds.[258] It was further affirmed elsewhere by the World Conferences against Racism, UNESCO recommendations and the International Labour Organization Indigenous and Tribal Peoples Convention that the content of ethnic equality should be reflected in school textbooks, educational aids and curricula in order to confront racism, racial prejudice and stereotyping.[259]

In 2009 the Secretary-General of the United Nations confirmed that, according to international human rights treaties, States are not only responsible for preventing and eliminating negative attitudes to, and prejudice against, individuals and groups that prevent them from fully enjoying their human rights.[260] They also have a duty to report their educational programmes and public information campaigns to this end.[261] Occasionally, under the theme of racial discrimination, discrimination based on religion and discrimination against migrants, indigenous and tribal people are also discussed since they often associate with each other. Just as the intersectional theory suggested, oppressions within society – such as racism, sexism, xenophobia, belief-based bigotry and hostility towards indigenous people – do not act independently of one another.[262] In this regard, the United Nations, UNESCO, the International Labour Organization and regional mechanisms such as the Council of Europe tend to claim that States bear a duty to mould social attitudes in favour of equality, particularly on the issues of religious equality and the equality of migrants and indigenous and tribal people.

RELIGIOUS EQUALITY

Regarding discrimination based on religion, the Sub-Commission on Prevention of Discrimination and Protection of Minorities of the United Nations pronounced

257 The Programmes of Action of the Second (1983) World Conference to Combat Racism and Racial Discrimination, paras 16 and 17; the Declaration of the World Conference against Racism, Racial Discrimination, Xenophobia and Related Intolerance, para. 95.

258 The UNESCO Declaration of Principles on Tolerance, article 4 (1).

259 UNESCO recommendation concerning Education for International Understanding, Cooperation and Peace and Education relating to Human Rights and Fundamental Freedoms of 1974, para. 39; the programmes of action of the Second World Conference to Combat Racism and Racial Discrimination (1983), para. 16; The Programmes of Action of the World Conference against Racism, Racial Discrimination, Xenophobia and Related Intolerance (2001), para. 127; The International Labour Organization Indigenous and Tribal Peoples Convention, article 31.

260 UN Doc. HRI/GEN/2/Rev.6, p. 14.

261 UN Doc. HRI/GEN/2/Rev.6, p. 14.

262 Kimberle Crenshaw, 'Demarginalizing the Intersection of Race and Sex: A Black Feminist Critique of Antidiscrimination Doctrine, Feminist Theory and Antiracist Politics' (1989) 1 *University of Chicago Legal Forum* 139; Kathy Davis, 'Intersectionality as Buzzword: A Sociology of Science Perspective on What Makes a Feminist Theory Successful' (2008) 9 *Feminist Theory* 67.

a tentative rule in the 1950s and 1960s that '[e]very effort should be exerted by public authorities to educate public opinion and to create proper leadership for [the purpose of ending discrimination based on religion].'[263] On 25 November 1981 the General Assembly of the United Nations adopted the Declaration on the Elimination of All Forms of Intolerance and of Discrimination Based on Religion or Belief.[264] This Declaration appears to be similar to the UN Declaration on racial discrimination:

> Article 4
> 2. All States shall make all efforts to enact or rescind legislation where necessary to prohibit any such discrimination, and to take all appropriate measures to combat intolerance on the grounds of religion or other beliefs in this matter.
>
> Article 5
> 3. The Child . . . shall be brought up in a spirit of understanding, tolerance, friendship among peoples, peace and universal brotherhood, [and] respect for freedom of religion or belief of others.

In the discussion of the Sub-Commission on Prevention of Discrimination and Protection of Minorities, the role of education in the fight against discrimination based on religion or belief was continually emphasised.[265]

EQUALITY OF MIGRANTS

The issue of the rights of migrants does not fully coincide with the issue of racial discrimination. But this does not negate the fact that, in practice, some of the manifestations of racial discrimination are directed against migrant workers and members of their families.[266] Hence the two issues are gradually discussed together under many occasions. For instance, the International Convention on the Protection of the Rights of All Migrant Workers and Members of Their Families, which was adopted by the General Assembly of the United Nations in 1990, does not explicitly address the issue of discrimination or the obligation to influence public attitudes toward migrant workers. The only requirement of States is to inform migrant workers and their family members about their rights and obligations.[267] However, in 2001, the World Conference against Racism, Racial Discrimination, Xenophobia and Related Intolerance in Durban urged States to conduct education and information campaigns targeting public attitude,

263 UN Doc. E/CN.4/778, para. 61; UN Doc. E/CN.4/Sub.2/L.123/Add.1, para. 339.
264 UN Doc. A/RES/36/55.
265 UN Doc. E/CN.4/1984/3, para. 241.
266 UN Doc. A/RES/53/133.
267 The International Convention on the Protection of the Rights of All Migrant Workers and Members of Their Families, article 33.

to 'ensure that the public receives accurate information regarding migrants and migration issues, including the positive contribution of migrants to the host society and the vulnerability of migrants, particularly those who are in an irregular situation'.[268]

In 2002 the Special Rapporteur on the Human Rights of Migrants appointed by the Commission on Human Rights welcomed Ecuador's national plan to carry out training, publicity and awareness creation among the population with regard to the rights of migrants, foreigners and refugees, and encouraged its implementation.[269] In 2007 the Committee on the Protection of the Rights of All Migrant Workers and Members of Their Families also encouraged Ecuador to:

> Strengthen its awareness-raising efforts by promoting information campaigns for public officials working in the main areas of immigration, including at the local level, and for the general public on the elimination of discrimination against migrants, and combat their social marginalization and stigmatization, including via the media.[270]

Interestingly, the Committee in question developed such a recommendation whereas the UN convention on migrant workers of 1990 does not mention the State duty to change public attitudes toward migrant workers. As a regional human rights mechanism, the Council of Europe Commissioner for Human Rights addressed Germany in 2007, proposing policy responses to right-wing extremist and xenophobic attitudes, encouraging the avoidance of stigmatising migrants, asylum seekers and ethnic or religious groups in the context of political discourse and explicitly acknowledging the positive contribution of immigrants in society.[271]

EQUALITY OF INDIGENOUS AND TRIBAL PEOPLES

The Convention concerning Indigenous and Tribal Peoples in Independent Countries, adopted by the International Labour Organization in 1989, demands States target prejudice against indigenous and tribal peoples.[272] In that regard, history textbooks and other educational materials are asked to provide accurate portrayal of these people:

> Article 31
> Educational measures shall be taken among all sections of the national community, and particularly among those that are in most direct contact with

268 The Durban Programme of Action in the World Conference against Racism, Racial Discrimination, Xenophobia and Related Intolerance, para. 27.
269 The Operational Plan relating to the Human Rights of Migrants, Foreigners and Refugees, UN Doc. E/CN.4/2002/94/Add.1, para. 81.
270 UN Doc. CMW/C/ECU/CO/1, para. 20.
271 UN Doc. A/HRC/WG.6/4/DEU/3, para. 18; Comm DH (2007) 14, paras 17–22.
272 The International Labour Organization Indigenous and Tribal Peoples Convention, article 31.

> the peoples concerned, with the object of eliminating prejudices that they may harbour in respect of these peoples. To this end, efforts shall be made to ensure that history textbooks and other educational materials provide a fair, accurate and informative portrayal of the societies and cultures of these peoples.[273]

The General Assembly of the United Nations adopted the United Nations Declaration of the Rights of Indigenous Peoples in October 2007.[274] The long-awaited Declaration appealed that cultures, traditions, histories and aspirations of indigenous peoples be appropriately reflected in education and public information,[275] urging States to ensure that State- and privately-owned media duly reflect indigenous cultural diversity.[276] More importantly, the UN Declaration requests the elimination of prejudice and the promotion of tolerance and understanding among all segments of society:

> Article 15
> States shall take effective measures, in consultation and cooperation with the indigenous peoples concerned, to combat prejudice and eliminate discrimination and to promote tolerance, understanding and good relations among indigenous peoples and all other segments of society.[277]

Both the International Labour Organization convention and the UN declaration strongly advise States to address prejudice in society and to take educational measures with a view to moulding social attitudes in favour of equality for indigenous people.

STATE COMPLIANCE

In the Universal Periodic Review, States such as Finland, Germany, Italy and the Netherlands have admitted that, in order to eradicate racial discrimination, a change of social attitudes is necessary.[278] For its part, Belgium agreed to condemn through political statements any manifestation of racism, discrimination, xenophobia and Islamophobia.[279] Some States have accepted suggestions derived from the interactive dialogues of the Universal Periodic Review and have agreed to target racial prejudice, stereotyping, xenophobia and hostile attitudes among their general public. These States included Belgium,[280] Bhutan,[281] Croatia,[282]

273 The International Labour Organization Indigenous and Tribal Peoples Convention, article 31.
274 UN Doc. A/RES/61/295.
275 The United Nations Declaration on the Rights of Indigenous Peoples, article 15 (1).
276 The United Nations Declaration on the Rights of Indigenous Peoples, article 16 (2).
277 The United Nations Declaration on the Rights of Indigenous Peoples, article 15 (2).
278 UN Doc. A/HRC/8/24, para. 25; UN Doc. A/HRC/WG.6/4/DEU/1, para. 30; UN Doc. A/HRC/14/4, para. 15; UN Doc. A/HRC/WG.6/13/NLD/1, para. 74.
279 UN Doc. A/HRC/18/3, para. 100, recommendation 7.
280 UN Doc. A/HRC/18/3, para. 100, recommendations 7, 31 and 33.
281 UN Doc. A/HRC/13/11, para. 101, recommendation 17.
282 UN Doc. A/HRC/16/13, para. 97, recommendation 27.

Denmark,[283] Lithuania,[284] Sweden[285] and Turkey.[286] Some showed willingness to work with the media, with a view to raising awareness and deepening understanding of human rights and racism, among them Belarus,[287] Belgium,[288] Bulgaria[289] and Nicaragua.[290] Some others assented to the request of providing human rights education and training for their population. These countries included Belgium,[291] Bhutan,[292] Bosnia and Herzegovina,[293] Brunei Darussalam,[294] Bulgaria,[295] Italy[296] and Lithuania.[297] More States have received similar recommendations at the very least.[298]

Under the Universal Periodic Review, a vast number of States have reported their progress in conducting educational measures to inform public opinion and fight against racial attitudes. Italy[299] and Switzerland[300] understood that governmental work for a successful interaction among cultures and beliefs is equally as important as legal measures to confront discriminatory attitudes. Portugal reported in 2009 that it had taken initiatives to raise mass media awareness on the topic of integration and the stigmatisation of immigrants and ethnic minorities; to increase the public awareness on tolerance and diversity through actions within the social, cultural, artistic and sporting arenas; and to raise public awareness in favour of integration and the promotion of interculturalism through weekly TV shows and radio programmes.[301] Greece and Slovakia both valued the power of the mass media in the formation of public opinion and subsequently sponsored media campaigns in the hope of having a positive impact on public opinion.[302] Some States have also developed programmes to combat racial attitudes, stereotypes, stigmatisation and prejudices, including the Czech Republic,[303] Denmark,[304]

283 UN Doc. A/HRC/18/4, para. 106, recommendation 71; UN Doc. A/HRC/18/4/Add.1, p. 7.
284 UN Doc. A/HRC/19/15, para. 88, recommendation 21.
285 UN Doc. A/HRC/15/11, para. 95, recommendation 29.
286 UN Doc. A/HRC/15/13, para. 101, recommendation 1.
287 UN Doc. A/HRC/15/16, para. 95, recommendation 51.
288 UN Doc. A/HRC/18/3, para. 100, recommendation 7.
289 UN Doc. A/HRC/16/9, para. 80, recommendation 84; UN Doc. A/HRC/16/9/Add.1, p. 2.
290 UN Doc. A/HRC/14/3, para. 90, recommendation 21.
291 UN Doc. A/HRC/18/3, para.100, recommendation 27.
292 UN Doc. A/HRC/13/11/Add.1, p. 3.
293 UN Doc. A/HRC/14/16, para. 90, recommendation 30; UN Doc. A/HRC/14/16/Add.1, para. 11.
294 UN Doc. A/HRC/13/14, para. 89, recommendation 9.
295 UN Doc. A/HRC/16/9, para. 80, recommendation 84; UN Doc. A/HRC/16/9/Add.1, p. 2.
296 UN Doc. A/HRC/14/4, para. 84, recommendation 30; UN Doc. A/HRC/14/4/Add.1, p.2.
297 UN Doc. A/HRC/19/15, para. 88, recommendation 22.
298 UN Doc. A/HRC/8/49, para. 58, recommendation 14; UN Doc. A/HRC/12/8, para. 49; UN Doc. A/HRC/21/9, para. 110, recommendation 59; UN Doc. A/HRC/12/8, para. 49; UN Doc. A/HRC/8/24, para. 46.
299 UN Doc. A/HRC/WG.6/7/ITA/1, para. 79.
300 UN Doc. A/HRC/WG.6/2/CHE/1, para. 39.
301 UN Doc. A/HRC/WG.6/6/PRT/1, para. 82.
302 UN Doc. CEDAW/C/GRC/6, Annex A, para. 2; UN Doc. CERD/C/419/Add.2, para. 53.
303 UN Doc. A/HRC/WG.6/14/CZE/1, paras 10 and 17.
304 UN Doc. A/HRC/18/4/Add.1, p. 6.

Finland,[305] Germany,[306] the Netherlands,[307] Romania,[308] Slovakia,[309] Slovenia[310] and Switzerland.[311]

It has increasingly been reported that such work was not just carried out merely on an *ad hoc* basis, but instead was deemed to be a long-term task for governmental bodies. In a self-evaluation of the Chamber of the Council of the Government of the Czech Republic for Roma Community Affairs of 2008, the Chamber expressed its contribution to the changing of public opinion and the creation of public support for the elimination of social exclusion, prejudice and stereotypes from the Roma community.[312] In 2011 the Czech Republic appointed crime prevention assistants in each municipal police force, tasked with helping to influence society's negative attitude toward socially excluded people.[313] Sweden designated a Discrimination Ombudsman, entrusting him with the task of altering public opinion and making it more tolerant.[314] By 2012 Finland had established seven regional Advisory Boards for Ethnic Relations, the functions of which are to assist and support regional and local authorities in building a favourable attitude climate.[315] As for Germany, one of the focal points of the German Federal Agency for Civil Education is tackling extremism through projects that encourage children and young people to actively influence the atmosphere in their schools, as expressed by the State in 2008.[316]

In a broader sense, Botswana envisages a better society in 2016 as a moral nation with high standards of tolerant social attitudes toward people of different ethnic traditions.[317] To date, many States have established national human rights institutions, with different mandates and roles. Some of them have been mandated to undertake measures designed to inform public opinion as is the case in Argentina,[318]

305 Finland Ministry of Education and Culture has supported a long-term No Racism (NoRa) Programme of Save the Children Finland. It is an anti-racism youth work web project with the goal to increase non-discrimination and to eradicate prejudice. UN Doc. CERD/C/FIN/20–22, para. 98; UN Doc. A/HRC/WG.6/13/FIN/2, para. 19; UN Doc. CERD/C/FIN/CO/19, para. 15.

306 UN Doc. A/HRC/WG.6/4/DEU/1, paras 30 and 36.

307 UN Doc. A/HRC/8/31, para. 11.

308 The government implemented SPER – Stop the Prejudices against the Roma Minority – Discrimination is Learned at Home, in 2004–2006. UN Doc. A/HRC/8/49/Add.1, para. 45.

309 UN Doc. A/HRC/12/17/Add.1, para. 19.

310 UN Doc. A/HRC/WG.6/7/SVN/1, para. 66.

311 UN Doc. A/HRC/WG.6/14/CHE/1, para. 65.

312 UN Doc. CCPR/C/CZE/CO/2/Add.1, para. 33.

313 UN Doc. A/HRC/WG.6/14/CZE/1, para. 17.

314 UN Doc. A/CONF.189/PC.1/8, para. 65.

315 UN Doc. A/HRC/WG.6/13/FIN/1, para. 69.

316 UN Doc. A/HRC/WG.6/4/DEU/1, para. 36.

317 UN Doc. A/HRC/WG.6/3/BWA/1, paras 119 and 120 (c).

318 Argentina National Institute to Combat Discrimination, Xenophobia and Racism (INADI) is endowed with the mandate to inform public opinion about discriminatory, xenophobic or racist attitudes or conduct on the part of public bodies or private persons.

Australia,[319] Fiji,[320] Germany,[321] Ghana,[322] Italy,[323] Mauritania[324] and Qatar.[325] Some can recommend their governments to do so, as is the case in Britain.[326]

Conclusions

International law requires States to take an independent stance on the issue of racial discrimination, as opposed to relying on the single majority opinion in society. It also endows States with legislative and educational means to tackle racial discrimination. These means play a large role in the leveraging of social attitudes toward ethnic equality. The principle of educating public opinion on ethnic equality was discussed in historical UN documents and was subsequently embodied in follow-up human rights instruments. According to the bodies that oversee the implementation of these instruments, it is clear that States have a duty to target racist attitudes, racial prejudice and stereotypes, and any other negative attitude based on ethnic background, and in fact possess an obligation to promote tolerance, understanding and the principle of ethnic equality in society. As to the extent States' acceptance of such a duty, considerable compliance and endorsement can be seen, although some States show a high degree of reservation about such a duty, in some cases bordering on overt neglect.

319 UN Doc. CERD/C/476/Add.2, para. 92.

320 UN Doc. A/HRC/WG.6/7/FJI/1, para. 24.

321 Germany considered the German Institute for Human Rights contributes substantially to the process of shaping public opinion on all issues relevant to the question of human rights. UN Doc. A/HRC/WG.6/4/EDU/1, para. 15.

322 UN Doc. A/HRC/WG.6/2/GHA/1, para. 19.

323 UN Doc. CERD/C/ITA/15, para. 315.

324 The National Commission for Human Rights of Mauritania is responsible for raising awareness of human rights and of the combat against all forms of discrimination and violations of human dignity, in particular racial discrimination, slavery like practices and discrimination against women, by sensitizing the public through information, communication and education and by using the media in all its forms. UN Doc. A/HRC/WG.6/9/MRT/1, para. 37.

325 Qatar reported its plan to establish the National Human Rights Committee with a function to educate public opinion in 2001. The Committee was set up in 2002. UN Doc. CERD/C/360/Add.1, para. 73; UN Doc. A/HRC/WG.6/7/QAT/1, p. 12.

326 The Equality and Human Rights Commission, Great Britain's National Human Rights Institution motivated by European Convention on Human Rights, recommend its governments to educate public opinion on the subject of prison system. UN Doc. A/HRC/13/NI/4, Annex, UK Government UPR Mid-Term Report: Report from the Equality and Human Rights Commission, Recommendation 1, para. 6.

3 Public opinion and women's equality

The United Nations declares its faith in gender equality in the preamble of its Charter that '[w]e the peoples of the United Nations determined [. . .] to reaffirm faith [. . .] in the equal rights of men and women.' Viewing public attitudes as a key factor in the progress toward or even the achievement of gender equality, the UN Sub-Commission and Commission on the Status of Women have encouraged member States to collaborate with and offer support to the UN in order to stimulate global public opinions on the matter since the late 1940s.[1] Between the 1950s and 1960s, the role of UN bodies and NGOs in moulding public opinion in favour of gender equality has consistently been stressed. This was initially seen in 1950 when the Economic and Social Council urged the Secretary-General of the United Nations and the Director-General of UNESCO to promote throughout the world perceptions that favoured equal education opportunities for both sexes.[2] The role of NGOs in creating informed public opinion with regard to women's equality was continuously acknowledged by the Commission on the Status of Women and the Economic and Social Council throughout the same period.[3] In 1960 the Economic and Social Council and the Commission on the Status of Women began to underline the significance of national advisory committees in providing education for public opinion based around questions relating to human rights.[4] The Economic and Social Council in 1961 stressed the importance of action taken to change social attitudes with regard to discrimination against women, specifically in the fields of employment and occupation.[5]

1 The Sub-Commission on the Status of Women was established in February 1946 and was conferred with the status of a full commission four months later. UN Doc. E/20, p. 4; UN Doc. E/27, p. 3; UN Doc. E/90; UN Doc. E/84, para. 6.
2 UN Doc. E/Res/304(XI), p. 32; UN Doc. E/1849, p. 32.
3 Subjects cover working mothers with family responsibilities, equal pay for equal work and the advancement of women in developing countries, etc. UN Doc. E/Res/445(XIV), E; UN Doc. E/Res/504(XVI), G; UN Doc. E/Res/587(XX), C; UN Doc. E/Res/680(XXVI), C; UN Doc. E/Res/884(XXXIV), E.
4 The draft resolution was presented by seven States: Austria, Denmark, France, Lebanon, the Philippines, the United Kingdom and Venezuela. UN Doc. E/3335, para. 43. The submission was adopted by the Commission on Human Rights and the Economic, Social and Cultural Council in UN Doc. E/Res/772(XXX), B; UNCHR Res 2 (XVI), UN Doc. E/3335, para. 50 and p. 30.
5 UN Doc. E/Res/821(XXXII), IV, A; UN Doc. E/Res/IV, p. 21.

The Declaration on the Elimination of Discrimination against Women, which was adopted by the General Assembly of the United Nations in 1967, expected full responsibility from States to engage in educating public opinion through the employment of all appropriate measures.[6] Following the Declaration's adoption, the Commission on the Status of Women adopted a series of resolutions in the 1970s, encouraging States to mobilise public opinion in support of raising women's status. In 1979 the Convention on the Elimination of All Forms of Discrimination against Women was adopted by the General Assembly of the United Nations,[7] declaring that the State has a duty to eliminate gender prejudice and the idea of the gender inferiority or stereotyped roles of women. After the Convention entered into force, its supervisory body, the Committee on the Elimination of Discrimination against Women, identified three areas of public opinion in which States were to take educational measures for the sake of raising public awareness and changing societal attitudes toward gender equality.

The areas of concern identified by the Committee on the Elimination of Discrimination against Women were supported by the Human Rights Committee and the Committee on the Rights of the Child. The three treaty bodies developed the same principles, based on various women's rights provisions, including: the principle of non-discrimination; the rights to health, life, liberty and security of the person; the participation of women in political and public life; and States' temporary special measures and their duty to eradicate prejudice and sex role stereotyping. This goes some way to suggest that the State's duty to lead public opinion on gender equality constitutes the logical consequence of upholding women's rights. Toward this understanding, States have demonstrated considerable compliance in various human rights mechanisms, including the newly established Universal Periodic Review.

Historic UN resolutions: a subsidiary role of States

To collaborate with and support the UN to stimulate world public opinion

Soon after its establishment in 1946, the Sub-Commission on the Status of Women proposed a policy to stimulate world public opinion in favour of promoting the status of women.[8] It expected full collaboration and support from member States of the United Nations.[9] The draft policy appealed to the notion:

> That world public opinion be stimulated in favour of raising the status of women as an instrument to further human rights and peace. The Sub-Commission also recommends that in view of the fact that the governments

6 The Declaration on the Elimination of Discrimination against Women, article 3. UN Doc. A/RES/2263.

7 The Convention on the Elimination of All Forms of Discrimination against Women, article 5 (a).

8 UN Doc. E/HR/18 and Rev.1, p. 5; UN Doc. E/38/Rev.1, pp. 18–19.

9 UN Doc. E/HR/18 and Rev.1, p. 5; UN Doc. E/38/Rev.1, pp. 18–19.

> of all the United Nations in signing the Charter recognized that one of its principal aims, as stated in the Preamble, was 'to reaffirm faith in fundamental human rights, in the dignity and worth of the human person, in the equal rights of men and women and of nations large and small', the Sub-Commission on the Status of Women expects the full collaboration and support of the governments of all the United Nations in their endeavours to raise the status of women throughout the world.[10]

States were clearly expected to play a subsidiary role to the Sub-Commission on the Status of Women in the stimulation of world public opinion through this formulation. To justify its expectation of State collaboration and support, the Sub-Commission stated that all the UN member States endorsed the UN Charter which, in its preamble, enshrines the principle of gender equality. In addition to the draft policy, the Sub-Commission also put forward a programme of work that intended to 'create a worldwide public opinion [favourable to women] through the media of the press, radio, publications, lectures, motion pictures, etc.'.[11]

The draft work programme was controversial. Members of the Commission on Human Rights questioned whether the Sub-Commission possessed the ability to undertake such an ambitious task.[12] René Cassin and Eleanor Roosevelt each submitted a draft resolution for the Commission on Human Rights to consider.[13] René Cassin recommended that the Economic and Social Council 'draw the attention of the government of all Member States to the principles stated in the report of the Sub-Commission', which included both the draft policy and the draft work programme.[14] This proposal was backed by the Chairman of the Sub-Commission on the Status of Women, who hoped that the draft work programme would be kept in the Sub-Commission's terms of reference.[15] Eleanor Roosevelt's other draft resolution omitted the work programmes proposed by the Sub-Commission.[16] The Commission on Human Rights and the Economic and Social Council adopted Roosevelt's proposal which did not include the work programme but granted the Sub-Commission on the Status of Women the mandate to stimulate world public opinion with the support of States.[17]

The Sub-Commission was soon conferred with the status of a full commission in 1946.[18] The Commission on the Status of Women reaffirmed its guiding principles and aims for future work, declaring:

10 UN Doc. E/HR/18 and Rev.1, p. 5; UN Doc. E/38/Rev.1, pp. 18–19.
11 UN Doc. E/HR/18, II. Programme, point 7, p. 6; UN Doc. E/HR/18/Rev.1, p. 7; UN Doc. E/38/Rev.1, p. 20.
12 UN Doc. E/HR/24, p. 3.
13 UN Doc. E/HR/25.
14 UN Doc. E/HR/25, Memorandum I, point 2 (c), p. 2; UN Doc. E/HR/25, Draft, recommendation 3, p. 6.
15 UN Doc. E/HR/24, pp. 3–4.
16 UN Doc. E/HR/25, Memorandum II, recommendation 1, p. 3.
17 UN Doc. E/38 and Rev.1, p. 12; UN Doc. A/125, pp. 35–36.
18 UN Doc. E/90; UN Doc. E/84, para. 6.

> [t]hat world public opinion be stimulated in favour of raising the status of women as an instrument for promoting human rights and peace . . . The Commission on the status of Women expects the full collaboration and support of the governments of all Member States of the United Nations in their endeavours to raise the status of women throughout the world.[19]

In judging the performance of the Commission on the Status of Women in 1962, Hernán Santa Cruz, the Special Rapporteur of the Sub-Commission on Prevention of Discrimination, deemed that the Commission had played a leading role in educating public opinion toward acceptance of the principles of women's political rights.[20]

Means of influencing public opinion

The Commission on the Status of Women issued a series of resolutions in the late 1940s in order to implement its policy of triggering world public opinion. These resolutions intensively discussed means of influencing public opinion and underlined the importance of disseminating relevant information. However, most recommendations were made to different UN bodies as each body was considered primarily responsible for its own task. For example, under the title of 'influencing public opinion' in 1948, the Commission recommended that the Economic and Social Council prepare a popular pamphlet on women's political rights and grant permission for the Commission to offer information assistance for women's groups in need.[21] Endorsing this recommendation, the Economic and Social Council considered 'the need to influence public opinion in favour of equality between men and women', subsequently requesting the Secretary-General to prepare such a pamphlet and provide information assistance.[22]

The theme of encouraging public opinion was raised again at the third session of the Commission on the Status of Women in 1949, where Mexico and Syria put forward draft resolutions on the issue. Mexico requested the Secretary-General to publish a quarterly bulletin containing all the relevant information, including:

> (a) all the resolutions and recommendations adopted by the various organs of the United Nations and its Specialized Agencies relating to the status of women;
> (b) the action taken by these organs and agencies on the subject; and
> (c) information about the progress of women in the different countries.[23]

Syria proposed that States prepare biographies of famous female figures in their countries and ensure that these biographies were disseminated through all

19 UN Doc. E/281/Rev.1, p. 14.
20 UN Doc. E/CN.4/Sub.2/213/Rev.1, p. 31.
21 UN Doc. E/615, para. 37.
22 UN Doc. A/625, paras 143–144 and 149.
23 UN Doc. E/CN.6/116.

available channels.[24] The Commission on the Status of Women adopted the recommendations of Mexico and Syria and forwarded them to member States of the United Nations and to the Secretary-General in 1949.[25] The Economic and Social Council reached a general consensus that it had previously authorised the UN Secretary-General to 'take adequate measures for influencing public opinion regarding the status of women'.[26] Accordingly, the Economic and Social Council decided to take no action on this matter in 1949.[27]

Although its predecessor, the Sub-Commission on the Status of Women, had not succeeded in including it in its terms of reference, the Commission on the Status of Women discussed the possibility of working with the media during the session concerned with 'influencing public opinion' in 1948.[28] The Commission and the Economic and Social Council, reiterating the priority of influencing world public opinion, both suggested that UN bodies 'call upon the world press, radio, film and other information agencies to help in removing . . . prejudices'.[29] The role of States was neglected in these resolutions and recommendations.

The Declaration on the Elimination of Discrimination against Women and its implementation: to educate public opinion

The Declaration: to take all appropriate measures to educate public opinion

In 1967, the Declaration on the Elimination of Discrimination against Women was adopted by the UN General Assembly after four years of negotiations.[30] Article 3 of the Declaration calls on States (as well as other stakeholders) to take all appropriate measures to educate public opinion, elevating their secondary role in stimulating world public opinion:

> Article 3, Declaration of the Elimination of Discrimination against Women: All appropriate measures shall be taken to educate public opinion and to direct national aspirations towards the eradication of prejudice and the abolition of customary and all other practices which are based on the idea of the inferiority of women.[31]

This poses two questions regarding public opinion: (1) Should governments educate public opinion, and (2) can the education of public opinion be considered as an international principle or merely a goal established for the future?

24 UN Doc. E/CN.6/117.
25 UN Doc. A/972, para. 246.
26 UN Doc. A/972, para. 246.
27 UN Doc. A/972, para. 246.
28 UN Doc. E/38 and Rev.1, pp. 12–13; UN Doc. A/125, pp. 35–36.
29 UN Doc. E/615, para. 37; UN Doc. A/625, para. 149.
30 UN Doc. A/Res/1921(XVIII); UN Doc. A/Res/2263(XXII).
31 UN Doc. A/Res/2263(XXII).

Whether States should educate public opinion

To incorporate the education of public opinion in the Declaration on the Elimination of Discrimination against Women was not a decision made easily. In the negotiation period, States' attitudes were quite divided. Some endorsed the practical value of educating public opinion, including the representative of the Netherlands who stated that issues such as prostitution cannot be resolved purely by legislation, but should be approached through the education of public opinion.[32] The representative also said that 'all legislative measures would remain ineffective unless backed by enlightened public opinion.'[33] As a result, the Netherlands called for a worldwide social movement to enlighten public opinion.[34] The Swedish representative also favoured an effort to influence minds through the use of all possible means to inform public opinion.[35] She stated:

> It was public opinion which was most to blame for the persistence of prejudice and discrimination . . . The fight to end discrimination against women was therefore primarily a psychological one. The battle had to be fought at the level of public opinion, the habits and ways of thinking which decisively influenced ways of life.[36]

Pakistan concluded that it possessed experience in mobilising public support through the scrapping of ancient taboos.[37] Sweden and Lesotho emphasised the importance of education and all kinds of media in leading public opinion.[38]

Objections were also expressed in the negotiation. India claimed that 'although the ultimate aim was clear, public opinion and the sentiment of various sectors of the population had to be respected and the climate prepared for changes.'[39] The representative further contended that '[a]ny social change should be brought about by a change in public opinion before being established by law.'[40] India's view found opposition from a number of States. Jamaica considered certain customs as 'so inhuman and degrading that their direct eradication by Governments was justified' without consulting public opinion.[41] Offering a different perspective, Tanzania asserted that time-honoured practices require 'patient action based on education, appeals to public opinion and persuasion'.[42]

The negotiations resulted in a final text of the Declaration on the Elimination of Discrimination against Women which appealed to all States, institutions and

32 UN Doc. A/C.3/SR.1442, para. 13.
33 UN Doc. A/C.3/SR.1442, para. 12.
34 UN Doc. A/C.3/SR.1442, para. 17.
35 UN Doc. A/C.3/SR.1442, para. 47.
36 UN Doc. A/C.3/SR.1442, para. 46.
37 UN Doc. A/C.3/SR.1470, para. 42.
38 UN Doc. A/C.3/SR.1442, para. 47; UN Doc. A/PV.1597, para. 81.
39 UN Doc. E/AC.7/SR.540, p. 10.
40 UN Doc. A/C.3/SR.1443, para. 31.
41 UN Doc. A/C.3/SR.1477, para. 7; UN Doc. A/C.3/SR.1471, para. 8.
42 UN Doc. E/AC.7/SR.542, p. 14.

individuals who saw fit to take appropriate measures in order to mobilise public opinion on gender equality. The Declaration itself was considered an excellent instrument in educating public opinion by the Commission on the Elimination of Discrimination against Women[43] and by a number of States including Côte d'Ivoire, Ghana, Iran, Luxembourg, Nepal and the United States.[44] It was envisaged that the Declaration would set high international standards and guide governments with respect to their responsibilities on a national level.[45] China, however, rejected the assertion that the purpose of the Declaration was to serve as a guide for domestic legislations in influencing public opinion through instruction and education.[46]

The education of public opinion: a principle or goal for the future

There existed a debate on whether the Declaration was to enumerate basic principles or to set goals for the future. At the 41st session of the Economic and Social Council in 1966, France and India questioned the style of the draft Declaration, considering it more suitable to a convention rather than a declaration which typically ought to be a collection of general principles.[47] Luxembourg disagreed with this view, convinced that the draft Declaration was 'universal, clear and simple', containing 'fundamental principles without going into too many details'.[48] Besides the question of its style, the crux of the matter was that if the Declaration only intended to set goals for the future, in practice, its use would be very limited as it was almost impossible to define when the 'future' began. The Soviet Union, the United States and the United Kingdom all argued about the value of the Declaration in creating goals for this ill-defined temporal scope.[49] According to their statements, the Declaration should 'rather look to the future and aim at setting standards to be achieved in all countries with the least possible delay'.[50] The United Kingdom further suggested that a preambular clause be added, as 'the achievement of its aims might take a long time in some countries'.[51] Furthermore, the United Kingdom did not think that a subsequent convention was needed.[52]

43 UN Doc. E/AC.7/SR.539, p. 9; UN Doc. E/4175, para. 21.
44 UN Doc. E/CN.6/447, pp. 5–6; UN Doc. E/AC.7/SR.540, p. 6; UN Doc. E/AC.7/SR.540, p. 12; UN Doc. A/C.3/SR.1443, para. 10; UN Doc. A/C.3/SR.1471, para. 36; UN Doc. A/C.3/SR.1480, para. 15.
45 UN Doc. A/6003, para. 510; UN Doc. A/6303, para. 499; UN Doc. E/AC.7/SR.540, pp. 6, 7, 10, 12 and 17; UN Doc. E/AC.7/SR.539, p. 10; UN Doc. E/AC.7/SR.539, p. 9; UN Doc. E/4175, para. 21.
46 UN Doc. A/C.3/SR.1475, para. 8.
47 UN Doc. E/AC.7/SR.540, p. 15.
48 UN Doc. E/AC.7/SR.540, p. 12.
49 UN Doc. A/6303, para. 500; UN Doc. E/AC.7/SR.542, p. 4; UN Doc. E/AC.7/SR.540, pp. 7 and 16.
50 UN Doc. A/6303, para. 500.
51 UN Doc. E/AC.7/SR.540, p. 16.
52 UN Doc. E/AC.7/SR.540, p. 17.

It is not necessary to conclude that the United Kingdom and its colleagues had any intention of delaying the implementation of the Declaration, although the subjective language of 'setting goals' or 'taking a long time' did leave the door open to interpretation. For this reason, the Declaration on the Elimination of Discrimination against Women did not adopt the suggestions put forward by these States. After the Declaration was adopted by the General Assembly of the United Nations in 1967, its provisions including article 3 became widely regarded as fundamental principles in protecting the promotion of women's rights.

Implementation: to mobilise public opinion in support of gender equality

The mobilisation of public opinion

Following the adoption of the Declaration on the Elimination of Discrimination against Women, the Commission on the Status of Women intensively discussed the mobilisation of public opinion and the use of the mass media therein throughout the 1970s. These statements and resolutions were strongly supported by member States of the United Nations. In 1972 the Chairman of the 24th session of the Commission on the Status of Women announced that '[a] concerted international effort was needed to mobilise public opinion in support of' women's equality in all fields.[53] Many States sided with the Chairman, including Canada,[54] Chile,[55] Costa Rica,[56] Egypt,[57] Iran,[58] Iraq,[59] Tunisia[60] and the United Kingdom,[61] which appealed for a change in public attitude toward births out of wedlock,[62] equal pay for equal work,[63] family planning,[64] male superiority[65] and other traditional discriminatory attitudes and cultural patterns against women.[66]

Specifically, Canada pleaded 'to bring about a balance in those social attitudes' toward social responsibility for births out of wedlock.[67] Egypt underlined 'the need to bring about a change in the psychological attitude of women themselves', regarding the notion of equal pay for equal work.[68] The United Kingdom agreed that 'there had to be a change in attitude toward women's work on the

53 UN Doc. E/CN.6/MIN., p. 11.
54 UN Doc. E/CN.6/MIN., p. 172.
55 UN Doc. E/CN.6/MIN., p. 80.
56 UN Doc. E/CN.6/MIN., p. 195.
57 UN Doc. E/CN.6/MIN., p. 56.
58 UN Doc. E/CN.6/MIN., p. 66.
59 UN Doc. E/CN.6/MIN., p. 138.
60 UN Doc. E/CN.6/MIN., p. 137.
61 UN Doc. E/CN.6/MIN., p. 57.
62 UN Doc. E/CN.6/MIN., p. 172.
63 UN Doc. E/CN.6/MIN., pp. 56 and 57.
64 UN Doc. E/CN.6/MIN., pp. 137, 138 and 195.
65 UN Doc. E/CN.6/MIN., pp. 137 and 195.
66 UN Doc. E/CN.6/MIN., pp. 66 and 80.
67 UN Doc. E/CN.6/MIN., p. 172.
68 UN Doc. E/CN.6/MIN., p. 56.

part of the public', while Iran opined that a key method to eradicate discrimination against women was to 'change the traditional attitudes which were deeply ingrained among both men and women'.[69] Chile considered that cultural patterns were responsible for attitudes toward women, possessing a secondary role that was subject to change.[70] Costa Rica,[71] Iraq[72] and Tunisia[73] commented on the necessity for a change in men's attitude towards family planning and male superiority. The role played by NGOs in the mobilisation of public opinion was also noted in the discussion.[74]

As early as 1968, the Economic and Social Council of the United Nations had invited States to promote the recognition of principles of the Declaration on the Elimination of Discrimination against Women and to design programmes to give effect to them.[75] The Council reviewed the progress of States in 1974 and commended their efforts in raising public awareness and understanding of the principles contained within the Declaration through the press and other mass media, as well as schools and educational institutions.[76] Compliance with the provisions of the Declaration through law and State practice was also encouraged.[77] The Economic and Social Council additionally held that prevailing societal attitudes toward stereotyped gender roles were serious obstacles to the implementation of the Declaration.[78]

The media

The media have played a central role in women's liberation movements since the 1970s.[79] The Economic and Social Council appointed a Special Rapporteur to study the impact of the mass media on the changing roles of men and women in 1978.[80] Prior to this, the Commission on the Status of Women reviewed the relationship between the media and the formulation of new attitudes toward women at its 24th and 25th sessions in 1972 and 1974 respectively. At its session in 1972, the Commission on the Status of Women dedicated a few sections to the topic, entitled 'influence of mass communication media on the formation of a new attitude toward the role of women in society'.[81] In these sections, Spain expressed doubts concerning the effectiveness of legal measures in the shaping

69 UN Doc. E/CN.6/MIN., pp. 57 and 66.
70 UN Doc. E/CN.6/MIN., p. 80.
71 UN Doc. E/CN.6/MIN., p. 195.
72 UN Doc. E/CN.6/MIN., p. 138.
73 UN Doc. E/CN.6/MIN., p. 137.
74 UN Doc. E/CN.6/MIN., p. 182.
75 ECOSOC Res 1325 (XLIV) (31 May 1968).
76 ECOSOC Res 1852 (LVI) (16 May 1974).
77 ECOSOC Res 1852 (LVI) (16 May 1974).
78 ECOSOC Res 1852 (LVI) (16 May 1974).
79 Carolyn M. Byerly and Karen Ross, *Women and Media: A Critical Introduction* (Blackwell Publishing 2006).
80 ECOSOC Dec 1978/36, UN Doc. E/1978/78, p. 38.
81 UN Doc. E/CN.6/MIN., pp. 88 and 176; UN Doc. E/CN.6/L.610, p. 1.

of irrational attitudes.[82] After a discussion on the matter, the Commission paid heed to the influence of mass communication media on the formation of a social attitude that leads to discrimination against women and, on the suggestion of Chile, Colombia, Costa Rica and the Dominican Republic, requested member States to conduct studies on this subject.[83]

The Commission on the Status of Women continued to analyse the relationship between the mass media and the formation of new attitudes toward women's role at its 25th session in 1974. A report from the Secretary-General of the United Nations revealed that the mass media not only reflected the most prevalent social conceptions within a community, but also instigated trends and exponents of new movements and changing values.[84] The United Kingdom found that the mass media were responsible for the waves of crime and violence throughout the world, referring to television in particular.[85] The Dominican Republic noted that unless the negative image of women portrayed by the mass media were modified, very little progress could be attained in the promotion of the status of women, although it realised that its opinion was controversial, in the sense that it opposed fundamental freedoms of expression.[86]

In endorsing the importance of the subject, States made suggestions on how the mass media might serve to influence public opinion with respect to gender equality.[87] Belgium,[88] the Dominican Republic,[89] Kenya,[90] Liberia,[91] Norway[92] and the Philippines[93] requested their fellow States to exert pressure on the media in order to mould public opinion. The United Kingdom favoured action at the national level since '[i]n the first instance it was up to Governments to influence attitudes toward women in the mass media by indirect means; that implied a gradual re-orientation of government attitudes toward specific problems: such as women and employment.'[94]

The Convention on the Elimination of All Forms of Discrimination against Women: to eliminate stereotypes and prejudice

The year 1979 was an important one for the protection and promotion of women's rights, witnessing the adoption of the Convention on the Elimination of All Forms of Discrimination against Women by the United Nations General Assembly. The

82 UN Doc. E/CN.6/MIN., p. 167.
83 UN Doc. E/CN.6/MIN., p. 80; UN Doc. E/CN.6/L.600, pp. 1–2.
84 UN Doc. E/CN.6/SR.623, p. 110.
85 UN Doc. E/CN.6/SR.624, p. 122.
86 UN Doc. E/CN.6/SR.624, p. 116.
87 UN Doc. E/CN.6/SR.623, pp. 109–110.
88 UN Doc. E/CN.6/SR.623, p. 110.
89 UN Doc. E/CN.6/SR.624, p. 116.
90 UN Doc. E/CN.6/SR.624, p. 118.
91 UN Doc. E/CN.6/SR.624, p. 117.
92 UN Doc. E/CN.6/SR.623, p. 111.
93 UN Doc. E/CN.6/SR.624, p. 115.
94 UN Doc. E/CN.6/SR.624, p. 122.

text of the Convention was prepared by working groups from the Commission on the Status of Women during 1976 and was also intensively deliberated on by a working group of the Third Committee of the General Assembly from 1977 to 1979.[95] The Convention entered into force in 1981, which was much more quickly than any previous human rights convention had done.[96] By April 2014, the Convention had 188 State parties, achieving nearly universal ratification.

The content of the Convention on the Elimination of All Forms of Discrimination against Women was described by analysts as 'universal in reach, comprehensive in scope and legally binding in character'.[97] According to the Committee on the Elimination of All Forms of Discrimination against Women, the supervisory body of the Convention on the Elimination of All Forms of Discrimination against Women, the Convention is the only human rights treaty that specifically targets culture and tradition as influential forces in shaping gender roles and family relations. In article 5 (a), it expects States to play an active role in the process of targeting gender prejudice and sex role stereotyping:

> States Parties shall take all appropriate measures:
> (a) To modify the social and cultural patterns of conduct of men and women, with a view to achieving the elimination of prejudices and customary and all other practices which are based on the idea of the inferiority or the superiority of either of the sexes or on stereotyped roles for men and women.

The Convention on the Elimination of All Forms of Discrimination against Women hereby delivers an essential message that 'the formal prohibition of discrimination is insufficient to redress its inherited consequences'.[98]

The disappearance of educating public opinion

The Convention on the Elimination of All Forms of Discrimination against Women had its genesis in the Declaration on the Elimination of Discrimination against Women yet the role of education in shaping public opinion was omitted. This was due to a clash in the negotiations between opposing blocs led by the Soviet Union and the United States. Prior to the clash, about 10 draft conventions were written, expressing the obligation that States should take all necessary measures to educate public opinion on women's rights. These drafts were submitted by Benin, Canada, Indonesia, Pakistan, the Philippines, the Soviet Union, the United Kingdom, the All-African Women's Conference and the Working Group of the Commission on the Status of Women.[99] Some of these

95 UN Doc. A/CONF.177/7, para. 12.
96 UN Doc. A/CONF.177/7, para. 13.
97 Rebecca J. Cook, 'Reservations to the Convention on the Elimination of All Forms of Discrimination against Women' (1990) 30 *Virginia Journal of International Law* 643, 643.
98 UN Doc. A/CONF.177/7, para. 20.
99 UN Doc. E/CN.6/AC.1/L.6, p. 3; UN Doc. E/CN.6/606, p. 2; UN Doc. E/CN.6/573, para. 96, Annex 1, p. 2; UN Doc. E/CN.6/AC.1/L.2, p. 4; UN Doc. E/CN.6/AC.1/L.4, p. 2; UN

States proposed the use of the same wording as article 3 of the Declaration on the Elimination of Discrimination against Women, including Benin, Indonesia, Pakistan, the United Kingdom and the All-African Women's Conference.[100] The Philippines and the Soviet Union rephrased the language but retained the expressions 'educating public opinion' and 'preparing public opinion'.[101] Under Canada's observation, the education of the general public had not been mentioned by existing conventions and should be dealt with by any new convention adopted.[102]

As the debate raged on, States became divided into two blocs headed by the Soviet Union and the United States. Mexico flatly objected to the text reading 'to educate public opinion', concluding that the acceptance of such a provision would nevertheless be difficult, at the 26th session of the Commission on the Status of Women in 1976.[103] Mexico presented an alternative text, which stated that:

> State Parties shall take all appropriate measures to modify the social and cultural patterns of conduct of men and women with a view to achieving the elimination of prejudices and customary and all other practices which are based on the idea of the inferiority or the superiority of either of the sexes or on stereotyped roles for men and women.[104]

Mexico's proposal was favoured by Belgium, Colombia, Cuba, Denmark, Egypt, France, India, Sweden, the United Kingdom and the United States.[105] Responding to the proposal, the Soviet Union did not insist on its own views on the text of educating public opinion; its focus was to add protection of motherhood to the same article.[106]

Doc. E/CN.6/AC.1/L.4/Corr.1; UN Doc. E/CN.6/591, pp. 84, 92, 101 and 112; UN Doc. E/CN.6/589, Annex III.

100 Pakistan only made a small grammar change. UN Doc. E/CN.6/AC.1/L.6, p. 3; UN Doc. E/CN.6/606, p. 2; UN Doc. E/CN.6/591, pp. 84, 92, 101 and 112.

101 Article 4 of the Philippines' draft convention:

> 1. States Parties undertake to adopt immediate, effective appropriate measures, particularly in the fields of teaching, education, culture and information, with a view to educating public opinion and to directing national aspirations towards the eradication of prejudice and the abolition of customary and all other practices which are based on the idea of inferiority of women.

UN Doc. E/CN.6/573, Annex 1, p. 2.

Article 6 of the Working Paper submitted by the Soviet Union:

> The State Parties shall adopt all necessary measures with a view to preparing public opinion for the complete eradication of prejudices, customs and all other practices based on the concept of the inferiority of women and for recognition of motherhood as a social function.

UN Doc. E/CN.6/AC.1/L.2, p. 4.

The Philippines and the Soviet Union jointly submitted two drafts of the Convention. One used the wording 'to preparing public opinion' and another one adopted the phrase 'to educating public opinion'. UN Doc. E/CN.6/AC.1/L.4, p. 2; UN Doc. E/CN.6/AC.1/L.4/Corr.1.

102 UN Doc. E/CN.6/573, paras 56 and 96.

103 UN Doc. E/CN.6/SR.636, para.2.

104 UN Doc. E/CN.6/SR.636, para.2.

105 UN Doc. E/CN.6/SR.636, paras 5, 7, 9, 10, 11, 13, 24, 18–20 and 23.

106 UN Doc. E/CN.6/SR.636, paras 6 and 9.

Egypt suggested that the use of educational measures be further specified in Mexico's proposal, and submitted alternative phrasings such as: 'States Parties shall take all appropriate educational measures to modify' or 'States Parties shall take all appropriate measures, notably educational, to modify'.[107] Egypt submitted the proposal on the legal basis of article 3 of the Declaration on the Elimination of Discrimination against Women on the State duty to direct national aspirations toward the eradication of prejudice.[108] Egypt's suggestion was objected to by some States, basing their opposition on the argument that education in a number of countries fell within the remit of local authorities, existing beyond the reach of the central government.[109] Mexico's amendment was adopted by the Commission on the Status of Women and the Working Group of the Third Committee of the UN General Assembly, an amendment which saw the provisions concerning the education of public opinion omitted from the Convention on the Elimination of All Forms of Discrimination against Women.[110] However, the Soviet Union in the negotiation, and academic commentators after the adoption of the Convention, still held that the principle of educating public opinion was embodied in article 5 of the Convention and constituted a central theme of the provision.[111]

In view of the drafting history, the phrase 'to educate public opinion' was deleted from article 5 because the majority of States were nervous about such wording. Nonetheless, they agreed on taking actions to deal with elements of public opinion that are inconsistent with the standard of women's equality. These include prejudice and the idea of the inferiority or the superiority of either of the sexes or on stereotyped roles for men and women. States also agreed on the promotion of a proper understanding of maternity as a social function and the recognition of the common responsibility of men and women in the upbringing and development of their children. Without naming public opinion, States adopted a less controversial way to voice that they bear a duty to influence public opinion for the purpose of targeting discrimination against women.

Sex role stereotyping and prejudice

Although the final text of the Convention on the Elimination of All Forms of Discrimination against Women fails to mention public opinion, it nevertheless demands States address gender stereotyping and prejudice, specifically in two respects. First, the social and cultural patterns of conduct of men and women should be modified, requiring States to exert their moral influence on tradition,

107 UN Doc. E/CN.6/SR.636, para. 27.

108 UN Doc. E/CN.6/SR.636, para. 40.

109 UN Doc. E/CN.6/SR.636, paras 33, 38 and 39.

110 UN Doc. E/CN.6/SR.636, paras 39 and 41; UN Doc. A/C.3/32/WG.1/CRP.7/Add.5; UN Doc. A/C.3/32/WG.1/CRP.9, pp. 7–8.

111 UN Doc. E/CN.6/SR.638, para. 4; Lars Adam Rehof, *Guide to the Travaux Préparatoires of the United Nations Convention on the Elimination of All Forms of Discrimination against Women* (Martinus Nijhoff 1993) 79.

culture and customs (article 5 (a)). Second, these gender role stereotypes and prejudice need to be broken through education, either in the form of school education (article 10 (c)) or family education (article 5 (c)). In these circumstances, States may occasionally find themselves challenged by the strength of tradition, culture and customs, but it is a matter of principle for the State to assert itself in the face of such obstacles if they contribute to the perpetration of sex role stereotypes and prejudice. States also have a duty to ensure that the idea of gender equality is included in family education. Although family education exists within the boundary of private life and concerns the rights of parents, this provision can hardly be construed as an infringement.

Tradition, culture and customs

The Convention on the Elimination of All Forms of Discrimination against Women stresses in its preamble that 'a change in the traditional role of men as well as the role of women in society and in the family is needed to achieve full equality between men and women'. It goes on to state in article 5 (a) that States shall 'modify the social and cultural patterns of conduct of men and women', in order to eliminate prejudices and customary and other practices based on the idea of the inferiority or stereotyped roles of women. The general thrust of these provisions gives formal recognition to the influence of culture, tradition and customs on the generation and continuation of gender prejudices and stereotyped sex roles. It acknowledges that culture, tradition and customs can give rise to the multitude of legal, political and economic constraints on the advancement of women in society, serving to restrict women's enjoyment of their fundamental rights.

TRADITION

Prior to the preparation of the Convention on the Elimination of All Forms of Discrimination against Women, the Economic and Social Council advised States in 1968 to study the rapid evolution of the traditional roles of men and women with regard to their participation in the family and society.[112] In 1974, the Economic and Social Council found that stereotyped sex roles were serious obstacles to the implementation of the Declaration on the Elimination of Discrimination against Women.[113] In the same year, Canada entreated the Convention on the Elimination of All Forms of Discrimination against Women to discontinue merely prohibiting advocacy on the inferiority of women, but to overtly oppose stereotyped roles for women.[114]

During the preparation of the Convention on the Elimination of All Forms of Discrimination against Women, a number of statements based on tradition were

112 ECOSOC Res 1325 (XLIV) (31 May 1968).
113 ESOCOC Res 1852 (LVI) (16 May 1974).
114 UN Doc. E/CN.6/AC.1/L.6, pp. 2–3.

not adopted. This includes the statement made by Iraq that equal employment opportunities between men and women weaken the family structure as established in Iraq and the statement of Iran that it is not compatible with Iranian law.[115] Preparation proceeded without Egypt and Iraq when the States claimed that they would not accept the draft convention if it conflicted with their traditions.[116] The Convention on the Elimination of All Forms of Discrimination against Women received a draft preambular paragraph from Sweden that asserted that 'the position of women cannot be changed without changing also the role of men in society and in the family'.[117] The suggestion was inspired by the Declaration on Equality of Opportunity and Treatment for Women Workers, adopted by the General Conference of the International Labour Organization in 1975.[118] After comprehensive consultation, Sweden's proposal became the 14th preambular paragraph of the Convention, which declares 'that a change in the traditional role of men as well as the role of women in society and in the family is needed to achieve full equality between men and women'.[119] In 1981, the International Labour Organization Convention concerning Equal Opportunities and Equal Treatment for Men and Women Workers: Workers with Family Responsibilities endorsed the expression of the Convention on the Elimination of All Forms of Discrimination against Women that States Parties are 'aware that a change in the traditional role of men as well as the role of women in society and in the family is needed to achieve full equality between men and women'.[120]

CULTURE AND CUSTOMS

The content of modifying the social and cultural patterns of all citizens relative to women's rights is present in early drafts of the Convention,[121] remaining after the language of educating public opinion was removed from article 5.[122] At that time, two opposing opinions emerged regarding the existence of and methods of regulating such a modification. One opinion urged the omitting of the subject of social and cultural patterns entirely, directly authorising States to eliminate prejudice and discriminatory customs and other practices with all appropriate measures.[123] The other opinion was to announce the modification of social and cultural patterns while also restraining the principle in a State's 'policies

115 UN Doc. E/CN.6/591, para. 123.
116 UN Doc. E/CN.6/591, para. 14.
117 UN Doc. A/32/218/Add.1, para. 16.
118 The International Labour Organization Declaration on Equality of Opportunity and Treatment for Women Workers, preamble.
119 UN Doc. A/C.3/34/14, p. 23; Annex I, p. 2.
120 The International Labour Organization Convention concerning Equal Opportunities and Equal Treatment for Men and Women Workers: Workers with Family Responsibilities, preamble.
121 Lars Adam Rehof, *Guide to the Travaux Préparatoires of the United Nations Convention on the Elimination of All Forms of Discrimination against Women* (Martinus Nijhoff 1993) 9–10.
122 UN Doc. A/C.3/32/WG.1/CRP.9, pp. 7–8.
123 UN Doc. A/C.3/32/WG.1/CRP.9, p. 8; UN Doc. A/C.3/32/WG.1/CPR.6/Add.1, p. 1.

for economic, social and cultural advancement'.[124] Neither of these opinions was adopted. This result showed that the Convention on the Elimination of All Forms of Discrimination against Women assumes a strong position in recognising the linkage between the social and cultural factors in the fomenting of prejudices and sex role stereotypes.

Concerning discriminatory customs against women, most States and institutions agreed in the *travaux préparatoires* of the Convention that States should be obliged to tackle discriminatory customs. Among those who publicly supported this were Benin, Indonesia, Pakistan, the Philippines, the Soviet Union, the United Kingdom, the All-African Women's Conference and the Working Group of the UN Commission on the Status of Women.[125] Sweden understood that 'there are areas which, because they touch on personal questions do not allow for legislative action, and that therefore discriminatory customs may persist.'[126] Alternatively, it proposed education and information campaigns from States to eradicate prejudice and other concrete government measures during transitional periods.[127] Austria found it 'extremely vague' to target 'customs' and 'practices', as 'existing social customs and practices can be influenced only to a small extent by public inference'.[128] After the discussion, the Working Group of the Commission on the Status of Women and the Third Committee of the UN General Assembly agreed that States are responsible to modify and abolish discriminatory customs and other practices that are based on the ideas of inferiority and stereotypes of women.[129]

The final text of the Convention on the Elimination of All Forms of Discrimination against Women recognises the interaction between discrimination against women and the ideology of the inferiority or stereotypes of women. Such discrimination will not disappear if important changes do not initially occur in social ideology. When prompting States to accelerate the development of tradition, culture and customs toward human rights (specifically in the realm of women's rights) the Convention on the Elimination of All Forms of Discrimination against Women reached the conclusion that tradition, culture and customs are not static, but rather they are evolutionary. The Convention does not take the

124 Mali proposed: Each State shall take within the framework of its policies for economic, social and cultural advancement, all appropriate measures including legislation, to modify or abolish existing laws and regulations which are discriminatory to women. UN Doc. A/C.3/32/WG.1/CRP.9, p. 7.

125 UN Doc. E/CN.6/606, p. 2; UN Doc. E/CN.6/573, para. 51; UN Doc. E/CN.6/AC.1/L.6, pp. 2–3; UN Doc. E/CN.6/591, Annex II, A. Draft Convention submitted by Benin, article 2, 4; B. Draft Convention submitted by Indonesia, article 4; C. Draft Convention submitted by the All-African Women's Conference, article 2 (d), article 5; Annex III, article 2 (d); UN Doc. E/CN.6/573, Annex I, article 4 (1); UN Doc. E/CN.6/AC.1/L.2, article 6; E/CN.6/AC.1/L.4, article 6; UN Doc. E/CN.6/AC.1/L.4/Corr.1, article 5.

126 UN Doc. E/CN.6/591, para. 35.

127 UN Doc. E/CN.6/591, para. 35.

128 UN Doc. E/CN.6/591, para. 37 and p. 54.

129 UN Doc. E/CN.6/605, p. 2; UN Doc. A/C.3/32/WG.1/CRP.9, p. 6; UN Doc. A/C.3/32/L.59, para. 88.

position that States should play a passive role in the process either if the fundamental principle of gender equality is in jeopardy. This is a rather progressive approach, representing a shift from the conventional arguments that tradition, culture and customs are conservative phenomena that serve to hold back social evolution instead of promoting it.

EDUCATION INCLUDING FAMILY EDUCATION

To eradicate stereotyped roles of men and women, the Convention on the Elimination of All Forms of Discrimination against Women requires States to take measures in education in the form of both school and family education. This second approach poses an alternative to the modification of social and cultural patterns of conducts of men and women. In the *travaux préparatoires* of the Convention on the Elimination of All Forms of Discrimination against Women and its prior UN Declaration, the importance of education toward the transformation of social attitude became highly regarded.[130] In one case, the representative of Sweden, considering the Declaration on the Elimination of Discrimination against Women in the Economic and Social Council in 1966, stated that education should create a state of mind which is likely to foster a partnership between men and women in the sphere of work, as well as in family and social life.[131] Scrutinising the Convention on the Elimination of All Forms of Discrimination against Women in the Commission on the Status of Women in 1974, the representative from France considered education and the mass media, concluding that education held more weight in enlightening the public since magazines are fundamentally dependent on consumer goods advertising.[132] Belgium,[133] Kenya,[134] Iran[135] and the United Kingdom[136] urged all States to avoid traditional avenues of education that offered a stereotyped image of the roles of men and women. In 1974 the United States detailed its experience of rewriting textbooks for primary schools and including women's studies in university curricula.[137]

EDUCATION

Regarding education, article 10 (c) of the Convention on the Elimination of All Forms of Discrimination against Women declares that States shall take all appropriate measures to ensure:

130 UN Doc. A/C.3/SR.1442, para. 47; UN Doc. A/PV.1597, para. 81; UN Doc. E/CN.6/SR.640, paras 74–75, 76–77 and 79–81.
131 UN Doc. E/AC.7/SR.542, p. 12.
132 UN Doc. E/CN.6/SR.624, p. 117.
133 UN Doc. E/CN.6/SR.640, paras 66–73.
134 UN Doc. A/C.3/32/WG.1/CRP.6/Add.2; UN Doc. A/C.3/32/WG.1/CRP.9, p. 12.
135 UN Doc. A/C.3/32/WG.1/CRP.2.
136 UN Doc. A/C.3/32/WG.1/CRP.9, p. 12.
137 UN Doc. E/CN.6/SR.624, p. 121.

> The elimination of any stereotyped concept of the roles of men and women at all levels and in all forms of education by encouraging coeducation and other types of education which will help to achieve this aim and, in particular, by the revision of textbooks and school programmes and the adaptation of teaching methods.

A working paper from the Secretary-General of the United Nations first proposed this article in 1976, promoting the view that States should take all appropriate measures to ensure '[t]he speedy achievement of co-education based on the identical nature of family and socio-economic roles, at all levels and in all forms of education'.[138] When the Commission on the Status of Women considered the draft convention, Hungary felt that this idea had already been reflected in article 5.[139] France amended the text to focus more on general education, resulting in its provision that called for '[t]he speedy achievement of co-education in order to eliminate any stereotyped concept of masculine and feminine roles at all levels and in all forms of education'.[140] The French amendment raised concerns among the United States and UNESCO because they felt that it suggested that co-education was the only way to eliminate the stereotyped image.[141]

The Commission on the Status of Women entertained a proposal from India which suggested that '[t]he speedy achievement of co-education [. . .] would also help to eliminate any stereotyped image of masculine and feminine roles at all levels and in all forms of education.'[142] When the draft convention came under the gaze of the Third Committee of the UN General Assembly in 1977, the United Kingdom further revised the text to conclude that: '[e]ducation [. . .] will help to eliminate any stereotyped concept of masculine and feminine roles, at all levels and in all forms of education.'[143] This version began to correspond with the final text of article 10 (c) that declared all forms of education as effective means with which to tackle stereotyped concepts of the roles of men and women.

FAMILY EDUCATION

Article 5 (b) also imposes a duty on the State to undertake educational action, requiring States to ensure that family education includes a proper

138 UN Doc. E/CN.6/591/Add.1, p. 5.
139 UN Doc. E/CN.6/SR. 640, para. 68.
140 UN Doc. E/CN.6/SR. 640, para. 71.
141 UN Doc. E/CN.6/SR. 640, paras 74–75.
142 UN Doc. E/CN.6/SR. 640, para. 80. Adopted text: The speedy achievement of co-education which will also help to eliminate any stereotyped concept of masculine and feminine roles at all levels and in all forms of education. UN Doc. E/CN.6/L.681/Add.1, para. 50; UN Doc. E/CN.6/SR.SR.640, paras 83–85.
143 UN Doc. A/C.3/32/WG.1/CRP.6/Add.3, p. 1; UN Doc. A/C.3/32/WG.1/CRP.9, p. 12.

understanding of maternity and shared parental responsibility. The text of article 5 (b) provides that:

> States Parties shall take all appropriate measures:
>
> . . .
>
> (b) to ensure that family education includes a proper understanding of maternity as a social function and the recognition of the common responsibility of men and women in the upbringing and development of their children, it being understood that the interest of the children is the primordial consideration in all cases.

Family is traditionally viewed as private, despite the fact that making the distinction of public and private *per se* contains some paradoxes.[144] The State has a long history of regulating and controlling issues such as marriage, divorce, abortion and the definition of 'legitimate relationships', for the purpose of preserving the family unit.[145] None of these regulations has gone to the degree of monitoring family education. Article 5 (b) of the Convention on the Elimination of All Forms of Discrimination against Women does. Touching as it does on the private sphere, the questions as to whether States should intervene in such a realm and whether parental function should be viewed as a social function were heatedly debated in the drafting process.[146]

Morocco disagreed with the interpretation of maternity as a social function in the discussion of the Third Committee on the UN General Assembly in 1977.[147] The United States preferred not to mention 'family education', instead preferring to phrase it as 'the education of men and women'.[148] These opinions did not prevail. According to the illustrations of Belgium, Cuba, Egypt, France and the United States in the negotiations, the content of family education (referred to by the United States as family responsibilities) included a proper understanding of motherhood as a social function and shared family responsibilities between mother and father.[149] The United States further regarded that the subjects of such education were the whole family, not just a mother and father.[150] The final text of the Convention on the Elimination of All Forms of Discrimination against Women adopted both the idea of maternity as denoting a social function as well as the term of family education.

144 Martha Albertson Fineman, 'Feminist Legal Theory' (2005) 13 (1) *Journal of Gender, Social Policy & the Law* 13, 22.

145 Ann Scales, 'Toward a Feminist Jurisprudence' (1978) 56 (2) *Indiana Law Journal* 375, 422–423; Martha Albertson Fineman, 'Feminist Legal Theory' (2005) 13 (1) *Journal of Gender, Social Policy & the Law* 13, 22.

146 UN Doc. E/CN.6/SR.636, paras 20–24.

147 UN Doc. A/C.3/32/L.59, para. 106.

148 UN Doc. A/C.3/32/L.59, para. 103.

149 UN Doc. E/CN.6/L.677, p. 1; UN Doc. E/CN.6/SR.636, para. 19; UN Doc. E/CN.6/SR.638, para. 20; UN Doc. E/CN.6/L.676.

150 UN Doc. E/CN.6/SR.636, para. 19.

Other attempts and possibilities

The media and advocacy of hatred or incitement to discrimination

The UN Economic and Social Council and the Commission on the Status of Women discussed the role of the media in influencing public opinion with regard to the recognition of gender equality and the fostering of positive images of women in the 1940s.[151] In the 1970s the Commission on the Status of Women paid heed to the significance of mass communication media once more when it encouraged States to comply with the UN Declaration on the Elimination of Discrimination against Women.[152] The Secretary-General of the United Nations adopted the stance that the mass media not only reflected prevalent concepts in a community, but were also an exponent of changing values, as outlined in a report of 1974.[153]

In the formulation of the Convention on the Elimination of All Forms of Discrimination against Women, Pakistan attempted to define the role of the mass media. It submitted a draft provision to the Commission on the Status of Women in 1976, which envisioned that '[t]he mass media shall be geared to adopt positive and constructive portrayals of women in their multiple roles in society'.[154] This proposal was not adopted. In the final text of the Convention on the Elimination of All Forms of Discrimination against Women, the only provision that has a connection with the media is article 2 (d). According to this provision, States have to ensure that public authorities and institutions do not engage in any act or practice of discrimination against women. In preparing this principle, the role of the media was taken into consideration. Sweden raised concerns to the UN Secretary-General in 1976 that this provision did not take into account the fact that public broadcasting corporations and other cultural and educational institutions enjoyed a high degree of autonomy and therefore it preferred a less mandatory expression over the existing language of 'ensure'.[155] This request was dismissed and the word 'ensure' was retained in the final text of article 2 (d).

The Philippines made another attempt to prohibit any advocacy of hatred that constitutes incitement to discrimination against women, in a proposal sent to the UN Secretary-General in 1973.[156] This proposal attempted to crystallise a norm in line with the pattern of article 4 of the UN Convention on racial discrimination which requires States to declare all dissemination of ideas based on racial hatred and incitement to racial discrimination an offence punishable by law. This suggestion was widely objected to by other States on the basis of freedom of expression

151 UN Doc. A/972, para. 246; UN Doc. E/615, Chapter XI, paras 37–38; UN Doc. E/615, para. 37; UN Doc. A/625, para. 149; UN Doc. A/972, para. 246.
152 UN Doc. E/CN.6/MIN., p. 80; UN Doc. E/CN.6/L.600, pp. 1–2.
153 UN Doc. E/CN.6/SR. 623, p. 110.
154 UN Doc. E/CN.6/606, p. 4.
155 UN Doc. E/CN.6/591, para. 36.
156 UN Doc. E/CN.6/573, Annex I, article 4, para. 2.

and the difficulty of demarcating the punishable offences in practice.[157] The United States merely agreed to prohibit 'incitement to discrimination' but not 'advocacy of the superiority'.[158]

A few States, particularly socialist countries, thought otherwise, as expressed in comments to the Secretary-General of the United Nations in 1976. For example, Ethiopia and Sierra Leone did not consider that the Philippines' motion was a limitation on freedom of expression.[159] Ethiopia recalled, 'fundamental freedoms, including freedom of speech are not generally granted to citizens without exceptions or bounds.'[160] The Soviet Socialist Republic of Byelorussia, the German Democratic Republic, Poland and the Soviet Union all expounded on the extreme importance of legislative prohibitions on the advocacy of the superiority of one sex over another.[161] They found that similar provisions existed in the United Nations Declaration on the Elimination of All Forms of Racial Discrimination, the International Convention on the Elimination of All Forms of Racial Discrimination and the International Covenant on Civil and Political Rights.[162] The Convention on the Elimination of All Forms of Discrimination against Women does not endorse the prohibition of 'incitement to discrimination' or 'advocacy of hatred and discrimination' in its final text. The difference reflects differing attitudes of States toward the issue of racial discrimination and discrimination against women. Racial discrimination, as announced in the UN declaration and convention on the topic, may jeopardise or disturb international peace and security.[163] But both the UN Declaration and the Convention on discrimination against women do not include a similar warning.

'All necessary/appropriate measures'

In addition to singling out specific means such as education and the modification of cultural and social patterns of the conduct of men and women, international law frequently prescribes 'all appropriate measures' and 'all necessary measures' for States to eliminate discrimination against women. This language

157 Afghanistan, Austria, Barbados, Benin, Canada, Colombia, Ecuador, Finland, Ireland, Germany (Federal Republic of), Indonesia, Italy, Japan, the Netherlands, Norway, Singapore, Sweden, the United States, the International Association for Social Progress, the World Union of Catholic Women's Organizations and the Associated Country Women of the World. UN Doc. E/CN.6/591, para. 73; UN Doc. E/CN.6/AC.1/L.12, p. 9; Lars Adam Rehof, *Guide to the Travaux Préparatoires of the United Nations Convention on the Elimination of All Forms of Discrimination against Women* (Martinus Nijhoff Publishers 1993) 80.

158 The United States' proposal: Actions that constitute incitement to discrimination against women shall be prohibited by law. UN Doc. E/CN.6/AC.1/L.6, p. 3.

159 UN Doc. E/CN.6/591, para. 73.

160 UN Doc. E/CN.6/591, para. 73.

161 UN Doc. E/CN.6/591, para. 74.

162 UN Doc. E/CN.6/591, para. 74.

163 The United Nations Declaration on the Elimination of All Forms of Racial Discrimination, preamble; the International Convention on the Elimination of All Forms of Racial Discrimination, preamble.

exists in 13 provisions of the Convention on the Elimination of All Forms of Discrimination against Women[164] and in six out of 11 articles of the Declaration on the Elimination of Discrimination against Women.[165] The use of this phrase has the capacity of accommodating all available measures taken by States with the purpose of creating a social atmosphere conducive toward women's rights and promoting the idea of gender equality in public opinion. Following the adoption of the Convention on the Elimination of All Forms of Discrimination against Women in 1979, the Second World Conference on Women (also known as the Copenhagen Conference) in 1980 repeated this expression and called on States to 'take all necessary measures' to effectively implement the Convention.[166]

Using the Convention on the Elimination of All Forms of Discrimination against Women by way of illustration, these 'appropriate' and 'necessary' measures can come in the form of legislation (articles 2 (b) (f), 3 and 6), sanctions (article 2 (b)), education (article 10 (c)) and actions taken in political, social, economic and cultural fields (article 3). Included are all kinds of other measures carried out in the context of targeting prejudice and practices based on ideas of inferiority and stereotypes of women (article 5 (a)); ensuring that family education includes maternity and shared parental responsibility (article 5 (b)); eradicating discrimination by individuals and organisations (article 2 (e)); raising women's status in education (article 10), employment (article 11), health care (article 12), economic, social, political and public life (articles 7, 8 and 13), marriage and family relations (article 16); and implementing the Convention (article 24) particularly in rural places (article 14).

The *travaux préparatoires* of the Convention on the Elimination of All Forms of Discrimination against Women indicate that States tried to define what these 'appropriate' or 'necessary' measures are. Mexico, the Philippines and the Soviet Union simply intended the term to encompass both legal and non-legal measures.[167] Mexico proposed a text of 'all necessary legislative and administrative measures', while Denmark expected the expression of all appropriate or necessary measures to stress that 'legislative measures should not be regarded as the only means of achieving the objectives of the convention'.[168] Occasionally debate arose between the choice of 'all appropriate measures' and 'all necessary measures'.

This occurred during the discussion in the Commission on the Status of Women in 1976 when the United Kingdom referred to the term 'all appropriate measures' in article 3 on the State duty to ensure the full development and advancement of women.[169] The United Kingdom considered the term logically correct in English and more appropriate than 'necessary' in given situations.[170]

164 Articles 2, 3, 5, 6, 7, 8, 10, 11, 12, 13, 14, 16 and 24.
165 UN Doc. A/RES/2263 (XXII).
166 UN Doc. A/CONF.94/35, p. 89.
167 UN Doc. E/CN.6/SR.634, para. 63; UN Doc. E/CN.6/573, para. 54; E/CN.6/AC.1/L.4.
168 UN Doc. E/CN.6/SR.634, paras 21, 52 and 61.
169 UN Doc. E/CN.6/SR.634, para. 64.
170 UN Doc. E/CN.6/SR.634, para. 64.

Hungary seconded that 'all appropriate measures' may include administrative means.[171] Benin, however, expressed doubts about the word 'appropriate' on the basis that it provided too much freedom of action and may give rise to abuse.[172] In light of the debate, France presented a compromise proposal in the form of 'all appropriate and necessary measures'.[173] Other alternatives were also submitted, including alternatives such as all 'preventive', 'effective' or 'concrete' measures. After much deliberation, 'appropriate' and 'necessary' were deemed as more defensive than 'preventive' and 'effective'[174] and stronger than 'concrete'.[175] Hence they were included in the Convention on the Elimination of All Forms of Discrimination against Women. States' steps in social, economic, cultural, political and legal fields were especially emphasised.[176] The prerequisite of 'when the circumstances so warrant' was deleted.[177]

The Convention on the Elimination of All Forms of Discrimination against Women does not explicitly mention the education of public opinion, but it does raise the issue of targeting prejudice and sex role stereotyping. To this end, it requires that States promote a change in tradition, culture and customs. It encourages State action in the realm of education, acknowledging that this occasionally touches on the private sphere. As to other effective means to achieve this goal, the Convention on the Elimination of All Forms of Discrimination against Women does not endorse restrictions on the media, neither does it prohibit advocacy of hatred or incitement to gender discrimination. Nevertheless, through the regular employment of the language of 'all necessary measures' and 'all appropriate measures', spatial and legal bases for further State action is provided.

Further interpretation and State compliance: to lead public opinion

The Convention on the Elimination of All Forms of Discrimination against Women was adopted by the General Assembly of the United Nations in 1979 and entered into force in 1981. Soon after that, the Committee on the Elimination of Discrimination against Women was set up to monitor implementation of the Convention.[178] The Committee considers State parties' regular reports as to the implementation of the rights of the Convention, voicing its concerns and making recommendations in the form of concluding observations.[179] It also formulates

171 UN Doc. E/CN.6/SR.634, para. 62.

172 UN Doc. E/CN.6/591, Annex I, Amendments and New Versions Proposed, p. 61.

173 UN Doc. E/CN.6/SR.634, para. 73.

174 UN Doc. A/C.3/33/L.47/Add.2, p. 13; UN Doc. E/CN.6/591/Add.1, p. 3; UN Doc. A/C.3/33/L.47/Add.2, p. 13; Lars Adam Rehof, *Guide to the Travaux Préparatoires of the United Nations Convention on the Elimination of All Forms of Discrimination against Women* (Martinus Nijhoff Publishers 1993) 59.

175 UN Doc. E/CN.6/573, p. 15, paras 48–55 and Annex I, p. 2.

176 UN Doc. E/CN.6/591/Add.1, p. 3; UN Doc. E/CN.6/SR.634, para. 36.

177 UN Doc. E/CN.6/573, p. 15, paras 48–55 and Annex I, p. 2; UN Doc. E/CN.6/591, paras 44 and 46.

178 The Convention on the Elimination of All Forms of Discrimination against Women, article 17.

179 The Convention on the Elimination of All Forms of Discrimination against Women, article 18.

general recommendations for all States concerning the articles and themes enshrined in the Convention.[180] Through these concluding observations and general recommendations, the Committee on the Elimination of Discrimination against Women has the opportunity to interpret the various principles within the Convention.

Similarly, the Human Rights Committee and the Committee on the Rights of the Child are also in a position to illustrate the rights of women and girls protected by the International Covenant on Civil and Political Rights and the Convention on the Rights of the Child in the form of recommendations and comments.[181] The three treaty bodies encourage States not to remain silent when public opinion is responsible for violations of women's rights, and to lead public opinion toward gender equality. The extent to which States accept and embrace their duty to lead public opinion in the direction of such a goal can be evidenced in their periodic reports made under major human rights treaties, their responses to recommendations and comments issued by treaty bodies and their interaction with other States' suggestions and concerns in the newly established mechanism of the Universal Periodic Review.

Interpretation by international human rights bodies

The Committee on the Elimination of Discrimination against Women

THREE AREAS OF PUBLIC OPINION

In its concluding observations to specific States and its issuance of general recommendations to all States, the Committee on the Elimination of Discrimination against Women urged them to work on influencing public opinion, which is attributable for various violations of women's rights. The Committee based this recommendation on article 5 (a) of the Convention on the Elimination of All Forms of Discrimination against Women, concerned with the State duty to eliminate prejudice and the stereotyping of sex roles. It also cited legal roots for such a recommendation in articles 2 (f), 7 (b), 10 (c) and 12 (1) concerning the elimination of discrimination against women's rights in education, health and political and public life, and States' active participation in the formulation of government policy concerning women's rights. This approach reflects a more progressive understanding than the limited text of article 5 (a) in the Convention on the Elimination of All Forms of Discrimination against Women. It can be argued that this progression constitutes a logical interpretation of human rights law, since gender prejudice and stereotypes adversely affect women's exercise of specific rights in the areas previously mentioned.

180 The Convention on the Elimination of All Forms of Discrimination against Women, article 21.

181 The International Covenant on Civil and Political Rights, article 45; The Convention on the Rights of the Child, article 40.

Generally speaking, three areas of public opinion are encouraged to become targets of the State by the Committee on the Elimination of Discrimination against Women. First, the Committee affirmed in general recommendation No. 3 (as well as suggestions made to specific States) that the deep entrenchment of patriarchal attitudes alongside pejorative stereotyping of women's roles in family and societal life are root causes of the disadvantaged position of women in the field of education, the labour market and in political life, manifesting as impediments to the implementation of the Convention on the Elimination of All Forms of Discrimination against Women.[182] The Committee urged States in general recommendation No. 25 to accelerate the modification and elimination of stereotypical attitudes that discriminate against or disadvantage women. In its concluding remarks to States' periodic reports, the Committee also called on States to modify the widely accepted prevalence of the subordination of women and to challenge the stereotypical roles of both sexes.[183] In doing so,

182 UN Doc. CEDAW/C/ARM/CO/4/Rev.1, para. 20; UN Doc. A/HRC/WG.6/3/BRB/2, para. 13; UN Doc. A/59/38, paras 167, 201, 245, 309 and 339, Annexe IV, paras 146, 292 and 332; UN Doc. A/55/38, Part Two, para. 53; UN Doc. A/HRC/WG.6/4/CHN/2, para. 12; UN Doc. CEDAW/C/CHN/CO/6, paras 5 and 17; UN Doc. A/HRC/WG.6/6/CYP/2, para. 15; UN Doc. CEDAW/C/CYP/CO/5, para. 17; UN Doc. A/HRC/WG.6/1/MAR/2, para. 11; UN Doc. CEDAW/C/MAR/CO/4, para. 18; UN Doc. A/57/38 (Part I), para. 138.

183 UN Doc. A/59/38, paras 116, 166, 194, 207, 252, 339–340, and Annexes IV, paras 54, 147, 242, 246, 293, 295 and 333; UN Doc. CEDAW/C/ARM/CO/4/Rev.1, para. 21; UN Doc. A/HRC/WG.6/3/BRB/2, para. 13; UN Doc. A/HRC/WG.6/8/BLR/2, para. 19; UN Doc. A/57/38 (Part I), paras 148, 193, 201, 289, 330 and 380; UN Doc. A/57/38 (Part II), paras 48, 104, 106, 137 and 334; UN Doc. A/HRC/WG.6/11/BEL/2, para. 23; UN Doc. CEDAW/C/BEL/CO/6, para. 24; UN Doc. A/HRC/WG.6/4/CMR/2, para. 11; UN Doc. A/55/38, Part Two, para. 54; UN Doc. A/HRC/WG.6/4/CUB/2, para. 17; UN Doc. CEDAW/C/CUB/CO/6, para. 18; UN Doc. A/HRC/WG.6/6/CYP/2, para. 15; UN Doc. CEDAW/C/CYP/CO/5, paras 17–18; UN Doc. A/HRC/WG.6/2/GAB/2, para. 13; UN Doc. CEDAW/C/GAB/CC/2–5, para. 31; UN Doc. A/HRC/WG.6/7/GMB/2, para. 15; UN Doc. A/HRC/WG.6/12/HTI/2, para. 22; UN Doc. CEDAW/C/HTI/CO/7, para. 21; UN Doc. A/HRC/WG.6/14/JPN/2, para. 18; UN Doc. CEDAW/C/JPN/CO/6, para. 30; UN Doc. A/HRC/WG.6/11/GRC/2, para. 11; UN Doc. CEDAW/C/GRC/CO/6, para. 14; UN Doc. A/HRC/WG.6/12/ISL/2, para. 21; UN Doc. A/63/38, para. 21; UN Doc. A/HRC/WG.6/9/LBR/2, para. 19; UN Doc. CEDAW/C/LBR/CO/6, para. 19; UN Doc. A/HRC/WG.6/3/LIE/2, para. 24; UN Doc. CEDAW/C/LIE/CO/3, para. 22; UN Doc. A/HRC/WG.6/3/LUX/2, para. 15; UN Doc. CEDAW/C/LUX/CO/5, para. 16; UN Doc. A/HRC/WG.6/9/MWI/2, para. 12; UN Doc. CEDAW/C/MWI/CO/6, para. 21; UN Doc. CEDAW/C/MDV/CO/3, para. 18; UN Doc. A/HRC/WG.6/4/MUS/2, para. 17; UN Doc. CEDAW/C/MAR/CO/5, para. 17; UN Doc. A/HRC/WG.6/10/MMR/2, para. 54; UN Doc. CEDAW/C/MMR/CO/3, para. 35; UN Doc. A/HRC/WG.6/10/KNA/2, para. 8; UN Doc. A/HRC/WG.6/11/SLE/2, para. 15; UN Doc. CEDAW/C/SLE/CO/5, para. 21; UN Doc. A/HRC/WG.6/12/THA/2, para. 13; UN Doc. CEDAW/C/THA/CO/5, para. 24; UN Doc. CEDAW/C/TZA/CO/6, para. 22; UN Doc. A/HRC/WG.6/12/TZA/2, paras 20 and 63; UN Doc. A/HRC/WG.6/13/ZAF/2, para. 17; UN Doc. CEDAW/C/ZAF/CO/4, para. 21 (a); UN Doc. A/60/38, Part One, para. 368; UN Doc. A/HRC/WG.6/1/MAR/2, para. 11; UN Doc. CEDAW/C/MAR/CO/4, para. 19; UN Doc. A/HRC/WG.6/11/SGP/2, para. 14; UN Doc. CEDAW/C/SGP/CO/3, para. 32; UN Doc. A/HRC/WG.6/5/URY/2, paras 15 and 28; UN Doc. CEDAW/C/URY/CO/7, paras 21, 30 and 31; UN Doc. A/

the Committee highlighted traditional attitudes that hamper women and girls' ambitions to exercise their right to education.[184]

Recommendations urging States to confront patriarchal attitudes and stereotyping of women were made to Angola, Armenia, Bangladesh, Barbados, Belarus, Belgium, Bhutan, Cameroon, Cyprus, Cuba, Denmark, Dominican Republic, Equatorial Guinea, Gabon, Gambia, Greece, Haiti, Iceland, Japan, Kyrgyzstan, Latvia, Liberia, Liechtenstein, Lithuania, Luxembourg, Madagascar, Malawi, Maldives, Mauritius, Morocco, Myanmar, Nepal, Portugal, Russia, Saint Kitts and Nevis, Saint Lucia, Sierra Leone, Singapore, South Africa, Spain, Sri Lanka, Suriname, Tanzania, Thailand, Timor-Leste, Trinidad and Tobago, Tunisia, Turkey, Uganda, Uruguay, Vanuatu, Viet Nam, Yemen and Zambia. The Committee ultimately expressed its regret that not every State had undertaken sustained programmes with the long-term view of changing social and cultural attitudes and patterns of behaviour that lead to stereotyping, citing the poor performance of Barbados in 2002 and Malawi in 2010.[185]

Second, the Committee highlighted the permissive societal attitudes contributing to violence and ill-treatment of women, including acid attacks, dowry deaths,[186] female circumcision, all kinds of family violence and abuse and forced marriage.[187] These violent practices were deemed to bear a close link to deeply rooted cultural and traditional attitudes that regard women as subordinate to men or as having stereotyped roles, leading to the perpetration of cycles of discrimination and ill-treatment.[188] The Committee encouraged States to identify the nature and prevalence of these attitudes in order that measures could be taken to overcome them.[189] It further offered suggestions to a vast number of States, calling on them to make certain preconceptions socially and morally unacceptable. These conceptions formed a long list which included, *inter alia*, female genital mutilation,[190] honour killings,[191] murders motivated by gender

HRC/WG.6/12/UGA/2, para. 75; UN Doc. A/HRC/WG.6/12/UGA/2, para. 17; UN Doc. CEDAW/C/UGA/CO/7, para. 21; UN Doc. A/HRC/WG.6/12/LTU/2, para. 22; CEDAW/C/LTU/CO/4, para. 15; UN Doc. A/HRC/WG.6/5/VUT/2, para. 15; UN Doc. CEDAW/C/VUT/CO/3, para. 23; UN Doc. A/CCPR/WG.6/5/VNM/2, para. 22; UN Doc. CEDAW/C/VNM/CO/6, para. 13; UN Doc. A/HRC/WG.6/5/YEM/2, para. 43; UN Doc. CEDAW/C/YEM/CO/6, para. 25; UN Doc. A/HRC/WG.6/14/ZMB/2, para. 12; UN Doc. CEDAW/C/ZMB/CO/5–6, para. 20; UN Doc. A/HRC/WG.6/7/MDG/2, para. 20; UN Doc. CEDAW/C/MDG/CO/5, para. 17; UN Doc. A/HRC/WG.6/10/LCA/2, para. 14; UN Doc. CEDAW/C/LCA/CO/6, para. 18; UN Doc. A/HRC/WG.6/12/TTO/2, para. 19; UN Doc. A/HRC/WG.6/13/TUN/2, para. 20; UN Doc. CEDAW/C/TUN/CO/6, para. 25.

184 UN Doc. A/HRC/WG.6/12/TLS/2, para. 62; UN Doc. CEDAW/C/TLS/CO/1, para. 36.

185 UN Doc. A/HRC/WG.6/3/BRB/2, para. 13; UN Doc. A/HRC/WG.6/9/MWI/2, para. 12; UN Doc. CEDAW/C/MWI/CO/6, para. 20.

186 Dowry deaths are the deaths of young women murdered or through suicide by continuous harassment and torture driven by husbands and in-laws in an effort to extort an increased dowry.

187 Committee general recommendations No. 14 and 19.

188 UN Doc. A/57/38 (Part I), para. 145; Committee general recommendations No. 14 and 19.

189 Committee general recommendation No. 19, para. 24 (e) and (f).

190 UN Doc. A/59/38, para. 252.

191 Honour killing is the homicide of a member of a family or social group by other members, on

prejudice,[192] traditional attitudes that discourage girls' education,[193] the stigmatisation of widows and other negative practices related to widowhood,[194] women being exclusively responsible for childrearing and housework,[195] violence against women including marital rape, physical chastisement of women family members and all forms of sexual abuse of women[196] among a number of other practices concerned with levirate marriage, inheritance, early and forced marriage and polygamy.[197]

Finally, States were urged to act on the promotion of the principle of gender equality and the fostering of a positive image of women, irrespective of the popular opinions on the topic. The Committee made it clear in general recommendation No. 23 that '[i]t is the Government's fundamental responsibility to encourage . . . initiatives to lead and guide public opinion and change attitudes that discriminate against women or discourage women's involvement in political and public life'.[198] It requested the conceptualisation of the role of women in society,[199] affirming articles of the Convention with the aim of compelling States into advancing the public understanding of parenting as a shared social responsibility of both mothers and fathers,[200] in addition to the idea of shared responsibility between men and women in family life and the workplace.[201] The Committee further recommended to States to increase public awareness on specific issues concerning women's rights, highlighting in general recommendation No. 15 the risk of HIV and AIDS in women, as well as their debilitating effects.[202]

the basis that the victim has brought dishonour on the family or community. Honour killing are directed mostly against women and girls. The Committee urged Iraq to make 'honour killings' socially and morally unacceptable. UN Doc. A/55/38, para. 179.

192 UN Doc. A/HRC/WG.6/7/SLV/2, para. 13; UN Doc. CEDAW/C/SLV/7, para. 24.

193 UN Doc. A/59/38, paras 194 and 304; UN Doc. A/HRC/WG.6/2/BEN/2, para. 26; UN Doc. A/HRC/WG.6/10/MMR/2, para. 54; UN Doc. CEDAW/C/MMR/CO/3, para. 35.

194 UN Doc. A/59/38, paras 207 and 252.

195 UN Doc. A/59/38, paras 309 and 339; UN Doc. A/57/38 (Part I), para. 193.

196 UN Doc. A/59/38, paras 79, 199; UN Doc. A/55/38, Part Two, paras 54; UN Doc. A/HRC/WG.6/4/CMR/2, para. 19; CESCR, E/C.12/1/Add. 40, paras 16 and 33; UN Doc. A/HRC/WG.6/4/CUB/2, para. 17; UN Doc. CEDAW/C/CUB/CO/6, para. 18; UN Doc. A/HRC/WG.6/12/THA/2, para. 13; UN Doc. CEDAW/C/THA/CO/5, para. 24

197 Recommendations were made to Bangladesh, Cameroon, Gabon, Gambia, Kyrgyzstan, Nepal, South Africa, Turkey, etc.
UN Doc. A/59/38, paras 168, 207, 252, Annexe IV, para. 147; UN Doc. A/55/38, Part Two, para. 54; UN Doc. A/HRC/WG.6/2/GAB/2, para. 13; UN Doc. CEDAW/C/GAB/CC/2–5, para. 31; UN Doc. A/HRC/WG.6/7/GMB/2, para. 15; UN Doc. A/HRC/WG.6/13/ZAF/2, para. 17; UN Doc. CEDAW/C/ZAF/CO/4, para. 21(a); UN Doc. A/60/38, Part One, para. 368.

198 Committee general recommendation No. 23.

199 UN Doc. A/57/38, Part One, para. 148.

200 UN Doc. A/59/38, paras. 168, 207, 252, Annexe IV, para. 333; UN Doc. A/HRC/WG.6/10/KNA/2, para. 8; UN Doc. A/57/38 (Part II), para. 104.

201 UN Doc. A/HRC/WG.6/12/ISL/2, para.45; UN Doc. A/63/38, para. 231; UN Doc. CEDAW/C/SGP/CO/3, para. 32.

202 Committee general recommendation No. 15.

EFFECTIVE MEANS

To effectively challenge public opinion and to promote cultural change, the Committee on the Status of Women emphasised the role of the media in promoting positive and non-stereotypical images of women and the value of gender equality for society as a whole.[203] The importance of training, awareness raising and educational campaigns was similarly noted.[204] The Committee urged States to comply with articles 2 (f) and 5 (a) of the Convention on the Elimination of All Forms of Discrimination against Women and to consider culture as a dynamic aspect of a country's social fabric and therefore being subject to change.[205] These statements were made in concluding observations to periodic reports submitted by Angola, Madagascar, Tanzania and Vanuatu from 2004 to 2008. The liberal interpretation and extension of the provisions of articles 2 (f) and 5 (a) of the Convention on the Elimination of All Forms of Discrimination against Women formed an integral part in adjusting cultural perceptions *vis-à-vis* human rights,

203 Committee general recommendation No. 19; UN Doc. CEDAW/C/ARM/CO/4/Rev.1, para. 21; UN Doc. A/HRC/WG.6/3/BRB/2, para. 13; UN Doc. A/57/38 (Part I), paras 289 and 330; UN Doc. A/57/38 (Part II), paras 48 and 334; UN Doc. A/59/38, paras 71, 116, 168, 207, 293 and 340, Annexe IV, paras 54, 147, 293 and 333; UN Doc. A/HRC/WG.6/14/JPN/2, para. 18; UN Doc. CEDAW/C/JPN/CO/6, para. 30; UN Doc. A/HRC/WG.6/12/ISL/2, para. 21; UN Doc. A/63/38, para. 21; UN Doc. CEDAW/C/LUX/CO/5, para. 16; UN Doc. A/HRC/WG.6/9/MDV/2/Rev.1, para. 16; UN Doc. CEDAW/C/MDV/CO/3, para. 18; UN Doc. CEDAW/C/TZA/CO.6, para. 22; UN Doc. A/HRC/WG.6/11/SUR/2, para. 13; UN Doc. CEDAW/C/SUR/CO/3, para. 18; UN Doc. A/60/38, Part One, para. 368; UN Doc. CEDAW/C/MAR/CO/4, para. 19; UN Doc. CEDAW/C/URY/CO/7, para. 21; UN Doc. CEDAW/C/LTU/CO/4, para. 15; UN Doc. A/HRC/WG.6/5/VUT/2, para. 15; UN Doc. CEDAW/C/VUT/CO/3, para. 23; UN Doc. A/HRC/WG.6/7/MDG/2, para. 20; UN Doc. CEDAW/C/MDG/CO/5, para. 17; UN Doc. CEDAW/C/LCA/CO/6, para. 18; UN Doc. CEDAW/C/VNM/CO/6, para. 13.

204 Committee general recommendations No. 14 and 19; UN Doc. CEDAW/C/ARM/CO/4/Rev.1, para. 20; UN Doc. A/HRC/WG.6/3/BRB/2, para. 13; UN Doc. A/57/38 (Part I), paras 54, 55, 106, 152 and 289; UN Doc. A/57/38 (Part II), paras 48, 334; UN Doc. A/59/38, paras 79, 199, 200, 201, 252, Annexe IV, para. 147, 333; UN Doc. A/55/38, Part Two, para. 54; UN Doc. A/HRC/WG.6/5/COG/2, para. 9; UN Doc. A/58/38, Part One, paras 164 and 165; UN Doc. A/HRC/WG.6/6/CYP/2, para. 15; UN Doc. CEDAW/C/CYP/CO/5, paras 17–18; UN Doc. A/HRC/WG.6/6/GNQ/2, para. 29; UN Doc. A/HRC/WG.6/7/FJI/2, para. 19; UN Doc. A/HRC/WG.6/2/GAB/2, para. 13; UN Doc. CEDAW/C/GAB/CC/2-5, para. 31; UN Doc. A/HRC/WG.6/14/JPN/2, para. 18; UN Doc. CEDAW/C/JPN/CO/6, para. 30; UN Doc. A/HRC/WG.6/8/KWT/2, para. 28; UN Doc. A/HRC/WG.6/11/GRC/2, para. 11; UN Doc. CEDAW/C/GRC/CO/6, para. 14; UN Doc. A/HRC/WG.6/12/ISL/2, para. 21; UN Doc. A/63/38, para. 21; UN Doc. A/HRC/WG.6/9/LBR/2, para. 19; UN Doc. CEDAW/C/LBR/CO/6, para. 19; UN Doc. CEDAW/C/LUX/CO/5, para. 16; UN Doc. A/HRC/WG.6/4/MUS/2, para. 17; UN Doc. CEDAW/C/MAR/CO/5, para. 17; UN Doc. A/60/38, Part One, para. 368; UN Doc. CEDAW/C/MAR/CO/4, para. 19; UN Doc. CEDAW/C/SGP/CO/3, para. 32; UN Doc. CEDAW/C/LTU/CO/4, para. 15; UN Doc. CEDAW/C/VNM/CO/6, para 13; UN Doc. CEDAW/C/LCA/CO/6, para. 18.

205 UN Doc. A/59/38, Annexe IV, para. 147; UN Doc. CEDAW/C/TZA/CO.6, para. 22; UN Doc. CEDAW/C/VUT/CO/3, para. 23; UN Doc. CEDAW/C/MDG/CO/5, para. 17.

specifically the rights of women. Campaigning to attain that goal, the Committee on the Elimination of Discrimination against Women further encouraged States to adopt comprehensive strategies, taking into consideration the roles of women and men at all levels of society.[206]

The Committee acknowledged the influence of certain figures in the conceptualisation of public opinion. It advised States to target particular groups, involving them in measures formulated in the pursuit of transforming public opinion and the culture of women's rights. Such groups included parliamentarians, decision-makers, community leaders, parents, teachers, officials, judges, journalists and the youth.[207] In one instance, the Committee called on States to encourage 'politicians, professionals, religious and community leaders at all levels' and include the media and the arts, to 'co-operate in influencing attitudes' toward the eradication of the practice of female circumcision, in its general recommendation No. 14.[208]

OTHER UN BODIES

The United Nations Entity for Gender Equality and the Empowerment of Women (also known as UN Women) agreed in 2011 that the deeply rooted patriarchal attitudes embedded in social and cultural infrastructures are responsible for violence against women.[209] The General Assembly of the United Nations adopted its first resolution on female genital mutilation in December 2012, through which the General Assembly called on States to enhance awareness-raising by means of formal, non-formal and informal education and training in order to mobilise the public against such practices.[210] It similarly aimed to ensure that all key actors, including government officials, community and religious leaders, teachers and media professionals became involved in this mobilisation aimed at eliminating attitudes that negatively affect girls.[211]

The Special Rapporteur in the field of cultural rights in 2012 and the Special Rapporteur on Violence against Women in 2007 submitted reports to the UN Secretary-General and the Human Rights Council, supporting the aim of modifying cultural perceptions of gender equality, entreating States to dispel the myth that culture is static, immutable or monolithic.[212] The Special Rapporteur in the field of cultural rights explained in its report to the UN General Assembly that

206 UN Doc. A/HRC/WG.6/12/HTI/2, para. 22; UN Doc. CEDAW/C/HTI/CO/7, para. 21; UN Doc. A/HRC/WG.6/11/SLE/2, para. 15; UN Doc. CEDAW/C/SLE/CO/5, para. 21.

207 UN Doc. CEDAW/C/ARM/CO/4/Rev.1, para. 21; UN Doc. A/59/38, para. 200, Annex IV, para. 295; UN Doc. A/55/38, Part Two, para. 54; UN Doc. CEDAW/C/MDV/CO/3, para. 18; UN Doc. CEDAW/C/TZA/CO.6, para. 22; UN Doc. A/60/38, Part One, para. 368; UN Doc. CEDAW/C/SGP/CO/3, para. 32; UN Doc. CEDAW/C/URY/CO/7, para. 21.

208 Committee general recommendation No. 14.

209 UN Doc. A/HRC/WG.6/12/TTO/2, para. 26.

210 UN Doc. A/Res/67/146.

211 UN Doc. A/Res/67/146.

212 UN Doc. A/67/287, paras 2 and 17; UN Doc. A/HRC/4/34, paras 51, 58 and 70.

'[c]ulture is created, contested and recreated within the social praxis of diverse groups interacting in economic, social and political arenas':[213]

> Delinking culture from the historical processes and contexts in which it is embedded essentializes cultures, which are then presumed to be static and immutable, homogenous and monolithic, apolitical and detached from prevailing power relations. [. . .] Viewing culture and attendant beliefs, including customs, traditions and religious interpretations, as 'static' obstructs the realization of women's human rights because it presupposes that particular values, practices and beliefs are 'intrinsic' to a given culture and, therefore, immutable.[214]

This examination concurred with the report of the Special Rapporteur on Violence against Women, which was submitted to the Human Rights Council in 2007.[215] The latter report also indicated that culture is diverse and dynamic in its response to differing and competing individual and collective needs and aspirations.[216] Therefore it is not correct to perceive culture as a collection of 'time-honoured "traditions" rather than the custom of some of those currently living within the culture'.[217]

The Human Rights Committee and the Committee on the Rights of the Child in interpreting their relevant treaty bodies both developed on the notion that it was the State's duty to exert a positive impact on public opinion with a view to protecting and promoting women's equality. Interestingly, the texts of the two relevant conventions, the International Covenant on Civil and Political Rights and the Convention on the Rights of the Child, barely mention public opinion, except that the latter mentions that the education of children should promote an understanding of human rights principles.[218] However, the two committees based their interpretations on the rights to equality, health, life, liberty and security of the person and the prohibition of cruel, inhuman and degrading treatment, in conformity with articles 2, 3, 7, 17, 23, 25 and 26 of the International Covenant on Civil and Political Rights, and articles 2 and 24 (3) of the Convention on the Rights of the Child.

Emboldened, the Human Rights Committee recommended in 2007 that Madagascar should strengthen its efforts in education and training so as to bring about genuine gender equality and to 'help to change mindsets and attitudes' in order to promote effective observance of the Covenant, when Madagascar presented its third periodic report.[219] It went on to encourage the former Yugoslav

213 UN Doc. A/67/287, para. 2.
214 UN Doc. A/67/287, paras 2 and 17.
215 UN Doc. A/HRC/4/34, paras 51, 58 and 70.
216 UN Doc. A/HRC/4/34, para. 51.
217 UN Doc. A/HRC/4/34, para. 58.
218 The Convention on the Rights of the Child, article 29 (d).
219 UN Doc. CCPR/C/MDG/CO/3, para. 8.

Republic of Macedonia to undertake educational campaigns designed to 'change the perception of women in stereotypical roles in the society', in concluding observations of 2008.[220] Similarly in 2009, the Committee advised Tanzania to 'step up its efforts to raise popular awareness of, and change, customary attitudes detrimental to women's rights'.[221]

The Committee on the Rights of the Child issued a recommendation to the United Arab Emirates in 2002 that sought to: reconcile the interpretation of Islamic texts with fundamental human rights; to prevent and combat negative societal attitudes in this regard, particularly within the family, by the means of comprehensive public education campaigns; to train members of the legal profession, especially the judiciary, in gender sensitivity; and to mobilise religious leaders in support of such efforts.[222] In 2003, the Committee on the Rights of the Child agreed with the Committee on the Rights of Women in response to the deep concern based on persistent discriminatory attitudes towards girls in Bangladesh, finding such discrimination firmly entrenched in traditional stereotypes.[223] Cyprus was encouraged to pursue information campaigns to eliminate stereotyping regarding the traditional roles of men and women in society when the Committee considered Cyprus' second report.[224] In 2006, it also recommended that Saudi Arabia take measures to break down stereotypical attitudes about the roles and responsibilities of women and men, when Saudi Arabia submitted its second periodic report.[225]

In the case of Bangladesh, in 2003 the Special Rapporteur on the Right to Food discovered a linkage between underweight births, the apparent persistence of social discrimination against women and the fact that women eat last and eat least.[226] The United Nations Children's Emergency Fund (UNICEF) also found in 2007 that social norms of Bangladesh often discourage or restrict women's mobility outside of the home and that those restrictions serve to compromise children's access to emergency health care by preventing women from travelling independently to shops, pharmacies or hospitals, and limiting women's direct contact with unrelated males, including doctors.[227]

The Committee on the Rights of the Child and the Human Rights Committee remain particularly concerned about the practice of female genital mutilation. The Committee on the Rights of the Child urged Senegal in 2006 and Niger in 2009 to strengthen awareness-raising campaigns and sensitisation activities for the general public, families, practitioners and traditional or religious leaders in order to encourage change in traditional attitudes and to discourage harmful

220 UN Doc. CCPR/C/MKD/CO/2, para. 9.
221 UN Doc. CCPR/C/TZA/CO/4, para. 9.
222 UN Doc. CRC/C/15/Add.183, para. 22.
223 UN Doc. CRC/C/15/Add.221, para. 28; UN Doc. A/59/38, para. 245.
224 UN Doc. CRC/C/15/Add.205, para. 28.
225 UN Doc. CRC/C/SAU/CO/2, para. 66.
226 UN Doc. E/CN.4/2004/10/Add.1, para. 39.
227 UNICEF, The State of the World's Children 2007, New York, 2006, p. 27.

practices.[228] In the case of domestic violence, the Committee on the Rights of the Child recommended in response to Ghana's second periodic report of 2006 that the State was required to raise awareness among the public with the aim of reversing public attitudes and traditions that inhibit victims, particularly women and girls, from reporting such violence.[229] The Human Rights Committee in 2006 called upon the Central African Republic to intensify its efforts in mobilising public opinion against female genital mutilation and to take measures to criminalise the act.[230]

State compliance

In response to the United Nations' inquiries on the protection and promotion of women's rights, States have answered that actions have been taken to lead public opinion. Australia declared in the Third Committee of the UN General Assembly in 1989 that in order to tackle violence against women, it had worked to 'change public opinion to produce a greater sense of community responsibility regarding the problem and to change attitudes throughout all groups, including aboriginal, islander and rural communities'.[231] In 2005, Armenia described to the Third Committee how it implemented the outcome of the Fourth World Conference on Women and the 23rd special session of the General Assembly, entitled 'Women 2000: gender equality, development and peace for the twenty-first century', stating that it had implemented a national plan for the prevention of human trafficking, including the creation of programmes intended to raise public awareness of the issue.[232] More frequently, States illustrated their attitudes and actions through the reporting procedures established by the Convention on the Elimination of All Forms of Discrimination against Women, the Convention on the Rights of the Child and the interactive dialogues of the Universal Periodic Review.

Treaty obligation

UNDER THE CONVENTION ON THE ELIMINATION OF DISCRIMINATION AGAINST WOMEN

Several States have made reservations and declarations to article 5 (a) of the Convention on the Elimination of Discrimination against Women. These States included France, India, Malaysia, Micronesia, Niger and Qatar. France declared that its application of article 5 will be subject to 'respect for article 17 of the International Covenant on Civil and Political Rights and article 8 of the European

228 UN Doc. CRC/C/SEN/CO/2, para. 51; UN Doc. CRC/C/NER/CO/2, para. 60.
229 UN Doc. CRC/C/GHA/CO/2, para. 45.
230 UN Doc. CCPR/C/CAF/CO/2, para. 11.
231 UN Doc. A/C.3/44/SR.22, para. 40.
232 UN Doc. A/C.3/59/SR.15, para. 41.

Convention for the Protection of Human Rights and Fundamental Freedoms'. India submitted that it shall abide by the provisions of article 5 (a) 'in conformity with its policy of non-interference in the personal affairs of any Community without its initiative and consent'. Malaysia did not consider itself bound by the provisions of article 5 (a), for the above provisions conflict with the Islamic Sharia law and the Federal Constitution of Malaysia. Micronesia did not apply the provisions of article 5 to 'the succession of certain well-established traditional titles, and to marital customs that divide tasks or decision-making in purely voluntary or consensual private conduct'. Additionally, Niger objected to the provision of 'modification of social and cultural patterns of conduct of men and women'.[233] There was a discussion about whether these reservations and declarations are compatible with the object and purpose of the Convention on the Elimination of Discrimination against Women.[234]

Some others entertained doubts but nevertheless were going to carry out action. For instance, the Czech Republic contended in its combined fourth and fifth periodic report in the Committee on the Elimination of Discrimination against Women in 2010 that:

> The main problem in effectively combating gender stereotypes lies in the fact that such stereotypes are widespread and rooted in broad layers of society, and that they largely reflect the true state of society . . . Nevertheless, . . . stereotypical thinking cannot possibly justify such an approach and it is necessary to try to change public opinion in this area.
>
> Another important factor which limits official authority's influence on public opinion is that some quarters of society are very critical about any Government effort to 'educate' the public – it is therefore difficult to find appropriate educational resources for the general public. This fact can be explained by the profoundly negative experience that the older generations, who remember the Communist regime before 1989, have of the promotion of 'correct' ideas from that era.[235]

To give effect to article 5 (a), the Czech Republic hosted the European Conference on New Ways to Overcome Gender Stereotypes in 2009, in which representatives of EU member States shared practices, tools and methods 'capable of achieving a positive change in public opinion'.[236] In 2007, Jordan implemented a programme to challenge female stereotypes by way of introducing the concepts of women's rights and gender equality at all levels of the education system, to preachers and imams, and through the use of the mass media and electronic games designed to

233 For the texts of the reservations and declarations, see United Nations Treaty Collection Databases.

234 Belinda Clark, 'The Vienna Convention Reservations Regime and the Convention on Discrimination against Women' (1991) 85 (2) *American Journal of International Law* 281.

235 UN Doc. CEDAW/C/CZE/Q/5/Add.1, paras 69–70.

236 UN Doc. CEDAW/C/CZE/Q/5/Add.1, para. 73.

communicate with the general public, in particular young men and women.[237] In 2006 the Greek General Secretariat for Gender Equality launched a campaign to inform public opinion, through a TV programme,[238] while in 2004 Kyrgyzstan made efforts to eliminate gender role stereotyping in the media.[239]

In 1995 Ukraine detailed to the UN General Assembly the major tasks of its national policy, including the informing of public opinion on the progression of international norms around women's rights, such as the advertising of the results of the Fourth World Conference on Women (the Beijing Conference).[240] In a report prepared by the Secretariat of the Committee on the Elimination of Discrimination against Women in 1992, Barbados had conducted research, presented in the media and worked with non-governmental organisations to raise community consciousness and diminish the idea of superiority of either of the sexes.[241] Canada launched a major public education campaign to 'educate the public' and to emphasise the seriousness of violence against women.[242] Burkina Faso, Canada, Germany and Jamaica carried out information campaigns to sensitise public opinion to the issue of prostitution.[243] Portugal conducted a media campaign in 1992 to increase awareness of violence within the family.[244]

UNDER THE CONVENTION ON THE RIGHTS OF THE CHILD

In the implementation of the Convention on the Rights of the Child, Ethiopia reported to its respective Committee through its third periodic review in 2006 that 'awareness-raising measures must [. . .] be taken to change public opinion in respect of educating girls'.[245] In this regard, the Ethiopian government had addressed the population and disseminated relevant information.[246] Sweden submitted in its third periodic review to the Committee on the Rights of the Child in 2004 on the topic of female genital mutilation that:

> Essentially, what is needed in the present situation is further preventive work in the form of a broad-based programme to educate public opinion along with the dissemination of information aimed at changing attitudes in the long term.[247]

These statements and actions demonstrate willingness on the part of States to promote and progress the rights of women and girls, accepting their duty to

237 UN Doc. CEDAW/C/SR.805 (A), paras 33–35.
238 UN Doc. CEDAW/C/GRC/Q/6/Add.1, para. 16, II, H.
239 UN Doc. A/59/38, para. 167.
240 UN Doc. A/C.3/50/SR.28, para. 51.
241 UN Doc. CEDAW/C/1992/4, para. 35.
242 UN Doc. CEDAW/C/1992/4, para. 36.
243 UN Doc. CEDAW/C/1992/4, para. 21.
244 UN Doc. CEDAW/C/1992/4, para. 49.
245 UN Doc. CRC/C/SR.1164, para. 59.
246 UN Doc. CRC/C/SR.1164, para. 59.
247 UN Doc. CRC/C/125/Add.1, para. 417.

lead public opinion in pursuit of equality. This is best illustrated in the continuous adherence of States to recommendations issued by the Committee on the Elimination of Discrimination against Women and the Committee on the Rights of the Child.

Customary obligation: the Universal Periodic Review

States not only report their actions to mobilise public opinion on women's status to the Committee on the Elimination of Discrimination against Women and the Committee on the Rights of the Child. They also submit national reports to the Human Rights Council and answer inquiries and recommendations from other States during the process of the Universal Periodic Review, the recently established mechanism which complements the work of human rights treaty bodies.[248] Interestingly, many States in the Universal Periodic Review have admitted to the necessity of changing public opinion on women's rights,[249] suggesting other States do so, or accepting recommendations of this kind without invoking their treaty obligations. The Human Rights Council in a resolution considers the Universal Declaration of Human Rights part of the basis of the Universal Periodic Review.[250] Because the Universal Declaration is widely regarded as a codification of customary law, the Human Rights Council's reference to it in the resolution means that the Council in effect is considering customary law and customary obligations of States. To this extent, the State duty to lead public opinion toward gender equality may have roots in customary law.

ACTIONS TAKEN

A number of States have worked on public opinion on violence against women through the aid of the Universal Periodic Review. In 2008, Finland campaigned to influence people's attitudes toward this issue.[251] Tajikistan's national policy for gender equality during the period of 2001 to 2010 set priorities for rallying of the general public and harnessing public opinion to combat violence against women.[252] Ukraine in 2008 identified changing social attitudes a task to work on and prohibited scenes of violence in the mass media, additionally considering the implementation of training courses in schools as a critical way to develop a new cultural approach.[253] Samoa in 2011 continued to conduct education and advocacy programmes in order to change mindsets and attitudes towards gender violence.[254] In 2011 Namibia implemented the 'Zero Tolerance

248 UN Doc. A/RES/60/251, para. 5 (e).
249 UN Doc. A/HRC/WG.6/3/LIE/1, para. 58; UN Doc. A/HRC/16/5, para. 50; UN Doc. A/HRC/19/19, para. 81.
250 UN Doc. A/HRC/RES/5/1, Annex, I, A, 1.
251 UN Doc. A/HRC/8/24/Add.1, para. 10; UN Doc. A/HRC/WG.6/1/FIN/1, para. 46.
252 UN Doc. A/HRC/WG.6/12/TJK/1, para. 46.
253 UN Doc. A/HRC/8/45, para. 12.
254 UN Doc. A/HRC/18/14, para. 63.

Campaign against Gender Based Violence, Including Human Trafficking' and ensured engagement at the highest political level in the campaign to highlight the unacceptability of violence against women in its addressing of the attitudes and stereotypes that perpetuate discriminatory practices that are harmful and violent toward women.[255]

Madagascar tried to involve all stakeholders in dialogues at local, regional and national levels, with a view to raising awareness and changing people's attitude toward 'moletry', a practice deemed by the Special Rapporteur on Contemporary Forms of Slavery as similar to slavery.[256] It urged traditional and religious leaders to join in and address the problem.[257] On the issue of female genital mutilation, Burkina Faso initiated major public education campaigns against the practice in the mid-1990s and then formally outlawed the practice in 1996.[258] In 2008, Mali said that its policy on female genital mutilation centred on awareness raising and education and was based on the belief that it was essential to obtain widespread public support for the eradication of such practices before adopting legislation.[259]

In the same year, Benin submitted that it had already banned the practice of female genital mutilation in 2003 and had implemented training programmes for public opinion leaders and practitioners of female genital mutilation, as well as awareness-raising actions for members of the judiciary, police officers and the population.[260] Norway initiated a four-year action plan (2008–2011) focused on changing public attitudes toward female genital mutilation through means of dialogues involving the groups concerned.[261] In 2009, the Central African Republic reported its efforts to mobilise public opinion against female genital mutilation.[262] Eritrea said in 2010 that it had campaigned extensively to educate the public on the issue of female genital mutilation and had committed to wiping out the practice from traditional culture.[263] Ghana even enacted laws that not only criminalised acts of female genital mutilation, but also outlawed pejorative attitudes toward that practice, alongside Trokosi and forced child marriages, as revealed in 2012.[264]

255 UN Doc. A/HRC/17/14, para. 97, recommendation 10.

256 Moletry is the conclusion of an engagement contract obliging an underage girl to behave irreproachably throughout the probationary one-year term of the marriage contract on pain of losing the agreed dowry (a maximum of three oxen and/or money). UN Doc. A/HRC/WG.6/7/MDG/1, para. 156; A/HRC/24/43/Add.2, para. 125.

257 UN Doc. A/HRC/WG.6/7/MDG/1, para. 156.

258 UN Doc. A/HRC/WG.6/3/BFA/2, para. 20.

259 UN Doc. A/HRC/8/50, para. 30.

260 UN Doc. A/HRC/8/39, para. 31.

261 UN Doc. A/HRC/13/5, para. 99.

262 UN Doc. A/HRC/12/2, para. 23.

263 UN Doc. A/HRC/13/2, para. 72.

264 Trokosi is a practice that traditional religious shrines take human beings, usually young virgin girls, in payment for services or in religious atonement for alleged misdeeds of a family member, almost always a male. UN Doc. A/HRC/WG.6/14/GHA/1, para. 85.

Regarding negative perceptions and stereotypes of women, Cambodia,[265] Liechtenstein,[266] Luxembourg,[267] Poland,[268] Thailand[269] and Ukraine[270] all carried out national strategies and specific initiatives, including workshops in schools and awareness-raising activities in society to eliminate such prejudices.[271] Ghana took aim at negative religious attitudes that hindered girls' education.[272] It said in 2012 that it had succeeded in changing some communal and religious leaders' perception and had moved them to encourage girls' education.[273] Andorra enacted the Act on Public Broadcasting and Television and the Incorporation of the Public Company Ràdioi Televisiód' Andorra SA of 13 April 2000, incorporating equality and non-discrimination as principles of public radio and television channels.[274] Latvia was of the view that '[p]ositive changes towards gender equality can be facilitated by deepening society's understanding and changing its attitude on certain issues.'[275] Therefore, it paid special attention between 2005 and 2008 to informative and educational activities for different target groups – employers, schoolchildren, teachers, judges, local government employees and politicians.[276]

SUGGESTIONS ACCEPTED

Some states, while not taking action, have accepted recommendations and made commitments to tackle negative attitudes toward women. These States are Afghanistan,[277] Andorra,[278] Angola,[279] Belgium,[280] Bulgaria,[281] Cambodia,[282] Greece,[283] Hungary,[284] Iceland,[285] Liechtenstein,[286] Lithuania,[287] Madagascar,[288]

265 UN Doc. A/HRC/WG.6/6/KHM/1, para. 81.
266 UN Doc. A/HRC/10/77, para. 37.
267 UN Doc. A/HRC/10/72, para. 8.
268 UN Doc. A/HRC/8/30, para. 7.
269 UN Doc. A/HRC/19/8, para. 73.
270 UN Doc. A/HRC/WG.6/2/UKR/1, para. 52.
271 UN Doc. A/HRC/10/77, para. 37.
272 UN Doc. A/HRC/WG.6/14/GHA/1, para. 85.
273 UN Doc. A/HRC/WG.6/14/GHA/1, para. 85.
274 UN Doc. A/HRC/WG.6/9/AND/1, para. 54.
275 UN Doc. A/HRC/WG.6/11/LVA/1, para. 65.
276 UN Doc. A/HRC/WG.6/11/LVA/1, para. 65.
277 UN Doc. A/HRC/12/9, para. 95, points 29 and 36.
278 UN Doc. A/HRC/16/8, para. 83, point 17.
279 UN Doc. A/HRC/14/11, para. 87, recommendation 49; UN Doc. A/HRC/14/L.10, para. 473.
280 UN Doc. A/HRC/18/3, para. 100, recommendation 28.
281 UN Doc. A/HRC/16/9, para. 80, recommendation 28; UN Doc. A/HRC/16/9/Add.1, p. 2.
282 UN Doc. A/HRC/13/4, para. 82, recommendation 30; UN Doc. A/HRC/13/56, para. 356.
283 UN Doc. A/HRC/18/13, para. 83, recommendations 18 and 19.
284 UN Doc. A/HRC/18/17, para. 94, recommendation 42.
285 UN Doc. A/HRC/19/13, para. 62, recommendations 3 and 4.
286 UN Doc. A/HRC/10/77, para. 37.
287 UN Doc. A/HRC/19/15, para. 88, recommendations 27–29.
288 UN Doc. A/HRC/14/13, para. 72, recommendations 26 and 27.

Namibia,[289] Norway,[290] Pakistan,[291] Saint Lucia,[292] Singapore,[293] Slovenia,[294] Spain,[295] Suriname,[296] Tajikistan,[297] Tanzania,[298] Thailand,[299] Trinidad and Tobago,[300] Tunisia,[301] Uganda[302] and Vanuatu.[303] They agreed to take up educational measures to battle against negative perceptions that derive from tradition, customs, culture and stereotypes.[304] These educational measures included reviewing school curricula and raising public awareness in society.[305] Target groups included the general public, opinion leaders and others whose opinions were important to the formulation of public opinion, namely religious leaders, politicians, public officers, teachers, parents and children.[306]

To promote the idea of gender equality and non-discrimination, Albania in 2010 endorsed the suggestion of providing training to law enforcement, judicial and other relevant authorities and conducting public awareness and education programmes with respect to issues related to sexual orientation and gender equality.[307] Australia agreed in 2011 to include human rights education in school and university curricula and to authorise action from national institutions and programmes.[308] A number of States favoured the suggestion of

289 UN Doc. A/HRC/17/14, para. 97, recommendation 10.
290 UN Doc. A/HRC/13/5, para. 105, recommendation 9.
291 UN Doc. A/HRC/8/42, para. 48.
292 UN Doc. A/HRC/17/6, para. 89, recommendation 59; UN Doc. A/HRC/17/6/Add.1, p. 5.
293 UN Doc. A/HRC/18/11, para. 95, recommendation 10.
294 UN Doc. A/HRC/14/15, para. 111, recommendation 25; UN Doc. A/HRC/14/15/Add.1, p. 3.
295 UN Doc. A/HRC/15/6, para. 84, recommendation 10.
296 UN Doc. A/HRC/18/12, para. 73, recommendations 28 and 29; UN Doc. A/HRC/18/12/Add.1, p. 3.
297 UN Doc. A/HRC/19/3, para. 88, recommendations 22 and 29.
298 UN Doc. A/HRC/19/4, para. 85, recommendations 23 and 29.
299 UN Doc. A/HRC/19/8, para. 88, recommendations 29 and 30.
300 UN Doc. A/HRC/19/7, para. 87, recommendation 5.
301 UN Doc. A/HRC/21/5, para. 114, recommendations 1 and 2.
302 UN Doc. A/HRC/19/16, para. 111, recommendation 4.
303 UN Doc. A/HRC/12/14, para. 56, recommendation 26; UN Doc. A/HRC/12/14/Add.1, p. 5.
304 These states include Andorra, Angola, Cambodia, Greece, Iceland, Liechtenstein, Lithuania, Spain and Suriname. UN Doc. A/HRC/16/8, para. 83, points 17 and 19; UN Doc. A/HRC/14/11, para. 87, recommendation 61; UN Doc. A/HRC/14/L.10, para. 473; UN Doc. A/HRC/13/4, para. 82, recommendation 30; UN Doc. A/HRC/13/56, para. 356; UN Doc. A/HRC/18/13, para. 83, recommendation 18; UN Doc. A/HRC/19/13, para. 62, recommendation 3; UN Doc. A/HRC/10/77, para. 37; UN Doc. A/HRC/19/15, para. 88, recommendation 27; UN Doc. A/HRC/8/42, para. 48; UN Doc. A/HRC/15/6, para. 84, recommendation 10; UN Doc. A/HRC/18/12, para. 73, recommendation 26; UN Doc. A/HRC/18/12/Add.1, p. 3.
305 Ibid.
306 UN Doc. A/HRC/14/11, para. 87, recommendation 61; UN Doc. A/HRC/14/L.10, para. 473; UN Doc. A/HRC/10/77, para. 37; UN Doc. A/HRC/12/9, para. 95, point 29.
307 UN Doc. A/HRC/13/6, para. 67, point 23.
308 UN Doc. A/HRC/17/10, para. 86, points 57, 58, 61 and 63; UN Doc. A/HRC/17/10/Add.1, pp. 2, 4 and 5.

tackling societal attitudes toward violence and harmful practices including sexual and psychological abuse of women,[309] female genital mutilation[310] and Wahaya (young women and girls being sold into sexual and domestic slavery).[311] These states were Andorra,[312] Costa Rica,[313] El Salvador,[314] Kenya,[315] Lithuania,[316] Niger,[317] Samoa,[318] Thailand[319] and Trinidad and Tobago.[320] Committed to the intensification of their cooperation with the media,[321] these States also determined to raise awareness and sensitise their general public and key persons such as practitioners, families and traditional and religious leaders through advocacy programmes.[322]

Conclusions

From merely expecting a subsidiary role to requiring full responsibility, international law has gone through remarkable achievements to establish the State duty to lead public opinion on gender equality. This State duty has been illustrated in numerous UN resolutions on the issue of mobilising public opinion in support of gender equality, stated as educating public opinion on the importance of the eradication of prejudice and the idea of the inferiority of women, according to the Declaration on the Elimination of Discrimination against Women. In the Convention on the Elimination of All Forms of Discrimination against Women, States have a duty to tackle gender role stereotyping and prejudice. In commentaries of human rights treaty bodies, States have the responsibility to make certain perceptions socially and culturally unacceptable, to eliminate the ideology that confers stereotypical roles on women or considers them inferior to men, and to advocate the idea of gender equality regardless of its support within society. The State duty to lead public opinion on gender equality was developed not only by the Committee on the Elimination of Discrimination against Women, but also

309 UN Doc. A/HRC/13/15, para. 91, recommendation 7; UN Doc. A/HRC/13/15/Add.1, p. 4.
310 UN Doc. A/HRC/15/8, para. 101, recommendation 53.
311 UN Doc. A/HRC/17/15, para. 76, recommendation 26.
312 UN Doc. A/HRC/16/8, para. 83, point 19.
313 UN Doc. A/HRC/13/15, para. 91, recommendation 7; UN Doc. A/HRC/13/15/Add.1, p. 4.
314 UN Doc. A/HRC/14/5, para. 81, recommendations 22, 28 and 30; UN Doc. A/HRC/14/5/Add.1, para. 9.
315 UN Doc. A/HRC/15/8, para. 101, recommendation 53.
316 UN Doc. A/HRC/19/15, para. 89, recommendation 40.
317 UN Doc. A/HRC/17/15, para. 76, recommendation 26.
318 UN Doc. A/HRC/18/14, para. 63.
319 UN Doc. A/HRC/19/8, para. 88, recommendations 31 and 32.
320 UN Doc. A/HRC/19/7, para. 87, recommendations 13 and 14.
321 UN Doc. A/HRC/16/8, para. 83, point 19; UN Doc. A/HRC/15/6, para. 84, recommendations 10 and 11.
322 UN Doc. A/HRC/15/8, para. 101, recommendation 53; UN Doc. A/HRC/17/15, para. 76, recommendation 26; UN Doc. A/HRC/18/14, para. 63.

by the Human Rights Committee and the Committee on the Rights of the Child even though the two governing treaties, the International Covenant on Civil and Political Rights and the Convention on the Rights of the Child, do not refer to public opinion at all. Considerable State compliance can be found within the different human rights mechanisms, particularly in the Universal Periodic Review where this duty was requested and obeyed without requiring the invocation of a human rights treaty provision. This may go some way to suggest that this duty has a basis in customary law.

4 Influencing public opinion via human rights education

To achieve ethnic and gender equality, States have a duty to influence public opinion through education. This requires States to utilise their powers to punish racist speech, eliminate sex role stereotyping and prejudice, and target any other ideas that breed discrimination. Yet ethnic and gender equality is not the only area in which public opinion presents an obstacle to the realisation and defence of human rights. This chapter discusses whether States have a general duty to educate and inform public opinion on human rights issues. The discussion starts with an analysis of the aim and content of education, continuing to the widespread educational measures prescribed in human rights instruments and finally progressing to State practices in educating the public in order to realise and establish adherence to human rights in society.

The aim and content of education: attitudes change emergence

The aims and contents of education were discussed by States in the 1940s when they contemplated the provisions of the Constitution of the United Nations Educational, Scientific and Cultural Organization and the Universal Declaration of Human Rights. The United Nations Educational, Scientific and Cultural Organization (UNESCO), established in 1945, is a specialised UN agency mandated to promote respect for human rights and fundamental freedoms.[1] According to its Constitution, education is the central working method to achieve that goal. The Universal Declaration of Human Rights was adopted by the United Nations General Assembly on 10 December 1948 and represents the first comprehensive global expression of the rights to which all human beings are inherently entitled.[2] It regards education as providing a driving impetus in the respect for human rights and freedoms, as well as understanding, tolerance and friendship.[3]

1 The Constitution of the United Nations Educational, Scientific and Cultural Organization, article 1 (1).
2 UNGA Res. 217 A (III), UN Doc. A/810.
3 The Universal Declaration of Human Rights, preamble and article 26.

The Constitution of the United Nations Educational, Scientific and Cultural Organization

The Constitution of UNESCO states in the first recital of the preamble that 'it is in the minds of men that the defences of peace must be constructed'.[4] The slogan presented on its official website stresses the ideal of '[b]uilding peace in the minds of men and women'. Contributing factors that often lead to wars according to UNESCO include 'ignorance of each other's ways and lives' which leads to suspicion and mistrust,[5] the denial of the principles of human rights such as 'the dignity, equality and mutual respect of men' and the propagation, 'through ignorance and prejudice, of the doctrine of the inequality of men and races'.[6]

These factors hold true with people's perception and highlight the importance of education in overcoming such conflict. The preamble of the Constitution of UNESCO appeals to States to diffuse culture, educate for justice, liberty and peace, and to consider these tasks to be a sacred duty of States.[7] The preamble further declares that States, in addition to the pursuit of full and equal opportunities in education for all, should aim to reach an objective truth and 'mutual understanding and a truer and more perfect knowledge of each other's lives'.[8] It is reasonable to assume that the Constitution of UNESCO considers that educational undertakings of a State should embody the spirit of human rights principles.

It must be acknowledged that these appeals and statements are located in the preamble and not included in the substantive provisions of the Constitution. The preamble of a treaty is deemed to form part of its context for the purposes of interpreting the treaty, a process regulated by article 31 (2) of the Vienna Convention on the Law of Treaties. Jann Kleffner has pointed out that there is nothing in the law of treaties to suggest that the provisions of a preamble have no legal force or even an inferior legal presence in relation to other provisions.[9] States, by endorsing the Constitution of UNESCO, show a considerable degree of acceptance of their duty of building peace, security and respect for human rights in people's minds. To facilitate States' realisation of such a duty, UNESCO

4 The Constitution of the United Nations Educational, Scientific and Cultural Organization, preamble.

5 The Constitution of the United Nations Educational, Scientific and Cultural Organization, preamble.

6 The Constitution of the United Nations Educational, Scientific and Cultural Organization, preamble.

7 The Constitution of the United Nations Educational, Scientific and Cultural Organization, preamble.

8 The Constitution of the United Nations Educational, Scientific and Cultural Organization, preamble.

9 Jann K. Kleffner, 'Auto-referrals and the Complementary Nature of the ICC', in Carsten Stahn and Göran Sluiter (eds), *The Emerging Practice of the International Criminal Court* (Brill 2009) 41, 45.

refers to educational methods as 'best suited to prepare the children of the world for the responsibilities of freedom'.[10]

The Universal Declaration of Human Rights: education to promote understanding, tolerance, friendship and respect for human rights

The Universal Declaration of Human Rights mentions education at two points, initially in its preamble which declares education as a general method with which to promote respect for human rights and freedoms,[11] and again in article 26 expressing the right to education. In the preamble, the Declaration pronounces education as a significant approach to instilling respect and understanding for human rights. In article 26, the Declaration embodies the instruction and dissemination of human rights as an aim and content of education, forming part of the meaning which defines the right to education. Hence, the right to education as established in the Declaration not only calls for States to ensure that '[e]veryone has the right to education', but also delineates the quality of education that everyone is entitled to. This second part is somewhat controversial and is a point often neglected by commentators and States.

Preamble

The preamble of the Universal Declaration of Human Rights considers education as an important way to promote respect for the rights and freedoms enshrined in the Declaration, as well as their recognition and observance, 'both among the peoples of Member States themselves and among the peoples of territories under their jurisdiction'.[12] The Drafting Committee of the Commission on Human Rights emphasised that education should enhance the widest possible respect for human rights, as opposed to resorting exclusively to enforcement measures.[13] The Chinese delegate even acknowledged that the emphasis of the Declaration was to educate people on 'voluntary recognition of the rights of others', not about enforcement measures to restrain them.[14] Agreeing with this argument, the United Kingdom noted that the path on which the achievement of the progressive extension and refinement of human rights for which the Universal Declaration constituted a valuable basis lay in was education, teaching and the influence of morals on mankind.[15]

10 The Constitution of the United Nations Educational, Scientific and Cultural Organization, paragraph 2 of article 1.
11 The Constitution of the United Nations Educational, Scientific and Cultural Organization, preamble.
12 The Constitution of the United Nations Educational, Scientific and Cultural Organization, preamble.
13 UN Doc. E/CN.4/AC.1/SR.18, p. 3.
14 UN Doc. E/CN.4/SR.51, pp. 5–6.
15 UN Doc. E/CN.4/SR.54, p. 5; UN Doc. E/CN.4/38, para. 3.

Eleanor Roosevelt, head of the United States delegation in the negotiations, agreed on the significance of education in propagating human rights. In her analysis of the Declaration and its preamble, she wrote that:

> [t]he draft declaration was not a treaty or international agreement and did not impose legal obligations. It was rather a statement of basic principles of inalienable human rights, setting up a common standard of achievement for all peoples and all nations. Although it was not legally binding, the declaration would nevertheless, have considerable weight. Its adoption would commit Member States, in the words of the preamble, 'to strive by teaching and education to promote respect for these rights and freedoms and by progressive measures, national and international, to secure the universal and effective recognition and observance, both among the peoples of Member States themselves and among the peoples of territories under their jurisdiction'.[16]

The wording of the preambular clause, invoking States 'to strive by teaching and education to promote respect for' and 'secure . . . recognition and observance' of human rights and freedoms, was endorsed by the majority of delegations, including those of France,[17] Greece,[18] Lebanon,[19] the Philippines[20] and the United Kingdom.[21] The delegation of Poland, by way of contrast, found it to be vague, rambling and surprisingly weak,[22] yet it did not deny that the Declaration had created a new standard for education.[23]

As already mentioned, States are responsible for deepening people's understanding and enhancing their respect for human rights through education. Regarding the boundaries of 'peoples', France proposed to include the peoples of member States of the United Nations and the peoples of territories under their jurisdiction, a proposal which was subsequently adopted.[24] The adoption of this interpretation logically concludes that if States bear a duty to mould respect for human rights, the recipients of States' educational measures should include not only their citizens but also those citizens of territories under their jurisdiction. The final text of this preambular paragraph:

> proclaims THIS UNIVERSAL DECLARATION OF HUMAN RIGHTS as a common standard of achievement for all peoples and all nations, to the end that every individual and every organ of society, keeping this Declaration

16 UN Doc. A/C.3/SR.89, pp. 32–33.
17 UN Doc. A/C.3/SC.4/21.
18 UN Doc. A/C.3/314/Rev.1/Add.2.
19 UN Doc. E/CN.4/132.
20 UN Doc. E/CN.4/143.
21 UN Doc. E/CN.4/124.
22 UN Doc. A/C.3/SR.165, p. 761.
23 UN Doc. E/SR.215, pp. 646–647.
24 UN Doc. A/C.3/SC.4/21.

constantly in mind, shall strive by teaching and education to promote respect for these rights and freedoms and by progressive measures, national and international, to secure their universal and effective recognition and observance, both among the peoples of Member States themselves and among the peoples of territories under their jurisdiction.[25]

Right to education

The right to education provision (article 26) of the Universal Declaration encompasses a certain standard of education, not merely accessible education for all. The second paragraph of article 26 points out that:

> Education shall be directed to the full development of the human personality and to the strengthening of respect for human rights and fundamental freedoms. It shall promote understanding, tolerance and friendship among all nations, racial or religious groups, and shall further the activities of the United Nations for the maintenance of peace.[26]

Compared to the UNESCO Constitution, such a direction encompasses a broader entrenchment of human rights within educational standards. In doing so, it links the aim of education to the promotion of respect for human rights and the increasing of understanding, tolerance and friendship among all national, racial and religious groups.

MEMBER STATES' CONSTITUTIONS

There was a fierce debate in the *travaux préparatoires* regarding the specification of the aim and content of education in the provision enshrining the right to education provision. To facilitate the debate, the constitutions of member States were utilised for the purposes of reference. Interestingly, almost all of the constitutions referred to had defined the aim and mandatory content of education therein. For instance:

> China, Constitution of, Article 158
> Education and culture shall have as its aim the development among citizens of national spirit, a democratic spirit, national morality, sound and healthy physique, of sciences and of the knowledge and ability to earn a living.[27]

> Mexico (United Mexican States), Constitution of, Article 3
> The education that the State imparts [. . .] shall combat fanaticism and

25 The Constitution of the United Nations Educational, Scientific and Cultural Organization, preamble.
26 The Universal Declaration of Human Rights, article 26.
27 UN Doc. E/CN.4/AC.1/3/Add.1, p. 293.

prejudices, for which purpose the school shall organize its instruction and activities in a form that may permit the creation in youth of a rational and exact concept of the universe and of social life.[28]

Nicaragua, Constitution of, Article 92
The moral education of youth will be fostered in all schools, as well as the development of civic sentiment and personal and professional honesty.[29]

Panama, Constitution of the Republic of, Article 77
The service of national education in its intellectual, moral, civic, and physical aspects is an essential duty of the State. National education will be inspired by democratic doctrine and ideals of national aggrandizement and human solidarity.

It is a function of the State to fix the bases of education, which will be organized in a form in which unity, articulation, and continuity exist in all its grades.[30]

Paraguay, Constitution of, Article 11
Care for . . . the moral, spiritual, and physical education of youth, are fundamental duties of the State.[31]

Peru, Constitution of the Republic of, Article 79
Moral and civic education of children is obligatory and shall necessarily be inspired by the national growth and human solidarity.[32]

Philippines, Constitution of, the Section 5
The Government shall establish and maintain a complete and adequate system of public education [. . .]. All schools shall aim to develop moral character, personal discipline, civil conscience, and vocational efficiency, and to teach the duties of citizenship.[33]

Syria, Constitution of, Article 20
Education shall be directed to raising the moral and intellectual standard of the people on lines best suited to the national characteristics, and the promoting concord and a fraternal spirit among all citizens.[34]

In these provisions, moral and spiritual development was frequently mentioned, as well as occasional mentions of democratic principles and the

28 UN Doc. E/CN.4/AC.1/3/Add.1, p. 300.
29 UN Doc. E/CN.4/AC.1/3/Add.1, p. 301.
30 UN Doc. E/CN.4/AC.1/3/Add.1, p. 301.
31 UN Doc. E/CN.4/AC.1/3/Add.1, p. 288.
32 UN Doc. E/CN.4/AC.1/3/Add.1, p. 304.
33 UN Doc. E/CN.4/AC.1/3/Add.1, pp. 305–306.
34 UN Doc. E/CN.4/AC.1/3/Add.1, p. 166.

combating of fanaticism and prejudices. These provisions provided grounds to support the argument of specifying the aim and content of education in the Universal Declaration.

WHETHER TO STATE THE AIM AND CONTENT OF EDUCATION

In the *travaux préparatoires*, a number of States and organisations seconded the promotion of identifying human rights as an aim and content of education in the aforementioned clause. The World Jewish Congress stated that the neglect of the spirit that governs education had been the root cause of two catastrophic wars.[35] UNESCO stated that the principle of the right of education for everyone had been adhered to in Germany and other fascist countries, but not the doctrines on which that education should be founded:

> If the Declaration failed to define the spirit in which future generations were to be educated, it would lose its value as a guide for humanity [.] It was necessary to stress the importance of the article (article 26) devoted to the spirit of education, which was possibly greater than that of all the other articles of the Declaration [.] [I]n Germany and in all other countries[,] it was necessary to work a change in the spirit of education.[36]

The Soviet Union stretched the point even further, maintaining that it should be made impossible for young people to be brought up in a spirit of hatred and intolerance, which it cited as one of the fundamental factors in the development of Nazism and fascism.[37]

Expressing similar views, China and the International Union of Catholic Women's Leagues stated that the Universal Declaration should not be silent on the aim and spirit of education.[38] Panama believed that education without the struggle against intolerance amounted to a mere form of training.[39] Lebanon agreed, opining that:

> It was not enough to say that everyone had the right to education; it was necessary to specify the nature of such education. That was the only possible guarantee that future generations would not be educated in a spirit contrary to the aims of the United Nations as defined in the Preamble to the Charter.[40]

At one stage in the negotiations, China, India, New Zealand and the United Kingdom expressed their opposition to the idea of stipulating the aim of education.[41] The United Kingdom warned of the dangers in summarising all the

35 UN Doc. E/CN.4/AC.2/SR.8, p. 4.
36 UN Doc. E/CN.4/SR.67, p. 13 (note added).
37 UN Doc. E/CN.4/SR.69, pp. 3–4.
38 UN Doc. E/CN.4/SR.67, p. 16; UN Doc. E/CN.4/SR.69, p. 5.
39 UN Doc. E/CN.4/AC.2/SR.8, p. 5.
40 UN Doc. E/CN.4/SR.67, p. 14.
41 UN Doc. E/CN.4/99, p. 7; UN Doc. E/CN.4/102, pp. 6 and 8; UN Doc. A/C.3/267, p. 2.

theories on the aims of education in three or four lines.[42] This warning was not shared by the majority of States. Ukraine, for instance, did not see any danger in 'stat[ing] the need for respecting all human rights and for developing international goodwill to prevent any kind of hatred'.[43] It explained its position that '[a]s far as the publishing of scientific discoveries was concerned, it was not a question of publicity or the lack of publicity, but of the way in which such publications were used in the education of young people.'[44] Others such as Cuba[45] and the Philippines[46] were also in favour of announcing the aim of education in the Universal Declaration of Human Rights.

WHAT IS THE AIM AND CONTENT OF EDUCATION?

As to the actual aim of education as expressed in the Universal Declaration, different suggestions came from China,[47] Cuba,[48] France,[49] Lebanon,[50] Mexico,[51] Panama,[52] the Philippines,[53] the Soviet Union,[54] Ukraine,[55] the United Kingdom,[56] the United States,[57] the World Jewish Congress[58] and UNESCO.[59] China, France, Mexico, the United Kingdom, the United States and the World Jewish Congress suggested that education should strengthen respect for human rights and fundamental freedoms.[60] France, the Soviet Union, Yugoslavia and the World Jewish Congress felt strongly that the aim of education should endeavour to combat or banish the spirit of intolerance and hatred against other nations, as well as racial or religious groups throughout the world.[61] France, Lebanon,

42 UN Doc. E/CN.4/SR.69, p. 4.
43 UN Doc. E/CN.4/SR.69, pp. 4–5.
44 UN Doc. E/CN.4/SR.69, pp. 4–5.
45 UN Doc. A/C.3/SR.146, p. 580.
46 UN Doc. E/CN.4/SR.68, p. 12.
47 UN Doc. E/CN.4/SR.67, p. 16; UN Doc. E/CN.4/SR.69, p. 9; UN Doc. A/C.3/SC.4/20.
48 UN Doc. E/CN.4/W.8, pp. 16–17; UN Doc. E/HR/1, p. 3; UN Doc. E/CN.4/AC.1/3/Add.1, p. 290.
49 UN Doc. E/CN.4/AC.2/SR.8, p. 5; UN Doc. E/CN.4/82/Add.8, p. 6; UN Doc. E/CN.4/95, p. 12; UN Doc. A/C.3/355.
50 UN Doc. E/CN.4/SR.69, p. 8.
51 UN Doc. E/CN.4/85, p. 44; UN Doc. A/C.3/266, p. 1; UN Doc. A/C.3/356.
52 UN Doc. E/CN.4/AC.2/SR.8, p. 5; UN Doc. E/CN.4/121; UN Doc. E/CN.4/SR.67, p. 10.
53 UN Doc. E/CN.4/SR.68, p. 12.
54 UN Doc. E/CN.4/SR.69, p. 2.
55 UN Doc. E/CN.4/SR.67, p. 17.
56 UN Doc. A/C.3/354.
57 UN Doc. A/C.3/356.
58 UN Doc. E/CN.4/AC.2/SR.8, pp. 3–4.
59 UN Doc. E/CN.4/AC.2/SR.8, p. 5.
60 UN Doc. E/CN.4/AC.2/SR.8, pp. 3–4; UN Doc. E/CN.4/82/Add.8, p. 6; UN Doc. E/CN.4/95, p. 12; UN Doc. E/CN.4/SR.68, p. 11; UN Doc. E/CN.4/SR.69, pp. 2, 8 and 9; UN Doc. E/CN.4/SR.67, p. 16; UN Doc. A/C.3/354; UN Doc. A/C.3/355; UN Doc. A/C.3/356; UN Doc. A/C.3/SC.4/20; UN Doc. E/CN.4/AC.2/SR.8, p. 5.
61 UN Doc. E/CN.4/AC.2/SR.8, pp. 3–4; UN Doc. E/CN.4/82/Add.8, p. 6; UN Doc. E/CN.4/95, p. 12; UN Doc. E/600, p. 18; UN Doc. E/CN.4/SR.69, pp. 2 and 9; UN Doc. E/

Mexico, the United Kingdom, the United States and UNESCO submitted that the aim include the promotion of understanding, tolerance, friendship and concord amongst peoples.[62] UNESCO stressed the view that a pacifist character and a spirit of tolerance should constitute the objectives of education.[63]

In addition, China proposed that education should pursue international good will.[64] Panama suggested that the foundation of education should be based on the principles of human freedom, morality and brotherhood or solidarity.[65] Cuba thought that education should lead to the 'sharing in all the material and spiritual benefits of civilization'.[66] In the view of the Soviet Union, education should be conducted on democratic lines, directed in a spirit of struggle against hatred, Nazism, fascism and the horrors of war and should be aimed toward a new international understanding.[67] The Philippines expressed the view that the objective of education should be to prevent the danger of governments pursuing anti-social aims.[68] It also thought that the objective of education should be compatible with the spirit of the UN Charter and the Constitution of UNESCO.[69]

When discussing the specific wording, Argentina questioned whether the term 'combating' the spirit of intolerance had an intolerant and aggressive rhetorical construction and whether intolerance and hatred should be done away with by means of peaceful persuasion and education.[70] After some discussion, the aim and content of education was confirmed in paragraph 2 of article 26 of the Universal Declaration as providing for the strengthening of respect for human rights and fundamental freedoms and the promotion of understanding, tolerance and friendship among all nations, racial or religious groups.[71] The combating of intolerance was omitted. Notably, the aim and content of education indicates factors that would favour the development of human personality, but does not set forth directives on the educational system itself.[72] This can be attributed to a debate on the right of the State in determining the educational system and the right of the family to choose what kind of education their child should receive. Concerning the right of the family, a third paragraph was added to article 26,

CN.4/148/Add.1, p. 4; UN Doc. E/800, p. 13; UN Doc. A/C.3/355; UN Doc. E/CN.4/AC.2/SR.8, p. 5.

62 UN Doc. E/CN.4/SR.68, p. 11; UN Doc. E/CN.4/85, p. 44; UN Doc. A/C.3/266, p. 1; UN Doc. A/C.3/354; UN Doc. A/C.3/355; UN Doc. A/C.3/356; UN Doc. A/C.3/364, p. 1; UN Doc. A/C.3/379, p. 4; UN Doc. A/C.3/SC.4/17, pp. 1–2; UN Doc. A/C.3/400, p. 13; UN Doc. A/777, para. 12; UN Doc. A/C.3/SC.4/20; UN Doc. A/C.3/SR.147, p. 598.

63 UN Doc. E/CN.4/AC.2/SR.8, p. 5.

64 UN Doc. E/CN.4/SR.69, pp. 2 and 9.

65 UN Doc. E/CN.4/121; UN Doc. E/CN.4/SR.67, p. 10.

66 UN Doc. E/CN.4/W.8, pp. 16–17; UN Doc. E/HR/1, p. 3; UN Doc. E/CN.4/AC.1/3/Add.1, p. 290.

67 UN Doc. E/CN.4/AC.2/SR.8, p. 4; UN Doc. E/CN.4/SR.69, pp. 3–4.

68 UN Doc. E/CN.4/SR.68, p. 12.

69 UN Doc. A/C.3/SR.147, p. 593.

70 UN Doc. A/C.3/SR.146, p. 581.

71 The Universal Declaration of Human Rights, article 26.

72 UN Doc. E/CN.4/SR.67, p. 15.

which provided that '[p]arents have a prior right to choose the kind of education that shall be given to their children.'

According to the Constitution of UNESCO, education should build defences for peace in the minds of men and, as such, it is a sacred duty of States to educate for justice, liberty and peace. The aim of education as envisioned in UNESCO's Constitution includes the pursuit of objective truths, mutual understanding and a truer and more perfect knowledge of each other's lives. The Universal Declaration of Human Rights defines the aim and content of education as the full development of the human personality, the strengthening of respect for human rights and fundamental freedoms, and the promotion of understanding, tolerance and friendship among all nations and racial or religious groups in conformity with paragraph 2 of article 26. The Universal Declaration also deems education as an essential means to facilitate the implementation of all the rights and freedoms of the Declaration, both among the peoples of member States themselves and among the peoples of territories under their jurisdiction.

Developing the aim and content of education

Reaffirming the aim and content of education

The Universal Declaration of Human Rights represents the first global expression of rights to which all human beings are inherently entitled. Articles of the Declaration have been elaborated in subsequent international treaties, regional human rights instruments and national legislation, including paragraph 2 of article 26 concerning the aim and content of education. Within the International Bill of Human Rights which consists of the Universal Declaration of Human Rights, the International Covenant on Economic, Social and Cultural Rights, the International Covenant on Civil and Political Rights and its two Optional Protocols, the aim and content of education is reaffirmed in paragraph 1 of article 13 of the International Covenant on Economic, Social and Cultural Rights:

> The States Parties to the present Covenant [. . .] agree that education shall be directed to the full development of the human personality and the sense of its dignity, and shall strengthen the respect for human rights and fundamental freedoms. They further agree that education shall [. . .] promote understanding, tolerance and friendship among all nations and all racial, ethnic or religious groups.[73]

Among other core human rights instruments, the Convention on the Rights of Persons with Disabilities declares that States shall foster at all levels of the education system an attitude of respect for the rights of persons with disabilities.[74] The UN Declaration of the Rights of the Child and the Declaration on the

73 The International Covenant on Economic, Social and Cultural Rights, article 13.

74 The Convention on the Rights of Persons with Disabilities, article 8.

Elimination of All Forms of Intolerance and of Discrimination Based on Religion or Belief both state that children 'shall be brought up in a spirit of understanding, tolerance, friendship among peoples, peace and universal brotherhood'.[75] The Convention on the Rights of the Child further defines the aim of education as providing for the development of respect for human rights and fundamental freedoms, as well as the promotion of the spirit of understanding, peace, tolerance, equality and friendship among all peoples, ethnic, national and religious groups and persons of indigenous origin, pursuant to article 29.[76] The Committee on the Rights of the Child, the supervisory body tasked with the implementation of the Convention on the Rights of the Child, emphasised that a child's right to education is a matter of content, not simply a matter of access.[77] The issues of content and access are located in two separate articles and are of equal importance.[78]

UNESCO adopted the same wording as the Universal Declaration of Human Rights with regard to the aim of education in its Convention against Discrimination in Education 1960 and its recommendation concerning Education for International Understanding, Co-operation and Peace and Education relating to Human Rights and Fundamental Freedoms of 1974.[79] The latter recommendation reiterates the role of education in promoting international understanding and respect for human rights and fundamental freedoms.[80] The UNESCO Declaration of Principles on Tolerance urges that education 'contribute to development of understanding, solidarity and tolerance among individuals as well as among ethnic, social, cultural, religious and linguistic groups and nations'.[81] The World Conference against Racism, Racial Discrimination, Xenophobia and Related Intolerance in 2001 reiterated that both the quality of education and access to free primary education are equally important.[82] Besides the UNESCO system, the Vienna Declaration and Programme of Action, adopted by the World Conference on Human Rights in Vienna on 25 June 1993, encourages States to 'direct education towards . . . the strengthening of respect for human rights and fundamental freedoms'.[83]

75 The Declaration of the Rights of the Child, article 10; the Declaration on the Elimination of All Forms of Intolerance and of Discrimination Based on Religion or Belief, article 5 (3).

76 The Convention on the Rights of the Child, article 29.

77 The Committee on the Rights of the Child Committee general comment no. 1, para. 3.

78 The Committee on the Rights of the Child Committee general comment no. 1, para. 9.

79 The UNESCO Convention against Discrimination in Education 1960, article 5; UNESCO recommendation concerning Education for International Understanding, Co-operation and Peace and Education relating to Human Rights and Fundamental Freedoms of 1974, para. 3.

80 UNESCO recommendation concerning Education for International Understanding, Co-operation and Peace and Education relating to Human Rights and Fundamental Freedoms of 1974, preamble.

81 The UNESCO Declaration of Principles on Tolerance, article 4.

82 The Declaration of the World Conference against Racism, Racial Discrimination, Xenophobia and Related Intolerance, para. 96.

83 The Vienna Declaration and Programme of Action, para. 79.

To raise awareness

Human rights principles

Article 7 of the International Convention on the Elimination of All Forms of Racial Discrimination has further iterated the content of education as including the principles of the Charter of the United Nations, the Universal Declaration of Human Rights and the UN Declaration and Convention on the Elimination of All Forms of Racial Discrimination.[84] The Convention on the Rights of the Child agrees on the inclusion of principles enshrined in the Charter of the United Nations.[85] UNESCO found States to assume responsibility in making human rights principles 'an integral part' of each individual through the means of education in a recommendation released in 1974.[86] The Vienna Declaration and Programme of Action adopted in the World Conference on Human Rights in Vienna on 25 June 1993 held the view that '[g]overnments should promote an increased awareness of human rights and mutual tolerance'.[87] The UNESCO Declaration of Principles on Tolerance (1995) reaffirms that the aim of States in educating citizens should be to provide the capability for individuals to 'appreciate the value of freedom, respectful of human dignity and differences'.[88]

International humanitarian law

The Committee on the Rights of the Child suggested in its general comment No. 1 that international humanitarian law ought to be included in the content of education.[89] The World Conference on Human Rights in Vienna on 25 June 1993 also recommended humanitarian law as a subject in the curricula of all learning institutions, alongside subjects on human rights, democracy and the rule of law.[90] In fact, as early as 1949, the four Geneva Conventions established standards of international humanitarian law through which they outlined the duty of States in disseminating the text of the Conventions throughout their respective territories in order to make the principles enshrined therein known to their populations.[91]

84 The International Convention on the Elimination of All Forms of Racial Discrimination, article 7.
85 The Convention on the Rights of the Child, article 29.
86 UNESCO recommendation concerning Education for International Understanding, Co-operation and Peace and Education relating to Human Rights and Fundamental Freedoms of 1974, para. 11.
87 The Vienna Declaration and Programme of Action, para. 82.
88 The UNESCO Declaration of Principles on Tolerance, article 4 (4).
89 The Committee on the Rights of the Child general comment no. 1, para. 16.
90 The Vienna Declaration and Programme of Action, para. 79.
91 Geneva Convention (I) for the Amelioration of the Condition of the Wounded and Sick in Armed Forces in the Field, article 47; Geneva Convention (II) for the Amelioration of the Condition of Wounded, Sick and Shipwrecked Members of Armed Forces at Sea, article 48; Convention (III) relative to the Treatment of Prisoners of War, article 127; Convention (IV) relative to the Protection of Civilian Persons in Time of War, article 144.

Human rights violations

In 1974, UNESCO recommended that education should address the inadmissibility of recourse to war for purposes of expansion, aggression and domination, in addition to the use of force and violence for purposes of repression.[92] It suggested that education draw attention to the conditions which perpetuate and aggravate human rights problems such as inequality and injustice, and measures of international cooperation which are likely to help solve them.[93] In the 1995 UNESCO Declaration of Principles on Tolerance, States are encouraged to address the cultural, social, economic, political and religious sources of intolerance that are major root causes of violence and exclusion.[94] Additionally, the 2001 World Conference against Racism, Racial Discrimination, Xenophobia and Related Intolerance in Durban urged States to promote awareness of the causes, consequences and evils of racism, racial discrimination, xenophobia and related intolerance through educational means.[95]

To change attitudes

Anti-discrimination

Education has also been tasked with the moulding of attitudes to create an atmosphere more conducive to the growth of human rights. The task of changing attitudes has been included as an aim of education in the International Convention on the Elimination of All Forms of Racial Discrimination,[96] a UNESCO recommendation of 1974[97] and the 2001 Declaration of the World Conference against Racism, Racial Discrimination, Xenophobia and Related Intolerance,[98] in which education was deemed to be a key tool in changing attitudes.[99]

The Convention on the Elimination of All Forms of Discrimination against Women outlines the State's obligation to eliminate gender prejudice and

92 UNESCO recommendation concerning Education for International Understanding, Co-operation and Peace and Education relating to Human Rights and Fundamental Freedoms of 1974, para. 6.

93 UNESCO recommendation concerning Education for International Understanding, Co-operation and Peace and Education relating to Human Rights and Fundamental Freedoms of 1974, para. 18.

94 The UNESCO Declaration of Principles on Tolerance, article 4 (2).

95 The Declaration and Programme of Action of the World Conference against Racism, Racial Discrimination, Xenophobia and Related Intolerance, paras 127 and 131.

96 The International Convention on the Elimination of All Forms of Racial Discrimination, article 7.

97 UNESCO recommendation concerning Education for International Understanding, Co-operation and Peace and Education relating to Human Rights and Fundamental Freedoms of 1974, para. 6.

98 The Declaration of the World Conference against Racism, Racial Discrimination, Xenophobia and Related Intolerance, paras 95 and 97.

99 The Declaration of the World Conference against Racism, Racial Discrimination, Xenophobia and Related Intolerance, para. 95.

stereotypical concepts of the roles of men and women through education.[100] In 1994 the UN Sub-Commission on Prevention of Discrimination and Protection of Minorities called on education to combat the discrimination, prejudice and stigma associated with those afflicted by HIV and AIDS.[101] Just over a decade later, the Working Group on Minorities of the UN Commission on Human Rights suggested in 2005 that education should promote religious tolerance.[102] The Convention on the Rights of Persons with Disabilities, adopted by the UN in 2006, demands that States foster an attitude of respect for the rights of persons with disabilities at all levels of the educational system.[103]

Cultural diversity

Cultural diversity has also been highlighted by UNESCO in 1974 as an aim and content of education.[104] UNESCO called for education to introduce different cultures, civilisations, values and ways of life, including domestic ethnic cultures and cultures of other nations.[105] It attached importance to the teaching of foreign languages, civilizations and cultural heritage as a means of promoting international and inter-cultural understanding.[106] The Convention on the Rights of the Child adopted in 1989 only requires education to enhance respect for a child's own cultural identity, language and values, and for the national values of the country in which the child is living and the country from which he or she may originate.[107] Nonetheless, the UNESCO system insisted that the mission of education include the cultivation of respect for different cultures, not only of one's own culture. Such a stance can also be found in the UNESCO Declaration of Principles on Tolerance of 1995, the Declaration and Programme of Action of the World Conference against Racism, Racial Discrimination, Xenophobia and Related Intolerance of 2001 and the UNESCO Universal Declaration on Cultural Diversity of 2001.[108]

100 The Convention on the Elimination of All Forms of Discrimination against Women, article 10 (c).
101 UN Doc. E/CN.4/Sub.2/1994/L.42.
102 UN Doc. E/CN.4/Sub.2/2005/27, para. 17.
103 The Convention on the Rights of Persons with Disabilities, article 8.
104 UNESCO recommendation concerning Education for International Understanding, Co-operation and Peace and Education relating to Human Rights and Fundamental Freedoms of 1974, para. 4.
105 UNESCO recommendation concerning Education for International Understanding, Co-operation and Peace and Education relating to Human Rights and Fundamental Freedoms of 1974, para. 4.
106 UNESCO recommendation concerning Education for International Understanding, Co-operation and Peace and Education relating to Human Rights and Fundamental Freedoms of 1974, para. 17.
107 The Convention on the Rights of the Child, article 29.
108 The Declaration and Programme of Action of the World Conference against Racism, Racial Discrimination, Xenophobia and Related Intolerance, paras. 95, 97 and 128; The UNESCO Universal Declaration on Cultural Diversity, Annex II; The Convention on the Rights of the Child, article 29; The UNESCO Declaration of Principles on Tolerance, article 4 (4).

A sense of belonging and a willingness to take positive actions

UNESCO suggested in 1974 that a child's school should contribute to improving and extending the child's sense of belonging to the family, the school and the local, national and world communities.[109] It further recommended that States harbour an attitude and willingness to take positive actions with regard to human rights.[110] To this end, it recommended that States provide teachers with a commitment to the ethics of human rights, the ability to shape attitudes based on the principle of non-discrimination and the ability to instil an appreciation of cultural diversity.[111]

Human rights education and States' educational duty

Human rights education

While human rights have become increasingly represented in concepts of international law concerning education, the notion of human rights education has also been developing alongside. To date the United Nations has released two World Programmes for Human Rights Education, the first taking place between 2005 and 2007, with the other occurring between 2010 and 2014.[112] Prior to that, it endorsed the United Nations Decade for Human Rights Education (1995–2004). In the two World Programmes, human rights education was defined as education, training and information aimed at building a universal culture of human rights.[113] Human rights education not only provides knowledge about human rights, but also develops values and reinforces attitudes that are necessary for the success of human rights.[114] Particularly, it aims at moulding attitudes in favour of:

(a) The strengthening of respect for human rights and fundamental freedoms;
(b) The combating of prejudices which lead to discrimination;

109 UNESCO recommendation concerning Education for International Understanding, Co-operation and Peace and Education relating to Human Rights and Fundamental Freedoms of 1974, para. 24.
110 UNESCO recommendation concerning Education for International Understanding, Co-operation and Peace and Education relating to Human Rights and Fundamental Freedoms of 1974, para. 30.
111 UNESCO recommendation concerning Education for International Understanding, Co-operation and Peace and Education relating to Human Rights and Fundamental Freedoms of 1974, para. 33; The Declaration and Programme of Action of the World Conference against Racism, Racial Discrimination, Xenophobia and Related Intolerance, para. 129.
112 UN Doc. A/59/525/Rev.1, para. 3; UN Doc. HR/PUB/12/3, pp. 2, 12 and 13; UN Doc. A/HRC/15/28, para. 3.
113 UN Doc. A/59/525/Rev.1, para. 3; UN Doc. HR/PUB/12/3, pp. 2, 12 and 13; UN Doc. A/HRC/15/28, para. 3.
114 UN Doc. A/59/525/Rev.1, paras 3–4; UN Doc. HR/PUB/12/3, p. 2; UN Doc. HR/PUB/12/3, pp. 12–13; UN Doc. A/HRC/15/28, para. 4.

(c) The promotion of understanding, tolerance, gender equality and friendship among all nations, indigenous peoples and racial, national, ethnic, religious and linguistic groups;
(d) The promotion of respect for cultural diversity.[115]

In 2005 the Secretary-General of the United Nations confirmed that human rights education is widely considered to be an integral part of the right to education.[116] UNESCO also states the same thing on its website. UNESCO further declares that human rights education is increasingly gaining recognition as a human right in itself. As stated by the Committee on the Rights of the Child in general comment No. 1, 'the education to which each child has a right is one designed . . . to promote a culture which is infused by appropriate human rights values.'[117] The content of human rights education has been suggested as encompassing peace, democracy, development, social justice, the provisions of human rights treaties and the reflection of human rights values in daily life and experience.[118]

There exists a growing consensus that human rights education contributes to the moulding of mutual understanding, tolerance and peace, a view conveyed by the World Conference on Human Rights in Vienna on 25 June 1993, the Secretary-General of the United Nations in 1997, the Commission on Human Rights in 2004, the General Assembly in 2005 and the Human Rights Council in 2010.[119] In 2009 the Outcome Document of the Durban Review Conference recognised States' efforts to sensitise the public at large and to foster respect for cultural diversity through human rights education.[120] The Human Rights Committee, the World Conference against Racism, Racial Discrimination, Xenophobia and Related Intolerance of 2001, the 2005 World Summit and the Outcome Document of the Durban Review Conference of 2009 all urged States to conduct human rights education.[121]

States' educational duty

Torture, slavery, violence, abuse and exploitation

Aside from the school textbooks and curricula found in formal educational systems, international law prescribes alternative educational measures with which

115 UN Doc. A/59/525/Rev.1, para. 3; UN Doc. HR/PUB/12/3, pp. 12–13.
116 UN Doc. A/59/525/Rev.1, para. 15.
117 The Committee on the Rights of the Child general comment No. 1, para. 2.
118 The Vienna Declaration and Programme of Action, para. 80; The Committee on the Rights of the Child general comment No. 1, para. 15.
119 UN Doc. A/52/469/Add.1, para. 12; UN Doc. HR/PUB/12/3, p. 12; UN Doc. E/CN.4/RES/2004/71; UN Doc. A/RES/59/113; The Vienna Declaration and Programme of Action, para. 78.
120 The Outcome Document of the Durban Review Conference in 2009, para. 22.
121 The Outcome Document of the Durban Review Conference in 2009, para. 107; UN Doc. A/60/L.1, para. 131; The Declaration and Programme of Action of the World Conference

States may address human rights issues. These measures are intended to target the whole population and influence the mindset of the people, thus providing for the inclusion of individuals who are not a part of the educational system. The prohibition on torture is an example of such an alternative provision of training, as the Torture Convention obliges States to educate law enforcement agents on the matter.[122] In 2000 the Special Rapporteur on Torture of the Commission on Human Rights, Sir Nigel Rodley, recommended that Cameroon become proactive in changing the atmosphere on this issue.[123] Rodley advised that the highest political authority of Cameroon should send a clear signal in public statements and internal governmental instructions that torture and other ill-treatment are not tolerated.[124]

On the matter of slavery, the 1993 Working Group on Contemporary Forms of Slavery of the Sub-Commission on Prevention of Discrimination and Protection of Minorities recommended that States provide education and disseminate information through national measures and strategies to prevent and eradicate all contemporary forms of slavery.[125] The Committee on the Rights of the Child in 2004 urged Mauritanian governments to launch an information and public awareness campaign to put an end to caste-based practice of slavery, which particularly impacted on girls in domestic service and boys forced to beg by marabouts.[126] Human rights institutions have consistently urged Japan to educate its public about the 'comfort women' of World War II, referring to the abuses against victims of Japan's military sexual slavery practices, in order to prevent hate speech and other practices that stigmatise these victims.[127] Appeals were made in this regard by the Human Rights Committee in 2008, the Committee on the Elimination of Discrimination against Women in 2009, and the Committee on Economic, Social and Cultural Rights and the Committee against Torture, both in 2013.[128]

The 1989 Convention on the Rights of the Child and the 2006 Convention on the Rights of Persons with Disabilities both prescribe educational measures for States to protect children and persons with disabilities from all forms of exploitation, violence and abuse, including sexual abuse.[129] The use of the mass

against Racism, Racial Discrimination, Xenophobia and Related Intolerance, para. 132; UN Doc. CCPR/C/KOR/CO/3, para. 20.

122 The Convention against Torture and Other Cruel, Inhuman or Degrading Treatment or Punishment, article 10.

123 UN Doc. A/HRC/WG.6/4/CMR/2, para. 22; UN Doc. E/CN.4/2000/9/Add.2, para. 78.

124 UN Doc. A/HRC/WG.6/4/CMR/2, para. 22; UN Doc. E/CN.4/2000/9/Add.2, para. 78.

125 UN Doc. E/CN.4/Sub.2/1993/30, Annex I, para. 5.

126 A marabout is a Muslim religious leader and teacher in West Africa. UN Doc. A/HRC/WG.6/9/MRT/2, para. 43; UN Doc. CERD/C/65/CO/5, para. 15.

127 UN Doc. CAT/C/JPN/CO/2, para. 19; UN Doc. CCPR/C/JPN/CO/5, para. 22; UN Doc. CEDAW/C/JPN/CO/6, para. 38; UN Doc. E/C.12/JPN/CO/3, para. 26.

128 UN Doc. CAT/C/JPN/CO/2, para. 19; UN Doc. CCPR/C/JPN/CO/5, para. 22; UN Doc. CEDAW/C/JPN/CO/6, para. 38; UN Doc. E/C.12/JPN/CO/3, para. 26.

129 The Convention on the Rights of Persons with Disabilities, article 16; The Convention on the Rights of the Child, article 19 (1).

media is included in these educational measures.[130] Prior to that, in 1995 the Working Group on Contemporary Forms of Slavery of the UN Commission on Human Rights insisted on the importance of education in combating sexual exploitation.[131] It urged States to introduce and reinforce education programmes that alert children to the risks and the harm caused by sexual exploitation.[132] In 2013, the Committee against Torture recommended that Japan broaden its public awareness-raising campaigns against all forms of gender-based violence after the State presented its second periodic report under the Convention against Torture.[133] Interestingly, such a recommendation was formulated despite the Convention against Torture only mentioning the States' duty to disseminate information among legal enforcement personnel.

In regional human rights law, Europe attaches considerable importance to the use of educational measures to tackle violence, exploitation and abuse. It first deploys education to combat violence in and associated with sports. The European Convention on Spectator Violence and Misbehaviour at Sports Events and in particular at Football Matches of 1985 requires States Parties to 'promot[e] the sporting idea through educational and other campaigns' and 'giv[e] support to the notion of fair play, especially among young people, so as to enhance mutual respect both amongst spectators and between sports players'.[134] In 2007, the Council of Europe adopted the Convention on the Protection of Children against Sexual Exploitation and Sexual Abuse. The Convention dedicates two articles to raising awareness among persons working with children (article 5) and among the general public (article 8), which states that '[e]ach Party shall promote or conduct awareness raising campaigns addressed to the general public providing information on the phenomenon of sexual exploitation and sexual abuse of children and on the preventive measures which can be taken.'

Children's rights

The Convention on the Rights of the Child affords a specific provision on the protection of children's rights in reference to States' educational duties, concerned with the prevention of violence, abuse and exploitation of children.[135] This differs from the UN conventions on racial discrimination and discrimination against women, which tackle discrimination, prejudice and stereotypes more generally among the population. In reviewing States' periodic reports,

130 The Convention on the Rights of the Child, article 17 (a).
131 UN Doc. E/CN.4/Sub.2/1995/28, para. 122.
132 UN Doc. E/CN.4/Sub.2/1995/28, para. 123, resolutions 3 and 4; UN Doc. E/CN.4/Sub.2/1999/17, para. 107, recommendation 3.
133 UN Doc. CAT/C/JPN/CO/2, para. 20.
134 The European Convention on Spectator Violence and Misbehaviour at Sports Events and in particular at Football Matches, article 3 (5).
135 The International Convention on the Elimination of All Forms of Racial Discrimination, article 7; The Convention on the Elimination of All Forms of Racial Discrimination, article 5; The Convention on the Rights of the Child, article 19 (1).

the Committee on the Rights of the Child expressed concerns over discriminatory attitudes toward children born out of wedlock,[136] children with disabilities, homeless children, child victims of sexual abuse and exploitation, and children coming from tribes and other vulnerable groups.[137] This Committee was also concerned with the public's attitude toward corporal punishment of children in homes and schools,[138] attitudes that limit the freedom of children to freely express their views and prevent their views from being fully respected[139] and the intolerance and negative attitudes toward adolescents in the media.[140]

Taking a step forward, the Committee on the Rights of the Child, concurring with the view of the Committee on the Elimination of Discrimination against Women, underlined the significance of education in shaping public attitudes toward the empowerment of girls and women.[141] The Committee on the Rights of the Child advised States to change societal attitudes against street children,[142] children with disabilities,[143] children born out of wedlock,[144] children from poor and rural families[145] or minority ethnic groups[146] and child victims of violence and sexual abuse including corporal punishment[147] and urged these States to change other discriminatory societal attitudes.[148]

Addressing corporal punishment, the Committee dedicated general comment No. 8 to the modification of public attitudes and the promotion of non-violent forms of discipline and childrearing. In its observations and comments to States as part of the periodic reporting process under the Convention on the Rights of the Child, the Committee pointed out that not only did societal attitudes need to change but also negative and discriminatory attitudes

136 UN Doc. A/HRC/WG.6/9/LBY/2, para. 40; UN Doc. CRC/C/15/Add.209, paras 23–24.

137 UN Doc. CRC/C/15/Add.221, para. 28; UN Doc. A/HRC/WG.6/4/BGD/2, para. 14.

138 UN Doc. A/HRC/WG.6/11/PLW/2, para. 35; UN Doc. CRC/C/15/Add.149, paras 44–45; UN Doc. A/HRC/WG.6/11/VCT/2, para. 31; UN Doc. CRC/C/15/Add.184, paras 28–29.

139 UN Doc. A/HRC/WG.6/4/SEN/2, para. 31; UN Doc. CRC/C/SEN/CO/2, para. 28; UN Doc. A/HRC/WG.6/11/PLW/2, para. 42; UN Doc. CRC/C/15/Add.149, paras 36–37; UN Doc. A/HRC/WG.6/3/ARE/2, para. 31; UN Doc. CRC/C/15/Add.183, paras 28 and 29.

140 UN Doc. CRC/C/GBR/CO/4, para. 24.

141 UN Doc. A/HRC/WG.6/5/VUT/2, para. 43; UN Doc. CRC/C/15/Add.111, para. 21; The Committee on the Rights of the Child, general comment No. 5, para. 12.

142 UN Doc. CRC/C/TZA/CO/2, para. 62.

143 UN Doc. CRC/C/15/Add.221, para. 56; UN Doc. A/HRC/WG.6/4/BGD/2, para. 14; UN Doc. A/HRC/WG.6/6/DMA/2, para. 13; UN Doc. CRC/C/15/Add.238, paras 36–37.

144 UN Doc. A/HRC/WG.6/3/ARE/2, para. 8; UN Doc. CRC/C/15/Add.183, para. 22; UN Doc. A/HRC/WG.6/9/LBY/2, para. 40; UN Doc. CRC/C/15/Add.209, paras 23–24.

145 UN Doc. A/HRC/WG.6/6/GNQ/2, para. 14; UN Doc. CRC/C/15/Add.245, para. 24.

146 UN Doc. A/HRC/WG.6/1/CZE/2, para. 24; UN Doc. CRC/C/15/Add.201, paras 39 and 41.

147 UN Doc. A/HRC/WG.6/6/CIV/2, para. 16; UN Doc. CRC/C/15/Add.155, para. 37; UN Doc. A/HRC/WG.6/3/BWA/2, para. 18; UN Doc. CRC/C/15/Add.242, para. 45; UN Doc. A/HRC/WG.6/5/MLT/2, para. 21; UN Doc. CRC/C/15/Add.129, paras 33–34; UN Doc. A/HRC/WG.6/6/BRN/2, para. 13; UN Doc. CRC/C/15/Add.219; para. 25 (a), (b) and (c).

148 UN Doc. A/HRC/WG.6/11/SGP/2, para. 18; UN Doc. CRC/C/C/SGP/CO/2–3, para. 30.

within families themselves.[149] In this respect, the respect for privacy should not be deemed absolute when it comes to the protection of certain core human rights. To achieve the aim of fostering a change in attitude, the Committee on the Rights of the Child recommended that States conduct national strategies,[150] training programmes,[151] public education,[152] awareness-raising campaigns[153] and other social mobilisation initiatives. [154] It encouraged States to involve opinion leaders, and even religious leaders, in these campaigns.[155] It also recommended that parents, guardians and professionals who work with children be sensitised and educated.[156] These recommendations have reached Bangladesh,[157] Belize,[158] Bhutan,[159] Botswana,[160] Brunei Darussalam,[161] Côte d'Ivoire,[162] Cyprus,[163] the Czech Republic,[164] Dominica,[165] the Emirates,[166]

149 UN Doc. A/HRC/WG.6/3/ARE/2, para. 8; UN Doc. CRC/C/15/Add.183, para. 22; UN Doc. A/HRC/WG.6/11/SGP/2, para. 22; UN Doc. CRC/C/SGP/CO/2-3, paras 39 and 40.

150 UN Doc. A/HRC/WG.6/6/GNQ/2, para. 14; UN Doc. CRC/C/15/Add.245, para. 24.

151 UN Doc. A/HRC/WG.6/1/CZE/2, para. 24; UN Doc. CRC/C/15/Add.201, paras 39 and 41.

152 UN Doc. A/HRC/WG.6/3/ARE/2, para. 8; UN Doc. CRC/C/15/Add.183, para. 22; UN Doc. A/HRC/WG.6/6/BRN/2, para. 13; UN Doc. CRC/C/15/Add.219; para. 25 (a), (b) and (c); UN Doc. A/HRC/WG.6/9/LBY/2, para. 40; UN Doc. CRC/C/15/Add.209, paras 23–24; UN Doc. A/HRC/WG.6/5/MLT/2, para. 21; UN Doc. CRC/C/15/Add.129, paras 33–34.

153 UN Doc. CRC/C/15/Add.221, para. 56; UN Doc. A/HRC/WG.6/4/BGD/2, para. 14; UN Doc. A/HRC/WG.6/10/PRY/2, para. 34; UN Doc. CRC/C/PRY/CO/3, para. 38; UN Doc. A/HRC/WG.6/10/LCA/2, para. 28; UN Doc. CRC/C/15/Add.258, para. 35; UN Doc. A/HRC/WG.6/4/SEN/2, para. 31; UN Doc. CRC/C/SEN/CO/2, para. 29; UN Doc. CRC/C/GBR/CO/4, para. 25.

154 UN Doc. A/HRC/WG.6/5/BLZ/2, para. 15; UN Doc. CRC/C/15/Add.252, para. 41; UN Doc. A/HRC/WG.6/6/BTN/2, para. 25; UN Doc. CRC/C/BTN/CO/2, para. 38; UN Doc. A/HRC/WG.6/6/CYP/2, para. 24; UN Doc. CRC/C/15/Add.205, paras 45–46; UN Doc. A/HRC/WG.6/10/OMN/2, para. 33; UN Doc. CRC/C/OMN/CO/2, paras 33–34; UN Doc. A/HRC/WG.6/11/PLW/2, para. 35; UN Doc. CRC/C/15/Add.149, paras 44–45; UN Doc. A/HRC/WG.6/11/VCT/2, para. 31; UN Doc. CRC/C/15/Add.184, paras 28–29.

155 UN Doc. A/HRC/WG.6/9/LBY/2, para. 40; UN Doc. CRC/C/15/Add.209, paras 23–24.

156 UN Doc. A/HRC/WG.6/11/SGP/2, para. 22; UN Doc. CRC/C/SGP/CO/2-3, paras 39 and 40; UN Doc. A/HRC/WG.6/3/ARE/2, para. 31; UN Doc. CRC/C/15/Add.183, paras 28 and 29.

157 UN Doc. CRC/C/15/Add.221, para. 56; UN Doc. A/HRC/WG.6/4/BGD/2, para. 14.

158 UN Doc. A/HRC/WG.6/5/BLZ/2, para. 15; UN Doc. CRC/C/15/Add.252, para. 41.

159 UN Doc. A/HRC/WG.6/6/BTN/2, para. 25; UN Doc. CRC/C/BTN/CO/2, para. 38.

160 UN Doc. A/HRC/WG.6/3/BWA/2, para. 18; UN Doc. CRC/C/15/Add.242, para. 45.

161 UN Doc. A/HRC/WG.6/6/BRN/2, para. 13; UN Doc. CRC/C/15/Add.219; para. 25 (a), (b) and (c).

162 UN Doc. A/HRC/WG.6/6/CIV/2, para. 16; UN Doc. CRC/C/15/Add.155, para. 37.

163 UN Doc. A/HRC/WG.6/6/CYP/2, para. 24; UN Doc. CRC/C/15/Add.205, paras 45–46.

164 UN Doc. A/HRC/WG.6/1/CZE/2, para. 24; UN Doc. CRC/C/15/Add.201, paras 39 and 41.

165 UN Doc. A/HRC/WG.6/6/DMA/2, para. 13; UN Doc. CRC/C/15/Add.238, paras 36–37.

166 UN Doc. A/HRC/WG.6/3/ARE/2, para. 31; UN Doc. CRC/C/15/Add.183, paras 28 and 29.

Equatorial Guinea,[167] Malta,[168] Oman,[169] Palau,[170] Paraguay,[171] Saint Lucia,[172] Saint Vincent and the Grenadines,[173] Senegal,[174] Singapore,[175] Tanzania[176] and the United Kingdom.[177]

The rights of persons with disabilities

To protect the rights of persons with disabilities, article 8 of the 2006 Convention on the Rights of Persons with Disabilities affirms that States have an obligation:

(a) To raise awareness throughout society, including at the family level and foster respect for the rights and dignity of persons with disabilities;
(b) To combat stereotypes and prejudices relating to persons with disabilities, including those based on sex and age, in all areas of life;
(c) To promote awareness of the capabilities and contributions of persons with disabilities.[178]

This provision continues to suggest specific measures:

(a) Initiating and maintaining effective public awareness campaigns designed:
    i. To nurture receptiveness to the rights of persons with disabilities;
    ii. To promote positive perceptions and greater social awareness towards persons with disabilities;
    iii. To promote recognition of the skills, merits and abilities of persons with disabilities, and of their contributions to the workplace and the labour market;
(b) Fostering at all levels of the education system, including in all children from an early age, an attitude of respect for the rights of persons with disabilities;
(c) Encouraging all organs of the media to portray persons with disabilities in a manner consistent with the purpose of the present Convention;
(d) Promoting awareness-training programmes regarding persons with disabilities and the rights of persons with disabilities.[179]

167 UN Doc. A/HRC/WG.6/6/GNQ/2, para. 14; UN Doc. CRC/C/15/Add.245, para. 24.
168 UN Doc. A/HRC/WG.6/5/MLT/2, para. 21; UN Doc. CRC/C/15/Add.129, paras 33–34.
169 UN Doc. A/HRC/WG.6/10/OMN/2, para. 33; UN Doc. CRC/C/OMN/CO/2, paras 33–34.
170 UN Doc. A/HRC/WG.6/11/PLW/2, para. 35; UN Doc. CRC/C/15/Add.149, paras 44–45.
171 UN Doc. A/HRC/WG.6/10/PRY/2, para. 34; UN Doc. CRC/C/PRY/CO/3, para. 38.
172 UN Doc. A/HRC/WG.6/10/LCA/2, para. 28; UN Doc. CRC/C/15/Add.258, para. 35.
173 UN Doc. A/HRC/WG.6/11/VCT/2, para. 31; UN Doc. CRC/C/15/Add.184, paras 28–29.
174 UN Doc. A/HRC/WG.6/4/SEN/2, para. 31; UN Doc. CRC/C/SEN/CO/2, para. 29.
175 UN Doc. A/HRC/WG.6/11/SGP/2, para. 22; UN Doc. CRC/C/SGP/CO/2–3, paras 39 and 40.
176 UN Doc. CRC/C/TZA/CO/2, para. 62.
177 UN Doc. CRC/C/GBR/CO/4, para. 25.
178 The Convention on the Rights of Persons with Disabilities, article 8.
179 The Convention on the Rights of Persons with Disabilities, article 8.

Addressing attitudes at the family level is also a notable aim, similar in nature to the protection of the rights of women and children.

Cultural rights and others

To defend various cultural rights, States are also urged to promote public awareness. For instance, the 2001 UNESCO Universal Declaration on Cultural Diversity recommends that States promote, through education, an awareness of the positive value of cultural diversity.[180] The UNESCO Convention for the Safeguarding of the Intangible Cultural Heritage of 2003 addresses the need to build greater awareness of the importance of intangible cultural heritage and its safeguarding, which requires States to conduct educational, awareness-raising and information programmes aimed at the general public and the communities and groups concerned.[181]

At the regional level, the 1985 European Convention on Offences relating to Cultural Property requires States Parties to enhance public awareness of the need to protect cultural property.[182] The Convention for the Protection of the Architectural Heritage of Europe of the same year describes the State duty in developing public awareness so as to conserve the value and heritage of architectural design.[183] Pursuant to the European Landscape Convention, States have a duty to 'increase awareness among the civil society, private organisations, and public authorities of the value of landscapes'.[184] Beyond cultural rights, equality in employment and occupation is monitored by the International Labour Organization Convention Concerning Discrimination in respect of Employment and Occupation of 1958 which also obliges States to carry out educational programmes.[185] Regionally, the African Charter on Human and People's Rights makes mention of the State duty to promote human rights through teaching, education and publication.[186]

State compliance

National human rights institutions

As early as 1960, the Commission on Human Rights issued recommendations that States establish a national advisory committee on human rights with a function to educate public opinion on human rights issues.[187] The motion

180 The UNESCO Universal Declaration on Cultural Diversity, Annex II.

181 The UNESCO Convention for the Safeguarding of the Intangible Cultural Heritage, article 14.

182 The European Convention on Offences relating to Cultural Property, article 4.

183 The Convention for the Protection of the Architectural Heritage of Europe, article 15 (1).

184 The European Landscape Convention, article 6 (A).

185 The Convention Concerning Discrimination in Respect of Employment and Occupation, article 3 (b).

186 The African Charter on Human and People's Rights, article 25.

187 UN Doc. E/3335, para. 43; UNCHR Res 2 (XVI), UN Doc. E/3335, para. 50 and p. 30.

was initiated by a collection of States, namely Austria, Denmark, France, Lebanon, the Philippines, the United Kingdom and Venezuela.[188] It was further endorsed by the Economic and Social Council.[189] The Paris Principles, which were adopted by UN General Assembly in resolution 48/134 of 1993, inaugurated core standards for the role and functions of national human rights institutions. Pursuant to these Principles, national human rights institutions are mandated with playing a significant role in developing and enhancing public awareness of human rights and freedoms through information, education and the use of the press.[190] They should '[a]ddress public opinion directly or through any press organ, particularly in order to publicize its opinions and recommendations'.[191] Such a role for national human rights institutions has been confirmed and endorsed by the Commission on Human Rights of the United Nations and its successor, the Human Rights Council, in addition to the General Assembly.[192]

At the national level, national human rights institutions have been formed in a large number of States. Some of these institutions are mandated to directly inform public opinion on human rights issues, as is the case in Australia,[193] Argentina,[194] Fiji,[195] Germany,[196] Ghana,[197] Italy,[198] Mauritania[199] and Qatar.[200] The Argentinean national human rights institution – the Argentinean National Institute to Combat Discrimination, Xenophobia and Racism (INADI) – informs public opinion about discriminatory, xenophobic or racist attitudes on the part of public bodies or private persons through its mandate.[201] Germany commended the work of its national human rights institution, the German Institute for Human Rights, as having substantially contributed to the process of shaping public opinion on all issues relevant to the question of human rights.[202] The National Commission for Human Rights of Mauritania has been endowed with the responsibility to raise awareness of human rights, sensitise the public and combat all forms of discrimination and violations of human dignity, in particular racial discrimination, practices similar to slavery and discrimination against

188 UN Doc. E/3335, para. 43.
189 UN Doc. E/Res/772 (XXX), p. 14.
190 UN Doc. A/RES/48/134.
191 UN Doc. A/RES/48/134.
192 UN Doc. E/CN.4/RES/2005/74; UN Doc. A/HRC/RES/20/14; UN Doc. A/RES/66/169; UN Doc. A/RES/63/172; UN Doc. A/RES/64/161.
193 UN Doc. A/HRC/WG.6/10/Aus/1, para. 24.
194 UN Doc. CERD/C/476/Add.2, para. 92.
195 UN Doc. A/HRC/WG.6/7/FJI/1, para. 24.
196 UN Doc. A/HRC/WG.6/4/EDU/1, para. 15.
197 UN Doc. A/HRC/WG.6/2/GHA/1, para. 19.
198 UN Doc. CERD/C/ITA/15, para. 315.
199 UN Doc. A/HRC/WG.6/9/MRT/1, para. 37.
200 UN Doc. CERD/C/360/Add.1, para.73; UN Doc. A/HRC/WG.6/7/QAT/1, p. 12.
201 UN Doc. CERD/C/476/Add.2, para. 92.
202 UN Doc. A/HRC/WG.6/4/EDU/1, para. 15.

women.[203] Qatar revealed a plan in 2002 to establish its national human rights committee with a function of educating public opinion.[204]

Some national human rights institutions, although lacking the mandate to enlighten public opinion, can make recommendations of their government to that effect. For example, in 2010 the British national human rights institution, the Equality and Human Rights Commission, recommended to the British government that it educate public opinion on the subject of the prison system.[205] The Committee on the Rights of the Child in general comment No. 2 encourages national human rights institutions to '[p]romote public understanding and awareness of the importance of children's rights and, for this purpose, work closely with the media and undertake or sponsor research and educational activities in the field'.[206]

State actions on public opinion

Besides the establishment of national human rights institutions, States have carried out all kinds of educational measures targeting public opinion on human rights. This can be interpreted as their response to the international calls for education to interact with, and subsequently mould, public opinion. According to its initial report under the Convention to the Committee on the Rights of the Child in 2001, in order to give effect to the Convention on the Rights of the Child, Mozambique initiated a national strategy designed to inform public opinion about the principles of the Convention and the importance of basic education.[207] Subsequent actions were then taken to mobilise public opinion in the hope of introducing changes to the educational system.[208] When Nigeria presented its initial report to the Committee on the Rights of the Child in 2001, the State summarised its actions in informing public opinion on the subject of domestic adoption via radio stations, panel discussion and the organisation of open days.[209] Nigeria had confirmed positive results derived from these measures.[210]

Established by the General Assembly in 2006, the Universal Periodic Review (UPR) has become a new and innovative mechanism to examine States' compliance with human rights obligations, in addition to treaty based human rights institutions.[211] The obligations examined in the Review derive from the Charter of the United Nations, the Universal Declaration of Human Rights, human rights instruments to which the State under review is a party and any voluntary

203 UN Doc. A/HRC/WG.6/9/MRT/1, para. 37.
204 UN Doc. CERD/C/360/Add.1, para.73; UN Doc. A/HRC/WG.6/7/QAT/1, p. 12.
205 UN Doc. A/HRC/13/NI/4, Annex, UK Government UPR Mid-Term Report: Report from the Equality and Human Rights Commission, Recommendation 1, para. 6.
206 The Committee on the Rights of the Child general comment No. 2, para. 19.
207 UN Doc. CRC/C/41/Add.11, paras 30, 473 and 474.
208 UN Doc. CRC/C/41/Add.11, paras 30, 473 and 474.
209 UN Doc. CRC/C/3/Add.29/Rev.1, para. 154.
210 UN Doc. CRC/C/3/Add.29/Rev.1, para. 154.
211 UN Doc. A/RES/60/251.

pledges and commitments made by the State in question.[212] During the review, several States, including Mali[213] and Lesotho,[214] admitted the necessity of sensitising and informing public opinion on the issue of child labour and national human rights institutions. In 2008 Ukraine deemed the alteration of social attitudes as a means of protecting and promoting human rights.[215] Notably, more States have asserted themselves in raising awareness and changing public attitudes toward human rights.

In particular, Botswana and Lesotho established directorates on corruption and economic offences in 2008 and 2010 respectively, with powers to educate the public against the consequences of corruption.[216] Antigua and Barbuda had formed an international treaties unit, entrusted with the duty of sensitising and shaping public opinion with regard to the State's international treaty obligations in 2011,[217] while in the same year, Denmark worked with the United Nations Children's Fund (UNICEF) to promote an attitude change throughout its nation toward the rights of children.[218] Poland aimed at shaping a positive attitude toward sports and eliminating prejudice and stereotypes associated therein when it hosted the 2012 UEFA European Championship.[219] Montenegro has already witnessed a positive change of social attitude, cited in 2008 as the result of adopting legislation on environment, space and natural assets.[220]

To reduce and eliminate domestic violence, Botswana reported to the Human Rights Council in 2009 that it had carried out a public education campaign involving the mass media and kgotla meetings[221] to educate and sensitise the public;[222] Slovenia had devised an awareness-raising training policy aimed at public attitude change in 2010;[223] while in 2011, Mongolia implemented public awareness campaigns to shape a culture of tolerance.[224] With regard to 'mob justice' and lynching, in 2008 Ghana reported a series of measures regarding its public education drive to mobilise the public in desisting from these unlawful acts via the mass media in the form of television, radio and newspaper publications.[225] Equatorial

212 UN Doc. A/HRC/RES/5/1, Annex, I, A, 1.
213 UN Doc. A/HRC/WG.6/2/MLI/1, para. 101.
214 UN Doc. A/HRC/15/7, para. 30.
215 UN Doc. A/HRC/8/45, para. 12.
216 UN Doc. A/HRC/WG.6/8/LSO/1, para. 30; UN Doc. A/HRC/WG.6/3/BWA/2, para. 4; World Bank, World Development Report 2005, Washington, DC, 2004, p. 42.
217 UN Doc. A/HRC/19/5, para. 21.
218 UN Doc. A/HRC/WG.6/11/DNK/1, para. 113.
219 UN Doc. A/HRC/WG.6/13/POL/1, para. 132.
220 UN Doc. A/HRC/WG.6/3/MNE/1, para. 65.
221 Kgotla meetings are the traditional governance system in Botswana in which men discussed matters of economic or political importance to the family or community. James Denbow and Phenyo C. Thebe, *Culture and Customs of Botswana* (Greenwood Press 2006) 21–22.
222 UN Doc. A/HRC/10/69, para. 15.
223 UN Doc. A/HRC/14/15, para. 111, recommendation 36; UN Doc. A/HRC/14/15/Add.1, p. 4.
224 UN Doc. A/HRC/16/5, para. 52.
225 UN Doc. A/HRC/WG.6/2/GHA/1, para. 74.

Guinea ran radio campaigns to change attitudes regarding the diseases of HIV/AIDS, malaria, river blindness and other forms of filariasis, leprosy or tuberculosis in 2009.[226] Thailand reported in 2011 that it was working to promote positive attitudes toward persons infected by HIV/AIDS so that they can live without stigmatisation and discrimination.[227] Further actions were reported by Albania,[228] Andorra,[229] Antigua and Barbuda,[230] Cameroon,[231] Finland,[232] New Zealand[233] and Ukraine.[234]

A number of States have also accepted suggestions of mobilising public opinion with regard to human rights during the process of the Universal Periodic Review, although no action has yet been taken. Sweden and the United States agreed to interact with public attitudes on the topics of domestic violence and stereotypes and violence against gays, lesbians, bisexuals and transsexuals.[235] Albania, Barbados, Ireland (partially accepted) and Timor-Leste committed to engaging with public attitude on the protection of children's rights, particularly focusing on child trafficking for sexual exploitation and forced labour,[236] the advantages of birth registration[237] and corporal punishment of children.[238] Azerbaijan was willing to foster dialogues between religions and to promote a culture of human rights among its society.[239] Botswana was determined to undertake educational awareness campaigns with a view to raising issues of sexual orientation, corporal punishment and the death penalty.[240]

More commitments were made by the Bahamas,[241] Belgium,[242] Brunei Darussalam,[243] Chile,[244] Dominica,[245] Germany,[246] Togo[247] and

226 UN Doc. A/HRC/WG.6/6/GNQ/1, para. 21 (c).
227 UN Doc. A/HRC/WG.6/12/THA/1, para. 51.
228 UN Doc. A/HRC/13/6, paras 44, 47 and 48.
229 UN Doc. A/HRC/WG.6/9/AND/1, para. 50.
230 UN Doc. A/HRC/19/5, para. 21.
231 UN Doc. A/HRC/WG.6/4/CMR/1, para. 37.
232 UN Doc. A/HRC/WG.6/13/FIN/1, paras 87–88.
233 UN Doc. A/HRC/WG.6/5/NZL/1, para. 57.
234 UN Doc. A/HRC/8/45, para. 12.
235 UN Doc. A/HRC/15/11, para. 95, recommendation 53; UN Doc. A/HRC/16/11, para. 92, recommendation 86; UN Doc. A/HRC/16/11/Add.1, para. 5.
236 UN Doc. A/HRC/13/6, para. 67, point 29.
237 UN Doc. A/HRC/19/17, para. 77, recommendation 41.
238 UN Doc. A/HRC/10/73/Add.1, para. 23; UN Doc. A/HRC/19/9, para. 107, recommendation 41; UN Doc. A/HRC/19/9/Add.1, para. 53.
239 UN Doc. A/HRC/11/20, para. 96, recommendation 19; UN Doc. A/HRC/11/20/Add.1, point 19; UN Doc. A/HRC/11/20, para. 96, recommendation 2; UN Doc. A/HRC/11/20/Add.1, point 2.
240 UN Doc. A/HRC/23/7, para. 92.
241 UN Doc. A/HRC/10/70, para. 52, point 4; UN Doc. A/HRC/10/70/Add.1, para. 2, point 4.
242 UN Doc. A/HRC/18/3, para. 100, recommendation 30.
243 UN Doc. A/HRC/13/14, para. 89, recommendation 15.
244 UN Doc. A/HRC/12/10, para. 96, recommendation 27.
245 UN Doc. A/HRC/13/12, para. 70, recommendation 27.
246 UN Doc. A/HRC/11/15, para. 81, recommendation 22; UN Doc. A/HRC/11/15/Add.1, para. 22.
247 UN Doc. A/HRC/19/10, para. 100, recommendation 37.

Uganda.[248] Inevitably, some States made reservations. Antigua and Barbuda hesitated to implement public awareness campaigns on discrimination based on sexual orientation.[249] Botswana did not accept the recommendation of conducting public awareness efforts to change the mindsets of people and their views regarding the corporal punishment of children, claiming to be concerned about 'the current pre-disposition of its people' and 'the norms of the society'.[250]

Conclusions

The right to education requires not only equal access to education but also demands education of a certain calibre, the latter element often being neglected. The right to education engulfs the aim and content of education, which includes the promotion of respect for human rights and the promotion of understanding, tolerance and other human rights values. This idea emerged in the 1940s when the United Nations drafted the Constitution of UNESCO and the Universal Declaration of Human Rights, finding subsequent endorsement and development from later human rights conventions and documents. As international human rights law has developed, the use of education has been encouraged to raise awareness of human rights principles, international humanitarian law and human rights violations. In doing so, education attempts to interact with and challenge people's attitudes, particularly toward discrimination, cultural diversity, a sense of belonging and a willingness to take positive actions on human rights. At the same time, the emergence of human rights education has increasingly gained recognition as an inherent constituent of the right to education.

States have often been called on to take various educational measures to protect and promote human rights. In many areas, deteriorated human rights situations cannot be comprehensively improved without a change addressing the mindset of the people involved. This has proved to be the case with the prohibition of torture, slavery, violence, abuse and exploitation. It is also relevant to the issues of the protection of the rights of children and persons with disabilities, cultural rights and racial and gender equality as discussed in the above chapters. At the national level, national human rights institutions have been established in many jurisdictions with a mandate to directly inform public opinion or to recommend their governments to do so. A large number of States have also carried out public education and awareness-raising programmes to influence public opinion on human rights, reporting such actions to human rights institutions that supervise the implementation of States' human rights obligations. This can be witnessed as State willingness to comply with their duty to educate public opinion with regard to human rights.

248 UN Doc. A/HRC/19/16, para. 111, recommendation 33.

249 UN Doc. A/HRC/19/5, para. 68, point 31; UN Doc. A/HRC/19/5/Add.1, p. 7.

250 UN Doc. A/HRC/10/69, para. 54 and para. 92, recommendation 20; UN Doc. A/HRC/10/69/Add.1, p. 7; UN Doc. A/HRC/19/5, para. 68, point 31; UN Doc. A/HRC/19/5/Add.1, p. 7.

5 Public opinion and the death penalty

Logically, in order to defend and support human rights, actions need to be taken to mobilise public opinion toward embracing core human rights standards. Legally speaking, from the analysis of the last three chapters, many international human rights treaties and declarations contain such a spirit. Education, as directed by international law, embodies an aim and content of promoting respect for human rights. States, in signing and/or implementing these treaties and declarations, are expected to take a positive role in moulding public opinion in order to protect and promote human rights. This request is particularly clear and strong in the implementation stage of human rights treaties and declarations. In responding, States rarely invoke public opinion to defend human rights violations such as discrimination and violence based on race, gender and other factors. They take actions to raise awareness and lead public opinion against these violations.

When it comes to the death penalty issue, matters are quite different. Many States claim that public opinion is the reason for their retaining the penalty, as if there is nothing they can do about it. But they do not do so to defend the existence of discrimination and other human rights violations. In States' defence, it can be argued that international law has not universally prohibited the death penalty, unlike the issues of discrimination and the protection of rights of children and persons with disabilities. However, there is an increasing consensus that the death penalty violates the right to life and the prohibition of cruel and inhuman treatment. With this in mind, the present chapter discusses whether the death penalty issue will follow the pattern of protecting other human rights issues. This chapter chooses the death penalty case to test the overall argument that States bear duties to inform and educate public opinion with regard to core human rights issues. By doing so, this chapter would challenge the legitimacy of the public opinion argument in the death penalty issue. It analyses whether principles in other fundamental human rights will inevitably apply in the death penalty issue.

Public opinion as a justification or excuse

Currently about 50 States and territories maintain the death penalty in law and practice; these States are referred to as retentionist countries.[1] The remaining States have abolished it either in law or in practice. About 100 States had terminated the death penalty as a matter of law by August 2016.[2] These States are referred to as abolitionist for all crimes. Fewer than ten countries are recognised as abolitionist for ordinary crimes,[3] with the death penalty reserved for instances of military offences in war time and crimes against the State such as treason, terrorism and armed insurrection.[4] About 30 States have not imposed the death sentence for more than ten years or have established an official moratorium.[5] These States are referred to as *de facto* abolitionist because they appear to have abolished the death penalty in practice, although it is possible for them to resume exercising the death penalty[6]

States that have not abolished the death penalty in law often invoke public opinion as a reason to uphold such punishment. In recent years public opinion is more frequently cited as other justifications or excuses have been gradually losing their credibility, including: the sovereign power of the State in choosing

1 Afghanistan, Antigua and Barbuda, the Bahamas, Bahrain, Bangladesh, Barbados, Belarus, Belize, Botswana, Chad, China, Comoros, Cuba, Democratic People's Republic of Korea, Democratic Republic of the Congo, Dominica, Egypt, Equatorial Guinea, Ethiopia, Gambia, Guatemala, Guinea, Guyana, Jamaica, India, Indonesia, Iran (Islamic Republic of), Iraq, Japan, Jordan, Kuwait, Lebanon, Lesotho, Libyan Arab Jamahiriya, Malaysia, Nigeria, Oman, Pakistan, Palestine, Qatar, Saint Kitts and Nevis, Saint Lucia, Saint Vincent and the Grenadines, Saudi Arabia, Singapore, Somalia, Sudan, Syrian Arab Republic, Taiwan, Thailand, Trinidad and Tobago, Uganda, United Arab Emirates, United States of America, Viet Nam, Yemen and Zimbabwe.

2 Albania, Andorra, Angola, Argentina, Armenia, Australia, Austria, Azerbaijan, Belgium, Bhutan, Bolivia (Plurinational State of), Bosnia and Herzegovina, Bulgaria, Burundi, Cambodia, Canada, Cape Verde, Colombia, Congo, Cook Islands, Costa Rica, Côte d'Ivoire, Croatia, Cyprus, Czech Republic, Denmark, Djibouti, Dominican Republic, Ecuador, Estonia, Fiji, Finland, France, Gabon, Georgia, Germany, Greece, Guinea-Bissau, Haiti, Holy See, Honduras, Hungary, Iceland, Ireland, Italy, Kiribati, Kyrgyzstan, Latvia, Liberia, Liechtenstein, Lithuania, Luxembourg, Madagascar, Malta, Marshall Islands, Mauritius, Mexico, Micronesia (Federated States of), Monaco, Montenegro, Mozambique, Namibia, Nauru, Nepal, the Netherlands, New Zealand, Nicaragua, Niue, Norway, Palau, Panama, Paraguay, Philippines, Poland, Portugal, Republic of Moldova, Romania, Rwanda, Samoa, San Marino, Sao Tome and Principe, Senegal, Serbia, Seychelles, Slovakia, Slovenia, Solomon Islands, South Africa, Spain, Suriname, Sweden, Switzerland, the former Yugoslav Republic of Macedonia, Timor-Leste, Togo, Turkey, Turkmenistan, Tuvalu, Ukraine, United Kingdom of Great Britain and Northern Island, Uruguay, Uzbekistan, Vanuatu, and Venezuela (Bolivarian Republic of).

3 Brazil, Chile, El Salvador, Israel, Kazakhstan and Peru.

4 UN Doc. E/2010/10, para. 3.

5 Algeria, Benin, Brunei Darussalam, Burkina Faso, Cameroon, Central African Republic, Eritrea, Ghana, Grenada, Kenya, Lao People's Democratic Republic, Malawi, Maldives, Mali, Mauritania, Mongolia, Morocco, Myanmar, Niger, Papua New Guinea, Republic of Korea, Russian Federation, Sierra Leone, Sri Lanka, Swaziland, Tajikistan, Tonga, Tunisia, United Republic of Tanzania and Zambia.

6 UN Doc. E/2010/10, para. 3.

whether or not and when to abolish the death penalty,[7] the deterrent effect of the death penalty and the nature of the issue as being subject to criminal justice or perceived as a human rights concern.[8] In some Muslim countries such as Kuwait and Libya, the application of the death penalty is upheld as part of Sharia law and thus the decision of maintaining the penalty is an exercise of the right to freedom of religious belief.[9]

The public opinion argument is particularly heard in two regions that actively enforce the death penalty, East Asia and the Americas. East Asia is considered as the next 'frontier for policy debate and legal change with respect to capital punishment'.[10] In the Americas, the United States seems to have relied on public opinion in determining the fate of capital punishment, unlike Western Europe, Canada, Australia and New Zealand, countries with which it shares similar political and legal values. This phenomenon is referred to as 'American exceptionalism'.[11] States often assert that they need to uphold 'the will of the people' and that abolition without public support would undermine confidence in law and may lead to private vengeance.[12] Occasionally, this argument enjoyed the support of abolitionist States. The Bolivarian Republic of Venezuela, for example, abolished capital punishment in the nineteenth century. However, in a reply to the Secretary-General of the United Nations on moratoriums on the use of capital punishment in 2008 it asserted that 'any process of change in respect of the death penalty must take into account the system of values and beliefs of the society concerned.'[13]

Retentionist States

Established by the UN General Assembly to examine States' compliance with human rights obligations,[14] the Universal Periodic Review found that a number of Asian countries linked their domestic public opinion to the retention of the death penalty. Despite not having ratified the International Covenant on Civil and Political Rights, China addressed the death penalty issue during two rounds of the Universal Periodic Review carried out by the Human Rights Council in 2009 and 2013.[15] In 2009 China declared that the current circumstances

7 UN Doc. A/63/293, para. 23.
8 UN Doc. A/HRC/WG.6/11/SGP/1, para. 120.
9 UN Doc. A/63/293, para. 25.
10 David T. Johnson and Franklin E. Zimring, *The Next Frontier, National Development, Political Change, and the Death Penalty in Asia* (Oxford University Press 2009) 3.
11 Roger Hood and Carolyn Hoyle, *The Death Penalty: A Worldwide Perspective* (Oxford University Press 2008) 354; Carole Steiker, 'Capital Punishment and American Exceptionalism' (2001) 97 *Oregon Law Review* 81, 114.
12 UN Doc. E/CN.4/Sub.2/1987/20, p. 24; G. Picca, 'La peine de mort: Un problème politique et social' (1987) 68 *Revue Internationalale de Droit Pénal* 435, 448.
13 UN Doc. A/63/293, para. 24.
14 UN Doc. A/RES/60/251.
15 UN Doc. A/HRC/11/25; UN Doc. A/HRC/25/5.

did not permit the abolition of the death penalty.[16] One condition was the overwhelming public support for the death penalty.[17] China confirmed in 2013 that it exercised 'strict control and caution in light of its current stage of social development'.[18] Japan submitted, in its first and second review in 2008 and 2012 respectively, that abolition would be inappropriate due to the majority opinion that the death penalty is 'unavoidable' for heinous crimes,[19] although it conceded in 2012 that there should be a broader discussion on the topic.[20] Lebanon, Malaysia and Singapore all cited public opinion as the reason for retaining the death penalty, during their periodic reviews in the Human Rights Council between 2008 and 2011.[21] Malaysia asserted that 'as a democratic state, the Government's policy must take into consideration the views of the majority of the electorates'.[22] Taiwan, although it does not present in the Universal Periodic Review, made a commitment in 2006 to abolish the death penalty when 80 per cent of its population held no objection to the abolition of capital punishment.[23]

During its interactive dialogue with the Universal Periodic Review in 2011, the United States commented that the matter of capital punishment is under earnest debate.[24] In an earlier reply to the Secretary-General of the United Nations with regard to capital punishment in 2005, it explained that '[a] majority of citizens have chosen, through their freely elected state and federal officials, to provide for the possibility of the death penalty for the most serious and aggravated crimes under federal, military, and most state laws' and that:

> in democratic societies the criminal justice system – including the punishment prescribed for the most serious and aggravated crimes – should reflect the will of the people freely expressed and appropriately implemented through their elected representatives.[25]

Saint Kitts and Nevis admitted that it was aware that the death penalty may not have played a role in deterrence, but it found difficult to '[justify] to its citizenry a decision to deprive the Court of that optional punishment' as

16 UN Doc. A/HRC/11/25.

17 Dietrich Oberwittler and Shenghui Qi, *Public Opinion on the Death Penalty in China* (Max-Plank Institute for Foreign and International Criminal Law, 2009) 6; Hu Yungteng, 'On the Death Penalty at the Turning of the Century', in Manfred Nowak and Xin Chunying (eds), 'EU-China Human Rights Dialogue: Proceedings of the Second EU-China Legal Experts' (2000) (Seminar held in Beijing on 19–20 October 1998) 88–94.

18 UN Doc. A/HRC/25/5, para. 84.

19 UN Doc. A/HRC/8/44, para. 9; UN Doc. A/HRC/22/14, paras 15 and 67.

20 UN Doc. A/HRC/22/14, para. 32.

21 UN Doc. A/HRC/18/11, para. 87; UN Doc. A/HRC/WG.6/9/LBN/1, para. 31; UN Doc. A/HRC/11/30, para. 55.

22 UN Doc. A/HRC/11/30, para. 55.

23 *Taipei Times*, 2 January 2006.

24 UN Doc. A/HRC/16/11, para. 55.

25 UN Doc. E/2005/3/Add.1, para. 17.

'there was a great demand by the society for it to remain', during its interactive dialogue of the Universal Periodic Review in the Human Rights Council in 2011.[26] Cuba was 'philosophically opposed to the death penalty' and it committed to its elimination 'when suitable conditions exist', as submitted in its national report under the Universal Periodic Review in 2013.[27] Barbados confirmed that public sentiment detected through opinion polls and surveys was the reason why it has not abolished the death penalty, as described in its own review in 2009.[28]

In Europe, Belarus is the only State that imposes the death penalty. It maintained that the decision to initiate abolition or a moratorium depends on whether a majority of public opinion comes to favour the abolition of the death penalty, in the Human Rights Council in 2010.[29] Belarus upheld the retention decision even when its Constitutional Court recommended otherwise.[30] In Africa, Botswana said in 2009 that it retained the death penalty because the authority 'is responsive to the needs of the people and it cannot undertake initiatives that are contrary to their interest'.[31] It confirmed in 2013 that public consultations showed that Botswana still prefers retention of capital punishment.[32] Guinea indicated in the Human Rights Council in 2010 that it was premature to envisage a discussion on capital punishment and that the discussion would be deferred to when 'the country returns to normal constitutional life'.[33] Finally, Tonga in Oceania chose to wait for the development of national debate regarding the issue of the death penalty, as revealed in its interactive dialogue with the Universal Periodic Review in 2008.[34]

De facto *abolitionist and abolitionist for ordinary crimes*

While the majority of States have either stopped imposing the death penalty in practice or have abolished it for ordinary crimes, some of them are reluctant to take a step forward, either through the establishment of a legal moratorium or through abandoning the death penalty for all crimes. Public opinion is cited as the primary deterrent for this. Despite not carrying out executions for more than ten years, Russia disagreed with the suggestion that the death penalty could and should be abolished when public opinion opposed it, as presented in its sixth periodic report for the Human Rights Committee under the International Covenant on Civil and Political Rights in 2010.[35] It stated that 'it is the duty of

26 UN Doc. A/HRC/17/12, paras 9 and 36.
27 UN Doc. A/HRC/WG.6/16/CUB/1, para. 98.
28 UN Doc. A/HRC/10/73/Add.1, para. 12.
29 UN Doc. A/HRC/15/16, para. 54; UN Doc. A/HRC/15/16/Add.1, paras 2, 46 and 47.
30 UN Doc. A/HRC/15/16, paras 45 and 53.
31 UN Doc. A/HRC/10/69, para. 9.
32 UN Doc. A/HRC/23/7/Add.1, para. 5.
33 UN Doc. A/HRC/15/4, para. 40; UN Doc. A/HRC/15/4/Add.1, paras 22–23.
34 UN Doc. A/HRC/8/48, para. 66.
35 UN Doc. CCPR/C/SR.2664, para. 5.

the head of state and the parliament to respect the sentiment of the people by not imposing things that they firmly opposed.'[36] During the Universal Periodic Review in 2009, Russia viewed that abolition depends on whether the majority of Russian public opinion will come to support it.[37]

Similarly, in East Asia, South Korean legislators found that public opinion was the most decisive factor for the retention of capital punishment as it can exert political pressure on the legislature.[38] The government indicated in the Human Rights Council in 2008 that abolition requires a national consensus-building process along with in-depth research, which take time.[39] Elsewhere, Kazakhstan pursued a gradual abolition policy as its national public opinion continued to be divided according to opinion polls, as cited in its national report under the Universal Periodic Review in 2009.[40]

In Africa, Cameroon has enforced a moratorium for over 20 years but still hesitated to fully abolish the death penalty. It stated in the Human Rights Council that '[t]he law was the expression of the general will and the Government was required to take into account its electorate, regardless of its convictions', during its second review under the Universal Periodic Review in 2013.[41] In its first review in 2009, Cameroon similarly opined that the death penalty was retained 'particularly because of the public's feelings toward certain offences'.[42] Zambia, in 2013, declined the suggestion of abolishing the death penalty or establishing a *de jure* moratorium based on public opinion,[43] explaining that '[t]he Government believes in democracy and is eager to respect the wishes of the people in this regard despite the fact the position of the Government may be different on this issue.'[44]

During the process of the Universal Periodic Review, Burkina Faso,[45] the Central African Republic,[46] Kenya,[47] Madagascar,[48] Mali,[49] Tanzania[50] and Tunisia[51] all listed public opinion as the reason for their not taking immediate actions toward abolition. The Democratic Republic of the Congo submitted the same argument to the Committee against Torture that the death penalty

36 UN Doc. CCPR/C/SR.2664, para. 5.
37 UN Doc. A/HRC/11/19/Add.1/Rev.1, p. 2.
38 LJC, 2006, 37.
39 UN Doc. A/HRC/8/40, paras 7 and 27.
40 UN Doc. A/HRC/WG.6/7/KAZ/1, paras 36 and 37.
41 UN Doc. A/HRC/24/15, para. 58.
42 UN Doc. A/HRC/11/21, para. 38.
43 UN Doc. A/HRC/8/43/Add.1, p. 2; UN Doc. A/HRC/8/43, para. 5; UN Doc. A/HRC/22/13/Add.1, para. 33.
44 UN Doc. A/HRC/22/13/Add.1, p. 6.
45 UN Doc. A/HRC/WG.6/BFA/1, para. 55; UN Doc. A/HRC/24/4, para. 64.
46 UN Doc. CCPR/C/CAF/CO/2, para. 13.
47 UN Doc. A/HRC/15/8, paras 49 and 104.
48 UN Doc. A/HRC/14/13/Add.1, para. 18.
49 UN Doc. A/HRC/WG.6/2/MLI/1, para. 118.
50 UN Doc. A/HRC/19/4, para. 23.
51 UN Doc. A/HRC/21/5, para. 39.

cannot be abolished because of public opinion when it presented its initial report under the Convention against Torture and Other Cruel, Inhuman or Degrading Treatment or Punishment in 2005.[52]

In the Americas, Guyana indicated to the Universal Periodic Review in 2010 that any change in the *status quo* would have to be accepted by the people.[53] Saint Lucia had observed a *de facto* moratorium for more than 15 years, but it was still not ready to establish a formal moratorium because its 'nationals have in fact been calling for a revival of use of the death penalty' and that 'in a democracy the Government acts with the consent of those being governed', as explained to the Human Rights Council in 2011.[54] Standing in the Human Rights Council in the same year, Jamaica found it unlikely to change its stance on the *de facto* moratorium since there was a public demand for the retention of the death penalty.[55] Barbados offered a similar reason in 2013 that 'there did not appear to be a national consensus or bipartisan support for the abolition of capital punishment.'[56]

Flaws of opinion polls

Elected politicians often hesitate to challenge the apparent will of their constituents no matter how uninformed they are, particularly on issues as emotive and prominent as crime and punishment.[57] Among the countries that invoke public opinion to retain the death penalty, many States refuse to acknowledge alternative opinions from those espoused by the public. Only Cameroon, Kenya and Zambia implied that they may not agree with public opinion but will enforce 'the will of the public' regardless.[58] How do States collect and identify the will of the people on the death penalty issue? Many States cite public opinion polls in their justification or explanation, although they do not address the extent to which these polls adequately reflect the will of the people.

Respondents of public opinion polls can be easily misled by leading questions and statistics gathered from polls are subject to various interpretations. Even if public opinion polls truthfully indicate a certain degree of public sentiment, they may not reveal peoples' conclusive attitudes toward the death penalty. For instance, France abolished the death penalty in 1981 when public opinion polls apparently supported it.[59] Politicians who made the so-called 'unpopular' decision, however, did not experience adverse consequences. President François Mitterrand was elected despite having revealed his preference for abolition

52 UN Doc. CAT/C/SR.687, para. 23.
53 UN Doc. A/HRC/15/14, paras 18 and 52.
54 UN Doc. A/HRC/17/6, paras 38 and 66.
55 UN Doc. A/HRC/16/14, para. 37.
56 UN Doc. A/HRC/23/11, para. 20.
57 David A Green, 'Public Opinion Versus Public Judgment: Correcting the "Comedy of Errors"' (2006) 46 *British Journal of Criminology* 131, 131.
58 UN Doc. A/HRC/15/8, paras. 49 and 104; UN Doc. A/HRC/22/13/Add.1, para. 33; A/HRC/24/15, para. 58.
59 Robert Badinter, *L'Abolition* (Fayard 2000) 301.

throughout his presidential campaign and was re-elected after the 'unpopular' bill was approved. Through democratic process, French people showed a collective and conclusive attitude toward capital punishment: although they did not favour abolition, they still supported the government that made the decision, because the issue was viewed by constituents as being of a lower priority than other issues.

Studies have affirmed the influence of public ignorance and 'off-the-top-of-the-head' opinions surrounding the issue of capital punishment. This situation can be aggravated by the mass media due to their partial and selective nature.[60] It can also be exacerbated by the oversimplified statements of governments that public opinion was in favour of the death penalty. The French case and other flaws in opinion polls raise questions regarding the conclusion that public opinion tends to support the death penalty. This also challenges the legitimacy of solely basing the death penalty policy on public opinion, which is hard to measure accurately. It can be further questioned to what extent States' educational duties to promote human rights can be extended to the issue of the death penalty or whether they may remain in a neutral position regarding the apparent support of the public for the death penalty.

The legitimacy of public opinion argument

Myths, hypothesis and empirical research

Myths of public opinion

Many governments use opinion polls to interpret public opinion. For instance, one year before France abolished the death penalty, the then French President Valéry Giscard d'Estaing expounded:

> I have a profound distaste for the death penalty . . . I believe that such a change can only take place in a peaceable society whose members are confident about their safety. And as long as this assurance is not felt, [abolition] would go against the deepest sensibilities of the French people.[61]

Michel Forst identified a problem with this statement, as Giscard mistakenly used opinion polls as the only way to understand public opinion. Forst questioned whether abolition is to go against the deepest sensibilities or to go against the polls.[62] There is more than one way to present public opinion, for instance

60 Stuart Henry, 'Newsmaking Criminology as Replacement Discourse' in Gregg Barak (ed.), *Media, Process, and the Social Construction of Crime: Studies in Newsmaking Criminology* (Garland 1995) 287–315.

61 Michel Forst, 'The Abolition of the Death Penalty in France', Council of Europe (ed.), *The Death Penalty Abolition in Europe* (Council of Europe Publishing 1999) 112.

62 Michel Forst, 'The Abolition of the Death Penalty in France', Council of Europe (ed.), *The Death Penalty Abolition in Europe* (Council of Europe Publishing 1999) 112.

through referendum, the development of national and international law, the jury's opinion and findings of prominent courts. William Bowers further pointed out that the public's expressed support for capital punishment through opinion polls is 'not a genuine but a spurious function of people's desire for harsh but meaningful punishment for convicted murderers'.[63] The nature of this support, according to Ellsworth and Gross, is highly emotional and symbolic and driven more and more by anger and retributive urges.[64]

Behind the logic of the public opinion argument lies the principle that majority rule is not just a characteristic of, but is in fact *equated with* democracy. Concerning this sentiment, the European Court of Human Rights concluded in *Young, James and Webster v. The United Kingdom* that 'democracy does not simply mean that the views of a majority must always prevail'.[65] The South African Constitutional Court further stated that the primacy of human rights should prevail over the consideration of public opinion with respect to the death penalty. In the case of *State v. Makwanyane*, Mr Justice Chaskalson stated the following:

> Public opinion may have some relevance to the enquiry, but in itself is no substitute for the duty vested in the Courts to interpret the Constitution and to uphold its provisions without fear or favour. If public opinion were to be decisive, there would be no need for constitutional adjudication. The protection of rights could then be left to parliament, which has a mandate from the public, and is answerable to the public for the way its mandate is exercised [.] The very reason [. . .] for vesting the power of judicial review in the courts, was to protect the rights of minorities and others who cannot protect their rights adequately through the democratic process. Those who are entitled to claim this protection include the social outcasts and marginalized people in our society. It is only if there is a willingness to protect the worst and weakest amongst us that all of us can be secure that our own rights will be protected.[66]

Public opinion does have an influence on State legislation, but to what degree depends on different political ideologies.[67] For instance, in the Western liberal

63 William Bowers, 'Capital Punishment and Contemporary Values: People's Misgivings and the Court's Misperceptions' (1993) 27 (1) *Law & Society Review* 157, 159.

64 Phoebe Ellsworth and Sam Gross, 'Hardening of the Attitudes: Americans' Views on the Death Penalty' (1994) 50 *Journal of Social Issues* 19; Phoebe Ellsworth and Lee Ross, 'Public Opinion and Capital Punishment: A Close Examination of the Views of Abolitionists and Retentionists' (1983) 29 (1) *Crime and Delinquency* 116; Robert Nolin, 'Simple Revenge Now Argument for Death Penalty', *Arizona Republic* 5 October 1997 A12.

65 *Young, James and Webster v. The United Kingdom*, Application no. 7601/76; 7806/77, European Court of Human Rights, para. 63.

66 *State v. Makwanyane* (1995) (3) SA 391, para. 88.

67 Roger Hood and Carolyn Hoyle, *The Death Penalty: A Worldwide Perspective* (Oxford University Press 2008) 352.

parliamentary democracies, laws are based on the mandate given to elected representatives. It is not incumbent on legislators to follow the majority view of the society. In comparison, some Middle Eastern and North African countries view that the death penalty is the commandment of Islam and it would appear that the abolition of capital punishment requires a challenge to the inherent political ideology of such States. But not every Muslim country has the same ideology. Malaysia, for instance, comprises approximately 65 per cent Muslim adherents and respects Islam as the 'religion of the Federation' according to its constitution, while the law and jurisprudence of the nation is based on English common law.[68] Thus Malaysia does not invoke Sharia law in the debate over capital punishment.

It is often heard that abolition without public support may lead to 'mob justice' or private vengeance. The Tanzanian government argued in the Tanzanian High Court that:

> [t]he court's and parliament's attitudes should not be radically different from those of society as a whole. It is very dangerous in fact to allow penal policy to jump too far ahead of the population, since it will result in the loss of public confidence in the criminal justice system and concomitantly in the alienation of the public from it. There is abundant evidence that members of the Tanzanian public often resort to mob justice in a situation in which they feel that the criminal justice system and/or its agencies lack the competence or the will to protect them against crimes. Therefore no civilised community should provoke such a situation in the name of a so-called 'progressive' penal policy.[69]

However, the authorities' articulation did not clarify whether there is a limit for States to carry out heavy punishment in order to maintain public confidence, or whether human rights should be introduced to prevent punishments that are increasingly recognised as cruel, inhuman and degrading. Before France became abolitionist for all crimes, French Minister of Justice M. Peyrefitte similarly warned of the danger of private vengeance.[70] Some legislators argued in the French parliamentary debate that led to abolition that '[w]e must not, in abolishing the death penalty at an inopportune moment, provoke the opposite of what we are trying to do; that is to say, push people to seek justice themselves.'[71] Despite such warnings, private vengeance did not happen in France after abolition.

68 The Constitution of Malaysia, article 3.

69 *Republic v. Mbushuu et al.* [1994] 2LRC. 335 (High Court of Tanzania), p. 349.

70 G. Picca, 'La peine de mort: Un problème politique et social' (1987) 68 *Revue Internationale de Droit Pénal* 435, 448.

71 Robert Badinter, *Abolition: One Man's Battle against the Death Penalty* (Northeastern University Press 2008) 111.

Empirical research and the Marshall Hypothesis

DOES PUBLIC OPINION FALL NATURALLY AFTER THE ABOLITION OF THE DEATH PENALTY?

Robert Badinter, a lawyer and politician who played a vital role in the abolition of the death penalty in France in 1981, suggested that the public would stop viewing the death penalty as useful or as connected with the level of homicide about ten to 15 years after its abolition.[72] In his analysis, public support for the death penalty may be likened to the pyramids at the Louvre in Paris, which were controversial before being constructed but were wholeheartedly accepted and seen as natural afterwards. Three years after the death penalty was abolished in France, the percentage supporting abolition (49 per cent) exceeded the percentage opposing it (46 per cent).[73]

Empirical research tends to back up Badinter's argument. Steven Stack's study across 17 countries observed that public support for the death penalty dropped every year after abolition.[74] Persons residing in a retentionist State were 2.88 times as likely to support the death penalty as persons residing in an abolitionist nation.[75] His analysis suggested that people tend to agree with what already exists in their culture and society, but they can adapt to a society that does not practise the death penalty. In other surveys, young people are inclined to think that the death penalty belongs in the past. For example, a Finnish survey in 2006 indicated that middle-aged Finns were the most likely to favour capital punishment, while only one in five students was in favour of executions.[76] Gallup surveys in the United States, the United Kingdom and Canada also found that support for the death penalty was lowest among those who were 18 to 29 years old.[77]

THE MARSHALL HYPOTHESIS

The Marshall Hypothesis constructs an alternative angle from which to view the relationship between public opinion and the death penalty. The Hypothesis argues that if the public is fully informed on the details of capital punishment, support for the death penalty will diminish. The US Supreme Court has rendered that the proscription of cruel and unusual punishments 'is not fastened to

72 Robert Badinter, Amnesty International lecture, 1 March 2007, Taylorian Institute, Oxford.

73 Michel Forst, 'The Abolition of the Death Penalty in France', Council of Europe (ed.), *The Death Penalty Abolition in Europe* (Council of Europe Publishing 1999) 115.

74 Steven Stack, 'Public Opinion on the Death Penalty: Analysis of Individual-level Data from 17 Nations' (2004) 14 *International Criminal Justice Review* 69, 69–98.

75 Steven Stack, 'Public Opinion on the Death Penalty: Analysis of Individual-level Data from 17 Nations' (2004) 14 *International Criminal Justice Review* 69, 86.

76 Death Penalty Information, Amnesty International Death Penalty Blog, 21 November 2006.

77 Gallup Poll press release, *Death Penalty Gets Less Support from Britons, Canadians than Americans*, 20 February 2006, cited by the DPIC.

the obsolete but may acquire meaning as public opinion becomes enlightened by a human justice'.[78] What is cruel and unusual punishment should be considered 'in the light of contemporary human knowledge'.[79] Most importantly, the meaning of 'cruel and unusual' 'must draw its meaning from the evolving standards of decency that mark the progress of maturing society', said the Court in *Trop v. Dulles*.[80]

United States Supreme Court Justice Thurgood Marshall concurred in *Furman v. Georgia* that a punishment may be invalid 'if popular sentiment abhors it' or if 'it shocks the conscience and sense of justice of the people'.[81] Concurrently, Marshall cast doubts on the use of opinion polls in determining public opinion or the 'evolving standards of decency'. Marshall wrote that 'whether or not a punishment is cruel and unusual depends, not on whether its mere mention "shocks the conscience and sense of justice of the people," but on whether people who were fully informed as to the purposes of the penalty and its liabilities would find the penalty shocking, unjust, and unacceptable.'[82] In conclusion, the Marshall Hypothesis holds that 'the great mass of citizens would conclude [. . .] that the death penalty is immoral and therefore unconstitutional' if they were fully enlightened.[83]

The Marshall Hypothesis does not contemplate that people could or should act rationally. It called for 'predictable subjective, emotional reactions of informed citizens'.[84] He even summarised information that will facilitate the opinion change, including the proposal that:

> [t]he death penalty is no more effective a deterrent than life imprisonment, that convicted murderers are rarely executed, but are usually sentenced to a term in prison; that convicted murderers usually are model prisoners, and that they almost always become law-abiding citizens upon their release from prison; that the costs of executing a capital offender exceed the costs of imprisoning him for life; that, while in prison, a convict under sentence of death performs none of the useful functions that life prisoners perform; that no attempt is made in the sentencing process to ferret out likely recidivists for execution; and that the death penalty may actually stimulate criminal activity.
>
> [C]apital punishment is imposed discriminatorily against certain identifiable classes of people; there is evidence that innocent people have been executed before their innocence can be proved; and the death penalty wreaks havoc with our entire criminal justice system.

78 Re Kemmler, 136 U.S. 436, p. 447; *Weems v. United States*, 217 U.S. 349 (1910), p. 378.
79 *Robinson v. California*, 370 U.S. 660 (1962), p. 370.
80 *Trop v. Dulles*, 356 U.S. 86 (1958), p. 101.
81 *Furman v. Georgia*, 408 U.S. 238 (1972), pp. 332 and 360.
82 *Furman v. Georgia*, 408 U.S. 238 (1972), p. 361.
83 *Furman v. Georgia*, 408 U.S. 238 (1972), pp. 363 and 232.
84 *Furman v. Georgia*, 408 U.S. 238 (1972), p. 362.

There exists rich literature that tests the Marshall Hypothesis,[85] with studies tending to find mixed but relatively consistent support for the Hypothesis.[86] These studies also presented additional findings. For instance, Bohm found that opinions on the death penalty may not be significantly influenced by increased knowledge about the subject or may only be influenced temporarily, at least if that knowledge is obtained in a 'college classroom'.[87] More findings include: information may polarise opinion; publicly announced opinions were more resistant to change; initial beliefs were not changed by information; and attitudes

85 Robert M. Bohm, 'The Effects of Classroom Instruction and Discussion on Death Penalty Opinions: A Teaching Note' (1989) 17 *Journal of Criminal Justice* 123; Robert M. Bohm, 'Death Penalty Opinions: Effects of a Classroom Experience and Public Commitment' (1990) 60 *Sociological Inquiry* 285; Robert M. Bohm, 'American Death Penalty Opinion: Past, Present, and Future', in James R. Acker, Robert M. Bohm and Charles S. Lanier (eds), *America's Experiment with Capital Punishment* (2nd edn, Carolina Academic Press 2003) 27–54; Robert M. Bohm, *Death Quest: An Introduction to the Theory and Practice of Capital Punishment in the United States* (4th edn, Anderson 2012); Robert M. Bohm, Louise J. Clark and Adrian F. Aveni, 'The Influence of Knowledge on Death Penalty Opinions: An Experimental Text' (1990) 7 *Justice Quarterly* 175; Robert M. Bohm, Louise J. Clark and Adrian F. Aveni, 'Knowledge and Death Penalty Opinion: A Test of the Marshall Hypotheses' (1991) 28 *Journal of Research in Crime and Delinquency* 360; Robert M. Bohm, Ronald E. Vogel and Albert A. Maisto, 'Knowledge and Death Penalty Opinions: A Panel Study' (1993) 21 *Journal of Criminal Justice* 29; Robert M. Bohm and Ronald E. Vogel, 'A Comparison of Factors Associated with Uninformed and Informed Death Penalty Opinions' (1994) 22 (2) *Journal of Criminal Justice* 125; Alan W. Clarke, Eric Lambert and Laurie Anne Whitt, 'Executing the Innocent: The Next Step in the Marshall Hypotheses' (2001) 26 (3) *Review of Law and Social Change* 309; Phoebe C. Ellsworth and Lee Ross, 'Public Opinion and Capital Punishment: A Close Examination of the Views of Abolitionists and Retentionists' (1983) 29 (1) *Crime and Delinquency* 116; Eric Lambert and Alan Clarke, 'The Impact of Information on an Individual's Support of the Death Penalty: A Partial Test of the Marshall Hypothesis among College Students' (2001) 12 *Criminal Justice Policy Review* 215; Dennis R. Longmire, 'Americans' Attitudes about the Ultimate Sanction Capital Punishment' in Timothy J. Flanagan and Dennis R. Longmire (eds), *Americans View Crime and Justice: A National Public Opinion Survey* (SAGE 1996) 93–108; Charles G. Lord, Lee Ross and Mark R. Lepper, 'Biased Assimilation and Attitude Polarization: The Effects of Prior Theories on Subsequently Considered Evidence' (1979) 37 *Journal of Personality and Social Psychology* 2098; Allan L. Patenaude, 'May God Have Mercy on Your Soul! Exploring and Teaching a Course on the Death Penalty' (2001) 12 *Journal of Criminal Justice Education* 405; Marla Sandys, 'Attitudinal Change among Students in a Capital Punishment Class: It May Be Possible' (1995) 20 *American Journal of Criminal Justice* 37; Austin Sarat and Neil Vidmar, 'Public Opinion, the Death Penalty, and the Eighth Amendment: Testing the Marshall Hypothesis' (1976) 17 *Wisconsin Law Review* 171; Neil Vidmar and Tony Dittenhoffer, 'Informed Public Opinion and Death Penalty Attitudes' (1981) 23 *Canadian Journal of Criminology* 43; Harold O. Wright, Robert M. Bohm and Katherine M. Jamieson, 'A Comparison of Uninformed and Informed Death Penalty Opinions: A Replication and Expansion' (1995) 20 *American Journal of Criminal Justice* 57; John K. Cochran and Mitchell B. Chamlin, 'Can Information Change Public Opinion? Another Test of the Marshall Hypotheses' (2005) 33 *Journal of Criminal Justice* 573.

86 John K. Cochran and Mitchell B. Chamlin, 'Can Information Change Public Opinion? Another Test of the Marshall Hypotheses' (2005) 33 *Journal of Criminal Justice* 573, 574.

87 Robert M. Bohm, 'American Death Penalty Opinion: Past, Present, and Future' in James R. Acker, Robert M. Bohm and Charles S. Lanier (eds), *America's Experiment with Capital Punishment* (2nd edn, Carolina Academic Press 2003) 44.

toward capital punishment were changed primarily due to information regarding racial disparities in justice and the execution of innocent persons.[88] The Marshall Hypothesis and related research have undermined the credibility of using opinion polls to determine public opinion and, more importantly, offered intellectual support for actions designed to change public opinion with regard to the death penalty.

Abolition without opinion poll support

Examples and updates

Besides France, quite a few States have ended capital punishment when public opinion, as measured by opinion polls and surveys, appeared to support it. These States include Canada,[89] Germany[90] and the United Kingdom.[91] Canada, Slovakia and the United Kingdom rejected the reintroduction of the death penalty while their public opinion seemed to call for it.[92] Slovakia replied to the Secretary-General of the United Nations in 2008 that the authority held firmly that reintroduction would be an unprecedented step against respect for human rights.[93] With regard to politicians that made the decision of abolition, the Parliamentary Assembly of the Council of Europe concluded that European officials did not suffer any backlash from public opinion.[94]

The French case, in particular, shows that abolition is a matter of political courage. In the French parliamentary debate that led to abolition, retentionist arguments were not dissimilar from those of today. It was argued that 'the time has not yet come',[95] that '[t]he chosen solution must respect the national sensibility' and that abolition may 'provoke the opposite of what we are trying to do' and 'push people to seek justice themselves'.[96] However, Robert Badinter questioned the motivation for politicians to oppose abolition, as such a decision 'appears to

88 John K. Cochran and Mitchell B. Chamlin, 'Can Information Change Public Opinion? Another Test of the Marshall Hypotheses' (2005) 33 *Journal of Criminal Justice* 573, 574.
89 Ezzat A. Fattah, 'Canada's Successful Experience with the Abolition of the Death Penalty' (1987) 25 *Canadian Journal of Criminology* 421, 421–431.
90 Richard J. Evans, *Rituals of Retribution: Capital Punishment in Germany 1600–1987* (Oxford University Press, 1966) 801–804; M. Mohrenschlager, 'The Abolition of Capital Punishment in the Federal Republic of Germany: The German Experience' (1987) 58 *Revue Internationale de Droit Pénal* 509, 513.
91 Roger Hood and Carolyn Hoyle, *The Death Penalty: A Worldwide Perspective* (Oxford University Press 2008) 352.
92 UN Doc. A/63/293, para. 26.
93 UN Doc. A/63/293, para. 26.
94 Parliamentary Assembly of Council of Europe Resolution 1807 (2011).
95 Michel Forst, 'The Abolition of the Death Penalty in France', Council of Europe (ed.), *The Death Penalty Abolition in Europe* (Council of Europe Publishing 1999) 112.
96 *Le Matin*, 11 December 1979; *Le Monde*, 21 December 1979; Robert Badinter, *Abolition: One Man's Battle against the Death Penalty* (Northeastern University Press 2008) 111 and 140.

be too politically risky'.[97] Addressing a television show during his presidential campaign in 1981, François Mitterrand stated:

> I am opposed to the death penalty. And I don't need to read the polls that tell me the opposite: a majority of the people are for the death penalty. And yes, I am a candidate for the presidency for the Republic [. . .] I say what I think, what I believe in, what is the foundation of my spiritual leanings, my faith, my concern for civilizations.[98]

He was subsequently elected and during his presidency the death penalty was abolished in France. This case illustrated that '[e]lections are not won by scrutinizing opinion polls but by proposing values that correspond to beliefs'.[99]

Unlike France and many other Western European countries, the United States imposes a distinct death penalty policy. This phenomenon used to be referred to as 'American exceptionalism'.[100] In 2002 Carol Steiker explored accounts for this difference and reviewed that 'American populism' as compared to European 'elitism' was most responsible.[101] Within a few years, this divergence between Europe and the United States has been observed as becoming blurred. The stereotype of accusing politicians who oppose capital punishment as siding with criminals and ignoring victims and law enforcement has gradually been changing.[102] Recent elections have seen a number of candidates elected who publicly challenged the death penalty, including governors in Maryland and Massachusetts and those who continued the moratorium in Illinois, New Jersey and Virginia.[103]

South Korea has moved from retentionist to *de facto* abolitionist since 2007. It could possibly be among the first States in Asia to abandon the death penalty. Kim Dae-jung, President of the Republic of Korea between 1998 and 2003, identified his commitment to abolishing the death penalty throughout his presidential

97 Robert Badinter, *Abolition: One Man's Battle against the Death Penalty* (Northeastern University Press 2008) 111.

98 Robert Badinter, *Abolition: One Man's Battle against the Death Penalty* (Northeastern University Press 2008) 172; François Mitterrand, *Politique 2, 1977–1981* (Fayard 1981) 255.

99 Michel Forst, 'The Abolition of the Death Penalty in France', Council of Europe (ed.), *The Death Penalty Abolition in Europe* (Council of Europe Publishing 1999) 113.

100 Roger Hood and Carolyn Hoyle, *The Death Penalty: A Worldwide Perspective* (Oxford University Press 2008) 354; Carole Steiker, 'Capital Punishment and American Exceptionalism' (2001) 97 *Oregon Law Review* 81, 114.

101 Carol Steiker, 'Capital Punishment and American Exceptionalism' (2002) 81 *Oregon Law Review* 97, 114.

102 Richard C. Dieter, 'Changing Views on the Death Penalty in the United States', Paper delivered in Beijing at the Conference on Alternatives to the Death Penalty in the USA and China, 7 October 2007, 7.

103 Richard C. Dieter, 'Changing Views on the Death Penalty in the United States', Paper delivered in Beijing at the Conference on Alternatives to the Death Penalty in the USA and China, 7 October 2007, 7.

election campaign and was elected.[104] Two consecutive presidents, Kim Dae-jung and Roh Moo-hyun, refused to sign death warrants and kept commuting death sentences.[105] Legislators of the country thrice presented bills aimed at abolition in 1999, 2001 and 2004, hoping to at least stimulate public debate.[106] Because of the direct involvement of politicians, the South Korean abolition movement was considered to be the result of political leadership.[107] These decisions, however, according to public opinion polls, were all unpopular.

Motivations

The decision to abolish the death penalty may come from various motivations. Germany, Italy, the Philippines, Romania and Spain used abolition to announce a new era after the fall of an authoritarian administration.[108] In 2012 Tunisia accepted the suggestion of abolishing the death penalty and ratifying the Second Optional Protocol to the ICCPR in its dialogue with the Universal Periodic Review in order to declare its disassociation with the past and a new start in its history in which authority is derived from an adherence to democracy and human rights.[109] An important background of the commitment was that Tunisia was undergoing a major revolution that broke out on 17 December 2010 and triggered a revolutionary wave of demonstrations and protests, riots and civil wars in the Arab world, which was referred to as the Arab Spring. In other countries, such as South Korea, capital punishment used to be closely linked to political crimes. Accordingly, abolition was considered in South Korea as an indicator of emergent political democracy.[110]

National death penalty policies can be influenced by foreign political forces to varying degrees. Direct influence can be found between colonies and their colonising countries. For example, Hong Kong and Macao are both abolitionist, despite the fact that the rest of China continues to impose the death penalty, primarily on account of the various regions' status as former colonies of the United Kingdom and Portugal. In Hong Kong, the death penalty was abolished by law in 1993, five years earlier than in the United Kingdom and four years before Hong Kong was handed over to China. The abolition decision was one of the rare cases in which the authority of the United Kingdom

104 Byung-Sun Cho, 'South Korea's Changing Capital Punishment Policy: The Road from De Facto to Formal Abolition' (2008) 10 (2) *Punishment & Society* 171, n. 16.

105 *Yonhap News*, 30 December 2007; Sangmin Bae, 'South Korea's De Facto Abolition of the Death Penalty' (2009) 82 (3) *Pacific Affairs* 407, 415.

106 Legislation and Judiciary Committee of South Korea, LJC, 2006, 26–27.

107 Byung-Sun Cho, 'South Korea's Changing Capital Punishment Policy: The Road from De Facto to Formal Abolition' (2008) 10 (2) *Punishment & Society* 171, 177.

108 Franklin Zimring, *The Contradictions of American Capital Punishment* (Oxford University Press 2003) 23.

109 UN Doc. A/HRC/21/5, paras 5 and 116, recommendations 6, 8, 9 and 10.

110 Byung-Sun Cho, 'South Korea's Changing Capital Punishment Policy: The Road from De Facto to Formal Abolition' (2008) 10(2) *Punishment & Society* 171, 177.

was enacted despite the opposition from the Hong Kong Chinese.[111] During the debate in the Hong Kong Legislative Council that led to abolition, some local legislators suspected that the decision was based on political motivations to confront China.[112]

Less directly, a number of States have been restricting their death penalty policies to win the respect of other countries, especially those that are referred to as 'the civilised world', 'advanced nations' and 'the international community'. In Japan, the Meiji Reformation (1868–1911) witnessed a 97 per cent decline in executions in order to earn the recognition and respect of 'the civilised world', which was then colonising Asia.[113] In recent decades, European governments and organisations have also had an impact on the low execution numbers of Japan.[114] The Parliamentary Assembly of the Council of Europe, for instance, has repeatedly threatened Japan with withdrawal of its observer status unless it made 'significant progress' on abolishing executions.[115] In South Korea, former President Kim Dae-jung announced during a public speech that the *de facto* abolitionist status of South Korea is a landmark in joining the advanced nations in terms of human rights.[116] The term 'civilised world' nowadays has gradually been replaced by the 'international community', with the intention of gaining the respect of 'advanced nations' or 'international community' helping to explain the decline of executions in China, Japan, South Korea and Taiwan.

In rare cases public opinion can directly trigger the abolition of the death penalty. Ireland put the issue of capital punishment into referendum in June 2001. The result was 62 per cent in favour of and 38 per cent against the proposal to remove all references to the death penalty and forbid the Houses of the Oireachtas (National Parliament) from enacting any law that provides for the imposition of the death penalty. After the referendum, a constitutional amendment was adopted to confirm the prohibition of the death penalty.[117] Alongside the referendum in Ireland, the Czech Republic and Romania revealed in written replies to the UN Secretary-General that their abolition decisions were made 'in response to public opinion', during the United Nations fifth quinquennial survey

111 Suy-kai Lau, *Society and Politics in Hong Kong* (Chinese University Press 1993) 31.

112 Hong Kong Legislative Council, Official Record of Proceedings (Chinese), 26 June 1991, p. 1966; Hong Kong Legislative Council, Official Record of Proceedings (English), 21 April 1993, p. 2937.

113 Kaoru Murano, *Nihon no Shikei* (Soshoku Shobo 1992) 53; David T. Johnson and Franklin E. Zimring, *The Next Frontier: National Development, Political Change, and the Death Penalty in Asia* (Oxford University Press 2009) 59.

114 Roger Hood, 'Capital Punishment: A Global Perspective' (2001) 3 *Punishment & Society* 331, 337; Sangmin Bae, *When the State No Longer Kills: International Human Rights Norms and Abolition of Capital Punishment* (State University of New York Press 2007).

115 The Parliamentary Assembly of the Council of Europe Resolution 1253, 25 June.

116 Kim Dae-jung, 'In Appreciation of the Announcement of Korea as a De Facto Abolitionist Country', speech at the Press Centre, 10 October 2007.

117 Twenty-First Amendment of the Constitution Act 2001 (Prohibition of death penalty and removal of references to death penalty). The death penalty was abolished in Ireland in 1990 through the Criminal Justice Act 1990.

on capital punishment in 1995.[118] During the same survey, Poland said that it repealed capital punishment for economic crimes on the grounds that public opinion did not accept it.[119]

A case of Chinese societies

China accounts for the majority of the world's executions. In Chinese society, public support for the death penalty is usually understood as a combination of Chinese culture and historical experience.[120] Arguing from culture and history, such an opinion seems to hold more weight and is becoming harder to change. However, among the four jurisdictions, China (or mainland China),[121] Hong Kong, Macao and Taiwan, Hong Kong abolished the death penalty in 1993 when public opinion polls suggested that Hong Kong Chinese were in favour of the penalty. Macao has had no executions for over a century. Taiwan has a relatively small number of executions, with none carried out between 2006 and 2009, whereas China continues actively to impose the death penalty. The four jurisdictions maintain separate attitudes toward the issue of public opinion regarding the death penalty.

Hong Kong and Macao

The abolition decision of Hong Kong and Macao was strongly influenced by the authorities of the United Kingdom and Portugal. Macao prohibited the use of the death penalty through its criminal code of 1995.[122] Prior to that, Macao had no executions for over a century, as it applied the Portugal 1886 Criminal Code, which did not legislate for the death penalty.[123] It is hard to detect to what extent public opinion was involved in the decision-making process, since the abolition happened a long time ago and, during the colonial era, ethnic Chinese were not considered among the political elite in spite of the fact that they comprised 97 per cent of Macao's population.[124]

Hong Kong went through a recorded debate to abolish the death penalty. In the Hong Kong Legislative Council in the early 1990s, public opinion was sometimes referred to as the 'Chinese opinion', whereas abolitionist opinion was called the 'British opinion'.[125] Some legislators argued that a responsive government should have considered the view of Hong Kong's population and Chinese ethics,

118 UN Doc. E/1995/78, paras 19 and 25.

119 UN Doc. E/1995/78, para. 26.

120 FIDH, The Death Penalty in Taiwan: Towards Abolition?, 2006, p. 6.

121 China (or mainland China) refers to the continental territory of the People's Republic of China, excluding Hong Kong and Macao.

122 Macao 1995 Criminal Code, article 39.

123 Amnesty International, 1997 report.

124 吴志良（编），*澳门华人政治文化* (澳门基金会出版社 1993).

125 Hong Kong Legislative Council, Official Record of Proceedings, 21 April 1993, pp. 1918, 1939, 2196 and 2198; Suy-kai Lau, *Society and Politics in Hong Kong* (Chinese University Press, 1993) 1.

but should not impose laws, ideologies and values of other countries, i.e. the United Kingdom.[126] In support of their argument, the case of the United States was invoked, questioning whether the abolition of capital punishment constitutes a necessary component of freedom, democracy and progressed civilisation, when 'the most civilised country' and 'world leader' still enforced the death penalty.[127]

Others asserted that legislators should use rational thought and not public opinion polls to address the death penalty, referring to the abolition cases of Canada and the United Kingdom.[128] It was said that '[paying] heed to the wishes of the public' does not mean 'follow[ing] public opinion polls on everything'.[129] They called for government officials and legislative councillors 'not to balk in the face of worked-up public emotions', but to grasp 'the foundation of knowledge and reason on which the democratic spirit depends' and 'explain to people and exercise leadership'.[130] After this debate, the Hong Kong Legislative Council repealed the death penalty through the Crimes (Amendment) (No. 3) Bill 1992. Around that time, statistics from public opinion polls showed that 71 per cent were in favour of retaining capital punishment in 1990, with 84 per cent believing so in 1992.

Taiwan

Taiwan is expected to be among the first Asian nations or territories to abandon the death penalty.[131] The Taiwanese administration promised to abolish the penalty when 80 per cent of Taiwanese supported it.[132] In 2005 the Ministry of Justice issued a gradual abolition policy and a plan to shape public opinion.[133] However, President Ma Ying-jeou twice confirmed (in 2010 and 2013) that abolition is a long-term goal, not what Taiwanese mainstream public opinion currently favours.[134] In 2010, Justice Minister Wang Ching-feng resigned because she publicly supported abolition and refused to sign death warrants.[135]

126 Hong Kong Legislative Council, Official Record of Proceeding, 26 June 1991, pp. 1918 and 1938–1939, 1944, 1945, 1946, 1949, 1960 and 1965–1966; Hong Kong Legislative Council, Official Record of Proceeding, 21 April 1993, pp. 2197 and 2198.

127 Hong Kong Legislative Council, Official Record of Proceeding, 21 April 1993, pp. 2196 and 2198; 26 June 1991, pp. 1945 and 1947.

128 Hong Kong Legislative Council, Official Record of Proceeding (Chinese), 26 June 1991, p. 1919.

129 Hong Kong Legislative Council, Official Record of Proceeding (Chinese), 26 June 1991, pp. 1925 and 1938.

130 Hong Kong Legislative Council, Official Record of Proceeding (Chinese), 26 June 1991, pp. 1938 and 1940.

131 Carsten Anckar, *Determinants of the Death Penalty: A Comparative Study of the World* (Routledge 2004) 4 ; David T. Johnson, 'The Death Penalty in Asia: Introduction to a Special Issue of Punishment & Society' (2008) 10 (2) *Punishment & Society* 99, 101.

132 *Taipei Times*, 2 January 2006; Ministry of Justice, The Policy of Gradual Abolition of the Death Penalty, 2005.

133 *Taipei Times*, 2 January 2006; Roger Hood and Carolyn Hoyle, *The Death Penalty: A Worldwide Perspective* (4th edn, Oxford University Press 2008) 351.

134 *United Daily News*, 12 March 2010; Central News Agency, 19 April 2013.

135 Central News Agency, 11 March 2010.

In conformity with the plan of shaping public opinion, the Taiwanese Ministry of Justice established a research and promotion team, mandated to inform the public and build consensus on abolition.[136] The Justice Ministry held a number of public hearings and commissioned relevant research.[137] In these hearings and research, information has been circulated with regard to the importance of informed public opinion, flaws in opinion polls and abolition cases, for instance in Hong Kong where capital punishment was abolished when opinion polls showed support for it.[138] The question remains whether the authority has exerted enough political energy to shape public opinion toward acceptance of abolition. By way of illustration, on the sensing of public opposition to the Economic Cooperation Framework Agreement with mainland China in 2009, the Taiwanese government mobilised all levels of government to campaign for the agreement and eventually had it approved.[139] The effort and commitment displayed in economic topics has not been matched in the death penalty case.

China

China has often stated that the time for abolition is not yet ripe and that the Chinese public overwhelmingly support the death penalty. However, the first empirical study on Chinese public opinion on the death penalty, conducted by the Max Planck Institute, Beijing Normal University and Wuhan University between 2007 and 2009, discovered that the public's enthusiasm for execution was overestimated.[140] The study found out that 58 per cent were in favour of the death penalty in general and that over one-quarter (28 per cent) were undecided about their attitude.[141] The level of knowledge and interest in the death penalty tended to be rather low among the majority of the Chinese population.[142]

Furthermore, respondents were likely to change their minds if alternatives were given or they were informed about the possibility of wrongful convictions and

136 法務部, 法務部暫緩執行死刑之說明, 11 March 2010, p. 3; Taiwan Alliance to End the Death Penalty, The Death Penalty Report of Taiwan 2010, p. 11.

137 法務部, 國內死刑相關議題之發展, 2010; 法務部, 死刑政策公聽會會議紀錄摘要, 2010; 法務部, 死刑政策公聽會討論議題之參考資料, 2010; 陳新民等，法務部委託研究計畫「廢除死刑暨替代方案之研究」期末報告.

138 法務部, 死刑政策公聽會會議紀錄摘要, 2010; 法務部, 死刑政策公聽會討論議題之參考資料, 2010; 陳新民等，法務部委託研究計畫「廢除死刑暨替代方案之研究」期末報告，pp. 56–66.

139 法務部, 死刑政策公聽會會議紀錄摘要, 2010.

140 Roger Hood, Research Survey on the Death Penalty in China, 2007–09: Introduction (Death Penalty Reform Project led by the Great Britain–China Centre and the College of Criminal Law Science of Beijing Normal University 2007–2009)4.

141 Dietrich Oberwittler and Qi Shenghui, Public Opinion on the Death Penalty in China: Results from a General Population Survey Conducted in Three Provinces in 2007–08 (Death Penalty Reform Project led by the Great Britain–China Centre and the College of Criminal Law Science of Beijing Normal University 2007–2009) 28.

142 Dietrich Oberwittler and Qi Shenghui, Public Opinion on the Death Penalty in China: Results from a General Population Survey Conducted in Three Provinces in 2007–08 (Death Penalty Reform Project led by the Great Britain–China Centre and the College of Criminal Law Science of Beijing Normal University 2007–2009) 22.

that capital punishment may not deter future crimes.[143] The study also revealed that a clear majority (64 per cent) agreed that the Chinese government should publish the number of yearly executions.[144] These findings are all indications that there is considerable space for education and enlightenment on the topic of capital punishment in China and that the public feels the need to be better informed.[145] Even legal professionals in China were found to be lacking in knowledge of international instruments and Chinese law concerning the safeguards against capital punishment.[146]

In order to build a national consensus on abolition, there exists a valuable resource that Chinese abolitionist movements can rely on, comprised of criminal law scholars, experts and jurists who have already reached a consensus on abolition. This community has already demonstrated its power to influence decision-makers toward the reduction in the use of capital punishment. They played a positive role in the contemplation and implementation of the eighth and ninth amendments to Criminal Law in 2011 and 2015, which repealed 13 and 9 capital crimes; the decision of the Supreme People's Court in 2007 to resume power to review capital cases, which triggered a major decline in executions;[147] and the criminal policy of 'justice tempered with mercy' and related guidelines since 2010, which encourages judicial discretion to limit death sentences[148] have proved to be a potential positive player in conceptualising a national opinion favouring abolition.

Recent decades have witnessed a range of innovative reforms undertaken in China. It is not uncommon for the Chinese administration to anticipate public opinion and to subsequently go against such popular sentiment. The best known case is the economic reform in 1978 through which China started to open to the West. This reform raised fundamental ideological questions between capitalism and socialism. Deng Xiaoping, 'the architect' of China's economic reforms, chose to engage in the debate and exert his personal impact. His famous cat theory – 'it doesn't matter if a cat is black or white, as long

143 Dietrich Oberwittler and Qi Shenghui, Public Opinion on the Death Penalty in China: Results from a General Population Survey Conducted in Three Provinces in 2007–08 (Death Penalty Reform Project led by the Great Britain–China Centre and the College of Criminal Law Science of Beijing Normal University 2007–2009) 22, 28 and 29.

144 Dietrich Oberwittler and Qi Shenghui, Public Opinion on the Death Penalty in China: Results from a General Population Survey Conducted in Three Provinces in 2007–08 (Death Penalty Reform Project led by the Great Britain–China Centre and the College of Criminal Law Science of Beijing Normal University 2007–2009) 17.

145 Roger Hood, Research Survey on the Death Penalty in China, 2007–09: Introduction (Death Penalty Reform Project led by the Great Britain–China Centre and the College of Criminal Law Science of Beijing Normal University 2007–2009) 3.

146 Roger Hood, Research Survey on the Death Penalty in China, 2007–09: Introduction (Death Penalty Reform Project led by the Great Britain–China Centre and the College of Criminal Law Science of Beijing Normal University 2007–2009) 2.

147 最高人民法院, 关于统一行使死刑案件核准权有关问题的决定, 1 January 2007.

148 最高人民法院, 《关于贯彻宽严相济刑事政策的若干意见》的通知, 2 August 2010; 最高人民法院、最高人民检察院、公安部、国家安全部和司法部, 《关于办理死刑案件审查判断证据若干问题的规定》和《关于办理刑事案件排除非法证据若干问题的规定》, 30 May 2010.

as it catches mice' – persuaded the Chinese to give more time for reform.[149] Subsequently, the Chinese began to endorse the reform when they saw positive results of it.

Historically, law was first publicised in China by Zi Chan around 500 BC.[150] Initially opposed by the public, this action gathered support three years after its introduction.[151] Shang Yang, who initiated a reform in 356 BC that paved the way for the first imperial dynasty of China, Qin (221 to 206 BC), lobbied the monarch Qin Xiao Gong prior to the reform that 'it will not be a wise choice to discuss with the public how and when to start a reform but it makes sense to share success with them. Success never comes if appealing to public opinion in every detail.'[152] Qin Xiao Gong agreed that 'wise people seldom accept emotional views in the name of tradition'.[153] Last but not least, Fei Yi, who aided Zhao Wu Ling Wang in changing the Han people's military culture to that of another ethnic group, the Hu, in 302 BC, commented before the reform that: '[g]reat success does not come through seeking agreements with the public in every detail [. . .] A fool is blinded by what already exists and the wise foresees results at an embryonic stage.'[154] The death penalty could well be a case in which the Chinese authority displays its political courage and commitment to human rights. To publicise yearly execution numbers and open a national debate in this regard could be the first step toward such a commitment.

Leading public opinion towards abolition

Does international law encourage States to lead public opinion toward the abolition of the death penalty? Discussion may be conducted in three dimensions: first, international law encourages States' educational measures to promote adherence to human rights. Given that the abolition of the death penalty is considered as a goal of international law and human rights, these educational measures may target the death penalty. Second, international law appeals for all necessary measures to achieve abolition, including measures which target public opinion. Third, in interpreting human rights obligations in treaties and customary norms, human rights regimes and international and regional intergovernmental organisations have been urging States that invoke public opinion in order to retain the death penalty to change their policies, particularly since the turn of the millennium. To a certain degree, States have accepted this suggestion and have taken action.

149 邓小平, *邓小平文选: 第一卷* (人民出版社 1993), p. 323.

150 Inspired by Zi Chan's action, Deng Xi composed a criminal code on bamboo in the state of Zheng in 501 BC. Zhao Yang and Xun Yin declared the Criminal Code of Jin on a special tripod in 501 BC. 张晋藩 (编), *中国法制通史：战国秦汉* (法律出版社 1999), p. 2.

151 左丘明, *左传: 襄公三十年*; 司马迁, *史记: 循吏列传*.

152 司马迁, *史记: 商君列传*.

153 司马迁, *史记: 商君列传*.

154 司马迁, *史记: 赵世家*.

To take educational measures to progress human rights

Connected to the development of the purpose and content of education, international law provides States with a duty to direct educational measures toward building a culture of human rights and moulding a friendly social attitude for human rights.[155] This duty is structured in order to uphold human rights, in particular the right to education, ethnic equality, economic, social and cultural rights, the rights of women, children, migrant workers and persons with disabilities, and the prohibition of torture and other cruel, inhuman or degrading treatment or punishment.[156] Should such a duty be extended to the death penalty issue when public opinion is cited as the justification or excuse for retention?

Under the UDHR

The Universal Declaration of Human Rights, adopted by the General Assembly of the United Nations on 10 December 1948, constitutes the cornerstone of contemporary human rights law.[157] It declares in its preamble that education is an important way to promote respect for human rights and freedoms. Concerning the right to education, the Universal Declaration defines the content and aim of education as including 'the strengthening of respect for human rights and fundamental freedoms'.[158] Bearing in mind the role of education envisaged in the Declaration, article 3 upholds the right to life without limitation or exception: '[e]veryone has the right to life, liberty and security of person.'[159]

In earlier documents, such as the working paper prepared by the Secretariat of the Sixth UN Congress on the Prevention of Crime and the Treatment of Offenders in 1980, article 3 was occasionally considered as taking a 'neutral' position on the death penalty.[160] More recent and prevailing opinions have

155 UN Doc. A/59/525/Rev.1, para. 3; UN Doc. HR/PUB/12/3, pp. 2, 12 and 13; UN Doc. A/HRC/15/28, para. 3; UN Doc. HR/PUB/12/3, p. 13: UN Doc. A/59/525/Rev.1, para. 4.

156 The Convention against Torture and Other Cruel, Inhuman or Degrading Treatment or Punishment, article 10; the International Convention on the Protection of the Rights of All Migrant Workers and Members of Their Families, article 33; the Convention on the Rights of Persons with Disabilities, articles 4 and 8; the Outcome Document of the Durban Review Conference, paras. 22 and 107; the 2005 World Summit Outcome, para. 131; the Universal Declaration of Human Rights, article 26; the International Covenant on Economic, Social and Cultural Rights, article 13; the Convention on the Rights of the Child, article 29; the Convention on the Elimination of All Forms of Discrimination against Women, article 10; the International Convention on the Elimination of All Forms of Racial Discrimination, article 7; the Vienna Declaration and Programme of Action, Part I, paras 33–34 and Part II, paras 78–82; the Declaration and Programme of Action of the World Conference against Racism, Racial Discrimination, Xenophobia and Related Intolerance, held in Durban, South Africa, in 2001, Declaration, paras 95–97 and Programme of Action, paras 129–139.

157 UNGA Res. 217 A (III), UN Doc. A/810.

158 The Universal Declaration of Human Rights, article 26.

159 The Universal Declaration of Human Rights, article 3.

160 William Schabas, *The Abolition of the Death Penalty in International Law* (3rd edn, Cambridge University Press 2002) 42–43; UN Doc. A/CONF.87/9, para. 5.

taken a different approach, with William Schabas construing article 3 as 'abolitionist in outlook' and '[b]y its silence on the matter of the death penalty, it envisages the abolition of capital punishment'.[161] This is the reason why 'article 3 has retained its pertinence during the evolution of more comprehensive abolitionist norms over subsequent decades.'[162] To fully achieve the right to life without limitation or exception, States' actions to raise awareness, clarify myths of the death penalty and propagate scientific findings and human rights norms can find support in article 26 of the Universal Declaration which directs education 'to the strengthening of respect for human rights and fundamental freedoms'.

To progress the right to life

The Universal Declaration of Human Rights was developed into four international treaties, the International Covenant on Civil and Political Rights, the International Covenant on Economic, Social and Cultural Rights, the Optional Protocol to the International Covenant on Civil and Political Rights adopted by the United Nations General Assembly on 16 December 1966[163] and the Second Optional Protocol to the International Covenant on Civil and Political Rights Aiming at the Abolition of the Death Penalty, adopted by the United Nations General Assembly in December 1989. The four instruments comprise the 'International Bill of Human Rights'.

Under this human rights system, the death penalty is specifically addressed in article 6 of the International Covenant on Civil and Political Rights; with regard to the right to life, the issue of abolition is upheld in the Second Optional Protocol aimed at abolition, while the International Covenant on Economic, Social and Cultural Rights confirms the promotion of respect for human rights through education. Realising that the two Covenants cannot be treated separately and human rights issues should be viewed from different angles, the aim and content of education as envisaged in the International Covenant on Economic, Social and Cultural Rights may shed light on the issue of capital punishment and public opinion.

The International Covenant on Civil and Political Rights strongly encourages abolition, declaring in paragraph 6 of article 6 that '[n]othing in this article shall be invoked to delay or to prevent the abolition of capital punishment by any State Party to the present Covenant.' This encouragement was reaffirmed by CCPR general comment No. 6 composed by the Human Rights Committee in 1982, and comments made by members of the Human Rights Committee when Barbados and Mali presented their periodic reports in conformity with the

161 William Schabas, *The Abolition of the Death Penalty in International Law* (3rd edn, Cambridge University Press 2002) 42–43.

162 William Schabas, *The Abolition of the Death Penalty in International Law* (3rd edn, Cambridge University Press 2002) 42–43.

163 UNGA Res. 2200A (XXI).

Covenant in 1981.[164] Designated as the supervisory body of the International Covenant on Civil and Political Rights, the general comments of the Human Rights Committee serve as official or authentic commentaries on the provisions of the Covenant.[165]

In general comment No. 6, the Human Rights Committee further stated that 'all measures of abolition should be considered as progress in the enjoyment of the right to life', although reports from States indicate that 'progress made towards abolishing or limiting the application of the death penalty is quite inadequate'.[166] When making concluding observations to Grenada in the absence of an initial report in 2009, the Human Rights Committee made it clear that 'all measures taken towards abolition of the death penalty are considered to be progress in the enjoyment of the right to life'.[167] The Second Optional Protocol expressed the same conviction in its preamble that 'all measures of abolition of the death penalty should be considered as progress in the enjoyment of the right to life'. The International Covenant on the Civil and Political Rights and its Second Protocol both require States to report their progress in the right to life to the Human Rights Committee.[168]

Based on the above analysis, abolition may be considered as a goal of human rights and measures taken toward this action progress the fundamental right to life. States' actions to lead public opinion can, first, find support from the right to education provision that directs the aim and content of education toward the promotion of respect for human rights, as outlined in article 13 of the International Covenant on Economic, Social and Cultural Rights. Second, although education is not directly dealt with in the International Covenant on Civil and Political Rights, the Human Rights Committee requires States Parties to promote human rights awareness among the general public and report back to the Committee, through guidelines that the Committee issued during the reporting procedure of the Covenant.[169]

Specifically, States need to submit in their periodical report information on the:

(e) Promotion of human rights awareness through educational programmes and Government-sponsored public information. Any measures taken to promote respect for human rights through education and training, including Government-sponsored public information campaigns . . .

164 UN Doc. CCPR/C/SR.264, para. 22; UN Doc. CCPR/C/SR.284, para. 20; CCPR general comment No. 6: Article 6 (Right to Life), Human Rights Committee, para. 6.

165 William Schabas, *The Abolition of the Death Penalty in International Law* (3rd edn, Cambridge University Press 2002) 94; purposes of these general comments can be found in: UN Doc. HRI/GEN/1/Rev.9 (Vol. I), pp. 172–173; UN Doc. A/36/40, Annex VII.

166 CCPR general comment no. 6: Article 6 (Right to Life), Human Rights Committee, para. 6.

167 UN Doc. CCPR/C/GRD/CO/114.

168 The International Covenant on Civil and Political Rights, article 40, para. 1; the Second optional Protocol to the International Covenant on Civil and Political Rights Aiming at the Abolition of the Death Penalty, article 3.

169 UN Doc. HRI/GEN/2/Rev.6, p. 12.

(f) Promotion of human rights awareness through the mass media. The role of the mass information media, such as the press, radio, television and internet, in publicizing and disseminating information about human rights, including the international human rights instruments.[170]

In the practice of the reporting procedure under the Covenant, Russia has been challenged on its governmental measures regarding educational curricula and the media to lay the groundwork for the change of abolition, contained in the sixth periodic review of the Human Rights Committee in 2009.[171]

To prohibit inhuman and degrading treatment or punishment

The death penalty has been declared by the European Court of Human Rights as a cruel, inhuman and degrading punishment.[172] The death row phenomenon, which refers to a combination of circumstances to which condemned persons are exposed, including inevitable ill-treatment due to special conditions on death row,[173] disproportionately long waiting periods prior to execution and methods of execution inflicting gratuitous suffering, has been held by the European Court of Human Rights and a number of other prominent constitutional courts as having violated fundamental human rights.[174]

In 2012 the Special Rapporteur on Torture and Other Cruel, Inhuman or Degrading Treatment or Punishment of the United Nations Human Rights Council not only confirmed the evolving standard of framing the debate about the death penalty within the context of the prohibition of torture and cruel, inhuman and degrading treatment or punishment, but also pointed out that this constitutes a new approach in examining the legality of the death penalty.[175] To date, the death penalty has been treated under provisions concerning the right to life and therein as an exception provided for by major human rights instruments, namely the International Covenant on Civil and Political Rights. However, the prohibition of torture and cruel, inhuman and degrading treatment or punishment does not permit any derogation under any circumstances. Under this approach, the pursuit of abolition is underdeveloped.

The Human Rights Committee, which monitors the implementation of the International Covenant on Civil and Political Rights, has not fully agreed with this approach. It does not support the assertion that the death row phenomenon

170 UN Doc. HRI/GEN/2/Rev.6, p. 12.
171 UN Doc. CCPR/C/SR.2664, para. 27.
172 *Öcalan v. Turkey* (App No. 46221/99, ECtHR, 12 March 2003).
173 *Francis v. Jamaica* (No. 320/1988), para. 12.4.
174 *Soering v. United Kingdom and Germany*, *Catholic Commission for Justice and Peace in Zimbabwe v. Attorney-General et al.*; *Pratt et al. v. Attorney General for Jamaica et al.*; *Andrews v. United States* (Case No. 11.139), Report No. 57/96, 6 December 1996; *United States v. Burns* [2001] 1 SCR 283.
175 UN Doc. A/67/279, para. 74.

per se constitutes cruel, inhuman or degrading treatment,[176] unless there exists 'some further compelling circumstances'[177] for example detention under harsh conditions that was protracted,[178] detention accompanied by serious medical consequences,[179] a lack of psychiatric treatment[180] or evidence of beatings and the destruction of belongings by jailers.[181] The Human Rights Committee assumed this approach because article 6 of the Covenant does not prohibit the death penalty and the Committee would hope that persons on death row be kept as long as possible.

In State practice, the Democratic Republic of the Congo answered questions in relation to the abolition of the death penalty under the Convention against Torture and Other Cruel, Inhuman or Degrading Treatment or Punishment, and welcomed suggestions on ways to influence public opinion, during the presentation of its initial report for the Committee against Torture in 2005.[182] The Convention itself does not address the topic of changing opinions of the public, as torture was directly caused by law enforcement officers and the prevention of torture requires a change of their mentality. Paragraph 1 of article 10 of the Convention provides a duty for the State to raise awareness and influence opinions among legal professionals through education, training and information. The Committee against Torture, through its general comment No. 2, encourages States to inform the public of the special gravity of this crime through the naming and definition of the crime of torture. Although it added conditions to recognise the death penalty as cruel, inhuman and degrading treatment, the Human Rights Committee suggests that all States Parties disseminate relevant information concerning the ban on cruel, inhuman and degrading treatment to the population at large and provide instruction and training to professionals involved in the custody or treatment of individuals subjected to any form of arrest, detention or imprisonment.[183]

176 *Pratt and Morgan v. Jamaica* (No. 210/1986 and 225/1987), para. 13.6; *Barrett and Sutcliffe v. Jamaica* (No. 271/1988), para. 8.4; *Kindler v. Canada* (No. 470/1991), para. 15.2.

177 *Simms v. Jamaica*, para. 6.5; *Berry v. Jamaica*, para. 11.8.

178 *Edwards v. Jamaica*, para. 8.3.

179 *Henry and Douglas v. Jamaica*, para. 9.5; *Brown v. Jamaica*, para. 6.13; *Whyte v. Jamaica*, para. 9.4; UN Doc.53/40, para. 458.

180 *Williams v. Jamaica*, para. 6.5.

181 *Collins v. Jamaica* (No. 240/1987), paras 8.6–8.7; *Francis v. Jamaica* (No. 320/1988), para. 12.4; *Bailey v. Jamaica* (No. 334/1988), para. 9.3; *Hylton v. Jamaica* (No. 407/1990), para. 9.3; *Raphael Thomas v. Jamaica* (No. 321/1988), UN Doc. A/49/40, Vol. II, p. 1, para. 9.2; *Sterling v. Jamaica*, paras 2.2–2.3, 3.2 and 8.2; *Spence v. Jamaica*, paras 3.2 and 7.2; *Reynolds v. Jamaica* (No. 587/1994), paras 10.2–10.4; *Walker and Richards v. Jamaica*, para. 8.1; *Young v. Jamaica*, para. 5.2; *McTaggart v. Jamaica*, para. 8.7; *Chung v. Jamaica*, para. 8.2; *Jones v. Jamaica*, para. 9.4; *Deidrick v. Jamaica*, para. 9.3; *Everton Morrison v. Jamaica*, para. 23.3; *Leslie v. Jamaica*, para. 9.2; *Whyte v. Jamaica*, para. 9.4; *Nicholas Henry v. Jamaica*, para. 7.3; *Colin Johnson v. Jamaica*, para. 8.1; *Floyd Howell v. Jamaica* (No. 798/1998), para. 6.2.

182 UN Doc. CAT/C/SR.687, para. 23.

183 CCPR general comment No. 20, para. 10.

To take all necessary measures to abolish the death penalty

Paragraph 2, article 2 of the International Covenant on Civil and Political Rights requires States to 'take the necessary steps' to bring into effect the rights recognised in the Covenant. The term 'take all necessary measures' allows for gradual realisation. Among the rights system, the right to life enjoys a pre-eminent position, variously described as 'the supreme right',[184] 'one of the most important rights',[185] 'the most fundamental of all rights',[186] 'the primordial right',[187] 'the foundation and fundamental of all rights'[188] and a right 'basic to all human rights'.[189] The content of the right to life is gradually incorporating the requirement of abolishing the death penalty, with the Human Rights Committee recognising the death penalty as an infringement of the prohibition of cruel, inhuman or degrading treatment, under 'some further compelling circumstances'.[190]

During the drafting of the International Covenant on Civil and Political Rights, there was a debate over whether it is appropriate and permissible to allow States to adjust their legislation after ratifying or acceding to an international convention, as opposed to implementing change before or at least by the time of the instrument's accession.[191] One side, supported by judgments and opinions of the Permanent Court of International Justice, argued that the adaptation of municipal law is not a premise for a State to be bound by an international covenant; they added that adaption after the ratification of or accession to a covenant is frequently how States practically assume responsibility, unless the treaty requires otherwise.[192] The opposing opinion questioned how much elasticity should be granted to States in the implementation of the Covenant. After discussion, paragraph 2, article 2 of the Covenant permits for its gradual realisation but does not allow excessive delay in implementation, as the phrase 'within a reasonable time' was deleted.[193]

184 Human Rights Committee general comment No. 6, UN Doc. HRI/GEN/1/Rev.9 (Vol. I), p. 176; UN Doc. A/37/40, p. 93; *de Guerrero v. Colombia* (Communication No. R. 11/45, 31 March 1982), para. 13.1; UN Doc. A/37/40, p. 137.

185 *Stewart v. United Kingdom* (App. No. 10044/82, ECtHR, 10 July 1984), p. 169.

186 Theo C. Van Boven, 'The Need to Stop Deliberate Violations of the Right to Life' in Daniel Prémont (ed.), *Essais sur le concept de 'droit de vivre' en mémoire de Yougindra Khushalani* (Bruylant 1988) 285.

187 Bertrand G. Ramcharan, 'The Concept and Dimensions of the Right to Life' in Bertrand G. Ramcharan (ed.), *The Right to Life in International Law* (Martinus Nijhoff 1985) 12.

188 Annual Report of the Inter-American Commission on Human Rights (1986–1987), OAS Doc. OEA/Ser.L/V/II.71, doc. 9 re. 1, p. 271.

189 General comment No. 14 (23), UN Doc. A/40/40, Annex XX; UN Doc. CCPR/C/SR.563, para. 1.

190 *Simms v. Jamaica*, para. 6.5; *Berry v. Jamaica*, para. 11.8.

191 UN Doc. E/CN.4/116, p. 2; UN Doc. E/CN.4/374.

192 The Advisory Opinion in the 'Case Relative to the Exchange of Greek and Turkish Populations', PCLJ, Series B, No. 10, p. 20; Advisory opinion on 'Jurisdiction of the Courts of Danzig', PCLJ, Series B, No. 15, pp. 4–47; Judgment in case concerning German interests in Upper Silesia, PCLJ, Series A, No. 7, p. 81; UN Doc. E/CN.4/116, para. 2.

193 UN Doc. E/1371, p. 28; UN Doc. A/2929, Chapter V, paras 8, 9 and 165.

The content of the right to life and the prohibition of cruel, inhuman or degrading treatment remains under development. '[A]ll necessary measures' to give effect to these rights and freedoms would accommodate State actions in building a favourable atmosphere toward their enjoyment, especially for those States that have held public opinion responsible for the maintenance of the death penalty. In developing the International Covenant on Civil and Political Rights, its Second Optional Protocol reaffirms the same notion that States shall 'take all necessary measures to abolish the death penalty'.[194]

Through the reporting procedure established by the Covenant, the Human Rights Committee has recommended to States such as Japan that invoke public opinion to retain the death penalty to take measures towards abolition.[195] During the process of the Universal Periodic Review, more States championing the death penalty argument were similarly recommended to pursue abolition, including Algeria, Barbados, Botswana, Burkina Faso, Cameroon, Cuba, Russia, South Korea, Tonga, Tunisia and Zambia.[196] Among these nations, Cuba accepted this recommendation in 2013.[197] In its 2012 review, Tunisia claimed that it constantly called for all stakeholders to engage in an open, frank and constructive debate on the subject.[198] If public opinion is the reason to impede abolition, measures that allow for open debate and the publication of relevant information may be included among the 'necessary measures'.

To lead public opinion on the death penalty

In 1980 the Sixth United Nations Congress on the Prevention of Crime and Treatment of Offenders identified the important role of governments in educating the public on the uncertainty of the deterrent effect of capital punishment, through a working paper prepared by its Secretariat.[199] This was the first time in the present research that international bodies recommended States to actively address public opinion with regard to the death penalty. More exciting developments arrived in the new millennium, with international bodies and States increasingly encouraging those who still invoke public opinion either to attempt to change that opinion or to raise awareness and open a debate around the issue.

194 The Second Optional Protocol to the International Covenant on Civil and Political Rights Aiming at the Abolition of the Death Penalty, article 1.

195 UN Doc. CCPR/C/79/Add.28, para. 18; UN Doc. CCPR/C/79/Add.102, para. 20.

196 UN Doc. A/HRC/23/11, para. 102, recommendation 64; UN Doc. A/HRC/24/4, para. 137, recommendations 13 and 15; UN Doc. A/HRC/24/14, para. 140, recommendation 100; UN Doc. A/HRC/24/15, para. 131, recommendation 92; UN Doc. A/HRC/24/16, para. 170, recommendation 134; UN Doc. A/HRC/22/10, para. 124, recommendation 35; UN Doc. A/HRC/22/13, para. 103, recommendation 38; UN Doc. A/HRC/21/5, para. 116, para. 8; UN Doc. A/HRC/21/13, para. 129, recommendation 90; UN Doc. A/HRC/23/4, para. 81, recommendations 15; UN Doc. A/HRC/23/7, para. 117, recommendation 4.

197 UN Doc. A/HRC/24/16/Add.1.

198 UN Doc. A/HRC/21/5/Add.1, para. 3.

199 UN Doc. A/CONF.87/9, para. 68.

Under the ICCPR

When Russia presented its sixth periodic report in the Human Rights Committee under the International Covenant on the Civil and Political Rights in 2010, Abdelfattah Amor of the Human Rights Committee suggested that 'it would not be undemocratic for a State to lead an attempt to change public opinion, rather than follow it.'[200] He further stated that '[t]he role of the State was vital because it was able to transform society and mentalities through legislation.'[201] Mongolian civil society representatives submitted a report to the Human Rights Committee, enquiring about the measures taken by the government to 'prevent negative reaction from the public' and 'raise awareness with regard to abolishing the death penalty', when Mongolia presented its fifth periodic report under the Covenant in 2010.[202]

A number of States have reported their actions regarding public opinion of the death penalty, which were limited to the mere identification of public views. These States include Botswana, Japan and South Korea, identified in Botswana's initial report under the International Covenant on the Civil and Political Rights in 2007,[203] Japan's fourth and fifth reports in 1997 and 2007 respectively[204] and South Korea's third report in 2005.[205] Taking a step forward, Kenya indicated during its third periodic report under the Covenant in 2010 that it had been 'educating the public on the need to abolish [the death penalty] in conformity with the international standards and trends'.[206] Mongolia expressed a willingness to 'introduce a culture of supporting abolition', which would 'require the President to play an essential role', during its fifth periodic review in 2011.[207] Zambia started the process of identifying public opinion in 1998 and saw it as the first step to encourage debate and achieve a national consensus on the issue.[208]

Through its concluding observations made to States' periodic reports, the Human Rights Committee made it clear that it disagreed with the public opinion argument in the death penalty issue. It raised its concern when the Central African Republic expressed the view that the death penalty cannot be abolished due to public opposition in 2006.[209] It recommended Japan to inform the public, regardless of opinion polls, about the desirability of abolition in 2008.[210] It suggested

200 UN Doc. CCPR/C/SR.2664, para. 27.
201 UN Doc. CCPR/C/SR.2664, para. 27.
202 Civil Society Report on the Implementation of the ICCPR (Replies to the List of Issues CCPR/C/MNG/Q/5), p. 8.
203 UN Doc. CCPR/C/BWA/1, para. 143.
204 UN Doc. CCPR/C/115/Add.3, para. 62; UN Doc. CCPR/C/JPN/5, para. 130.
205 UN Doc. CCPR/C/KOR/2005/3, para. 112.
206 UN Doc. CCPR/C/KEN/3, para. 38.
207 UN Doc. HR/CT/732.
208 UN Doc. CCPR/C/ZMB/3, para. 151.
209 UN Doc. CCPR/C/CAF/CO/2, para. 13.
210 UN Doc. CCPR/C/JPN/CO/5, para. 15.

to Kenya to intensify awareness campaigns with a view to changing the mindset of the public regarding the retention of the death penalty in 2012.[211] Regarding the existing public discussion on the death penalty in Zambia, the Human Rights Committee pointed out in 2007 that the debate had not been based on fully informed documentation.[212] The Committee recommended the government make sure that all aspects of the matter were presented accurately, especially concerning the importance of achieving progress for the enjoyment of the right to life and the desirability of eventual ratification of the Second Optional Protocol to the ICCPR.[213] The same recommendation was issued to Botswana in 2008.[214]

Under the UPR

The Universal Periodic Review was initiated by the United Nations General Assembly in 2006.[215] It examines treaty obligations from the Charter of the United Nations and human rights instruments to which a State is party, customary norms in the Universal Declaration of Human Rights, and voluntary pledges and commitments made by States.[216] The Universal Periodic Review has persuasively and effectively reflected recent updates on the death penalty. States in the process have exchanged their understanding and actions with regard to capital punishment and public opinion and have subsequently responded to the recommendation of addressing the issue of public opinion on the topic of capital punishment.

During the process of the Universal Periodic Review, a number of States have reported that they have been educating the public and encouraging a national debate on the abolition of the death penalty. In Africa, Burkina Faso cited in its national report under the Universal Periodic Review in 2013 that public opposition to the abolition of the death penalty and the public's unfamiliarity with human rights instruments was a constraining obstacle that hinders adherence to human rights.[217] Nevertheless, it had held consultations to prepare public opinion to accept abolition.[218] During its interactive dialogue in the Human Rights Council, Burkina Faso was further questioned about its measures to change the population's reaction to the abolition of the death penalty.[219] It was recommended to better prepare national opinion for the abolition of the death penalty through further consultations.[220] By July 2014 Burkina Faso had not yet responded to that recommendation.[221]

211 UN Doc. CCPR/C/KEN/CO/3, para. 10.
212 UN Doc. CCPR/C/ZMB/CO/3, para. 17.
213 UN Doc. CCPR/C/ZMB/CO/3, para. 17.
214 UN Doc. CCPR/C/BWA/CO/1, para 13.
215 UN Doc. A/RES/60/251.
216 UN Doc. A/HRC/RES/5/1, Annex, I, A, 1.
217 UN Doc. A/HRC/WG.6/16/BFA/1, para. 87.
218 UN Doc. A/HRC/WG.6/16/BFA/1, para. 55.
219 UN Doc. A/HRC/24/4, para. 61.
220 UN Doc. A/HRC/24/4, para. 137, recommendation 10.
221 UN Doc. A/HRC/24/4, para. 137, recommendation 10.

Kenya indicated during its 2010 Universal Periodic Review that it was working with its National Commission on Human Rights to create public support for abolition.[222] Mali said in the Human Rights Committee in 2013 that it had been educating its population about the abolition of the death penalty.[223] Botswana was recommended to educate the general public regarding the abolition of the death penalty in 2009.[224] Botswana subsequently committed to undertaking educational awareness campaigns regarding the death penalty before considering its abolition.[225] During its second evaluation in 2013, Botswana accepted the suggestion of opening and promoting public debate on the death penalty.[226]

Madagascar indicated in the Human Rights Council in 2010 that it intended to conduct awareness-raising campaigns and to organise a debate on the death penalty involving both the authorities and civil society before the presentation of a new bill.[227] Tunisia 'repeatedly called on all stakeholders to engage in an open, frank and constructive debate on the subject'.[228] It revealed willingness to consult and interact with all stakeholders in order to achieve consensus in 2012.[229] Morocco agreed to continue the debate on the death penalty in 2012.[230] Algeria confirmed that a public debate existed on the topic of the death penalty in 2012.[231] Zimbabwe took a different approach on the capital punishment and public opinion issue, declining the suggestion of pursuing the current debate on abolition in a transparent manner in 2011.[232]

In Asia, the government of Lebanon conducted an awareness campaign, targeted on public opinion toward the death penalty, according to its national report to the Human Rights Council in 2010.[233] Malaysia, in its national report of 2013, pledged to continue the engagement and consultation with the public on this matter, including the search for possible alternatives to the death penalty.[234] Thailand attached importance to a national consultation process on the death penalty in its national report in 2011.[235] During the interactive dialogues of the Universal Periodic Review, South Korea was questioned about its specific measures intended to advance the debate at the societal level of public opinion in 2008.[236] Norway welcomed public debate on capital punishment in India, stated

222 UN Doc. A/HRC/15/8, paras 49 and 104.
223 UN Doc. A/HRC/23/6, para. 15.
224 UN Doc. A/HRC/10/69, para. 63.
225 UN Doc. A/HRC/23/7/Add.1, para. 5.
226 UN Doc. A/HRC/23/7, para. 115, recommendation 59.
227 UN Doc. A/HRC/14/13, para. 34; A/HRC/14/13/Add.1, para. 20.
228 UN Doc. A/HRC/21/5/Add.1, para. 3.
229 UN Doc. A/HRC/21/5, paras 39 and 110.
230 UN Doc. A/HRC/21/3, para. 129, recommendation 59.
231 UN Doc. A/HRC/WG.6/13/DZA/1, para. 45.
232 UN Doc. A/HRC/19/14, para. 95, recommendation 25.
233 UN Doc. A/HRC/WG.6/9/LBN/1, para. 31.
234 UN Doc. A/HRC/WG.6/17/MYS/1, para. 46.
235 UN Doc. A/HRC/WG.6/12/THA/1, para. 33.
236 UN Doc. A/HRC/8/40, para. 38.

in the Human Rights Council in 2012.[237] Japan utilised the public opinion argument not just to oppose the abolition of the death penalty, but also to use any plan to establish a forum to discuss the death penalty system.[238] It rejected the suggestion of encouraging a deep nationwide dialogue on the death penalty, in the Human Rights Council in 2012.[239]

As the only State in Europe that imposes the death penalty, Belarus reported to the Human Rights Council that it initiated mass media and awareness-raising campaigns to influence public opinion, during the interactive dialogue of the Universal Periodic Review in 2010.[240] Belarus said that its State media regularly publicised information on the topic.[241] Among Caribbean nations, Antigua and Barbuda expressed its willingness to educate the public on the abolition of the death penalty, as revealed in its dialogue with the Universal Periodic Review in 2011.[242] In 2011 Saint Lucia also planned to discuss this matter with its population through a constitutional review.[243] Finally, in 2013 Barbados accepted the suggestion of opening and promoting public debate on the death penalty, made during the interactive dialogue of the Universal Periodic Review in the Human Rights Council.[244]

Under OSCE and the Council of Europe

European intergovernmental organisations urge their non-abolitionist participating States and observer States to educate the public and raise awareness regarding the death penalty issue. The Organization for Security and Cooperation in Europe (OSCE) appealed to its non-abolitionist participating States to launch public discussions with a view to promoting the abolition of the death penalty at its Supplementary Human Dimension Meeting on Human Rights and Inhuman Treatment in Vienna in March 2000.[245] The Organization for Security and Cooperation in Europe further recommended actions for States to take in order to lead public opinion on the death penalty:

- They should raise awareness of the fact that it is not proved that capital punishment deters crime.
- They should make efforts to educate the public about the issues surrounding the death penalty and the need for its abolition, e.g. by encouraging

237 UN Doc. A/HRC/21/10, para. 118.
238 UN Doc. A/HRC/22/14/Add.1, pp. 7 and 9.
239 UN Doc. A/HRC/22/14, paras 87, 92 and 147, recommendations 93 and 113; UN Doc. A/HRC/22/14/Add.1, pp. 7 and 9.
240 UN Doc. A/HRC/15/16, para. 54.
241 UN Doc. A/HRC/15/16/Add.1, para. 48.
242 UN Doc. A/HRC/19/5, para. 34.
243 UN Doc. A/HRC/17/6, para. 66.
244 UN Doc. A/HRC/23/11, para. 102, recommendation 70; UN Doc. A/HRC/23/11/Add.1, p. 3.
245 OSCE Supplementary Human Dimension Meeting on Human Rights and Inhuman Treatment or Punishment, March 2000, pp. 13–14.

respected public figures to make statements against the death penalty as a means of providing moral leadership.

- They should try to determine whether and under what circumstances the public would accept abolition, even where most people believe in the necessity of the death penalty.
- They should make efforts to determine how well public opinion is based on an understanding of criminal justice policy and international human rights standards.[246]

In 2009 the OSCE Parliamentary Assembly called on the retentionist participating States to encourage the organisation branches, in cooperation with the Council of Europe, 'to conduct awareness-raising activities against recourse to the death penalty, particularly with the media, law enforcement officials, policy-makers and the general public'.[247]

The Director-General of Human Rights of the Council of Europe concluded at the 56th session of the UN Commission on Human Rights in 2000 that, in the European experience, the abolition of the death penalty 'often required measures designed to make public opinion aware of it'.[248] The Parliamentary Assembly of the Council of Europe recognised in 2001 that public opinion in Japan and the United States, which are two observer States of the Council of Europe that continue to carry out executions, was an impediment to the abolition of the death penalty, but such an obstacle 'can and must be overcome'.[249] In the same year, the Committee on Legal Affairs and Human Rights and the Parliamentary Assembly of the Council of Europe authorised fact-finding missions to the United States and Japan, in the hope of finding ways to influence the attitude of the authorities and public opinion.[250] The report of this mission reaffirmed that 'it is necessary to lead, not follow public opinion'.[251] Renate Wohlwend, Rapporteur of the fact-finding missions and later chief of the Council of Europe delegation to Japan, suggested in 2003 that Japan propose an abolition bill – even if such a bill were rejected, it would help boost public opinion against the death penalty.[252] The suggestion enjoyed the support of Japan.[253]

246 OSCE Supplementary Human Dimension Meeting on Human Rights and Inhuman Treatment or Punishment, March 2000, pp. 13–14.
247 HDIM. OSCE. PA/0164/09, OSCE Parliamentary Assembly: Resolution on a Moratorium on the Death Penalty and Towards its Abolition, para. 44; the OSCE's Office for Democratic Institutions and Human Rights: The Death Penalty in the OSCE Area: Background Paper 2010, Annex I, p. 19.
248 UN Doc. E/CN.4/2000/SR.19, para. 7.
249 Parliamentary Assembly of the Council of Europe Resolution 1253 (2001), Abolition of the Death Penalty in Council of Europe Observer States.
250 Council of Europe Doc. 9115, IV, A, para. 5.
251 Council of Europe Doc. 9115, para. 23.
252 K. Kikuta, *Q&A: Shikei Mondai no Kiso Chishiki* (Akashi Shoten 2004) 87 and 88.
253 K. Kikuta, *Q&A: Shikei Mondai no Kiso Chishiki* (Akashi Shoten 2004) 87 and 88.

Conclusions

Many States invoke public opinion in order to retain the death penalty, but the legitimacy of this argument is disputed. An example of this exists in the unreliability of the methods used to measure public opinion, usually in the form of polls. Such polls may not reflect a population's accurate or comprehensive attitude toward capital punishment. This is reflected in a number of cases in which the death penalty was abolished despite enjoying popular support in the form of public opinion polls. Among four Chinese societies, China, Hong Kong, Macao and Taiwan, death penalty policies are vastly different despite their similar cultures and public opinion according to polls, further proof of the marginal relevance of public opinion in the death penalty issue. From a different perspective, the Marshall Hypothesis suggested that public opinion will turn against capital punishment when the population is fully informed on the issue, finding support from empirical research across nations. Concurring with the Marshall Hypothesis, the United Nations Seventh Survey on the death penalty received a submission from the Japan Federation of Bar Associations, which stated that '[o]ne of the main reasons' why capital punishment has not been abolished in Japan 'is the extraordinary secrecy about the death penalty system and the consequent lack of proper information to discuss the matter of abolition'.[254]

According to human rights norms, States have a duty to promote respect for human rights. This duty can be extended to the death penalty issue, since measures toward abolition are recognised as progress toward the enjoyment of the right to life and, concurrently, the death penalty has been increasingly deemed as a violation of the right to life and the prohibition of inhuman and degrading punishment. Educational actions such as informing the public and initiating and encouraging public debate on the issue can be construed as part of the 'necessary' measures needed to achieve the abolition of the death penalty. In practice, and particularly since 2000, States have frequently received recommendations from human rights treaty bodies, intergovernmental organisations and other States to shift public opinion with regard to the death penalty. Optimistically, there has been considerable State compliance with these recommendations.

254 Roger Hood and Carolyn Hoyle, *The Death Penalty: A Worldwide Perspective* (Oxford University Press 2008) 94.

6 Conclusions

Public opinion is a complex issue and how to divine conclusive public opinion requires dedicated studies. States easily invoke public opinion to hold back or delay the realisation of human rights, but it is highly questionable whether their public is truly against actions intended to protect and promote human rights, a conclusion based on a series of political and sociological studies. This book approaches this issue from the perspective of human rights law, arguing that States cannot blindly rely on public opinion to decide issues concerning fundamental human rights and freedoms. Instead, States should have an independent voice on these issues and lead public opinion to embrace core human rights standards.

Analysis of the study starts from the issue of racial discrimination, which fundamentally violates basic human rights. International law has long been aware of the importance of enlightening public opinion on ethnic equality. It established the principle of combating racial discrimination and guiding public opinion in the 1940s. Soon international law developed two main approaches to the issue of racial discrimination, which both have an effect of informing and educating public opinion. They are legal and educational measures: legal measures warn the public away from racism and racial discrimination; educational measures sway them by teaching, education, culture and information. As long as States' measures fully respect other fundamental rights and freedoms such as freedom of expression and association, international law encourages States to punish racial expressions, racist organisations and propaganda activities and combat racial prejudice and promote human rights values and principles through teaching, education, culture and information.

This book finds that public opinion is not immutable when it comes to ethnic equality. States are expected to play an active role. Concerning issues that manifest themselves through racial discrimination, this work also finds that similar principles apply, for instance in the rights of migrants, indigenous and tribal peoples, equality in education and the matters of political and religious rights. In practice, substantial numbers of States have carried out legal and educational measures that have had varied impacts on public opinion. Yet there are States that retain reservations. Sometimes they hold no objection but treat their duties with neglect, particularly on the promotion of ethnic equality through teaching, education, culture and information.

States are also expected to educate public opinion with regard to discrimination against women. United Nations recommendations and the Declaration on the Elimination of Discrimination against Women made it clear that '[a]ll appropriate measures shall be taken to educate public opinion' (article 3). When they drafted the Convention on the Elimination of All Forms of Discrimination against Women, States did not reach a consensus about the wording of 'educating public opinion'. But they were certain about what aspects of public opinion are not tolerated and what segments in public opinion should be encouraged. States agreed on eliminating prejudices and the idea of the inferiority or the superiority of either of the sexes and stereotyped roles for men and women. They also consented to the promotion, under States' auspices, of a proper understanding of maternity as a social function and the recognition of the common responsibility of men and women in the upbringing and development of their children.

In implementing the Convention on the Elimination of All Forms of Discrimination against Women, the Committee on the Elimination of Discrimination against Women further interpreted these principles. The Committee urged States to fight against patriarchal attitudes in society, lead public opinion against violence and other practices against women and promote the principle of gender equality and a positive image of women, regardless of the popularity of such views. Interestingly, the Human Rights Committee and the Committee on the Rights of the Child developed similar principles, while the International Covenant on Civil and Political Rights does not refer to public opinion at all and the Convention on the Rights of the Child merely mentions aims of education as developing respect for human rights and fundamental freedoms and values (article 29). States reveal considerable compliance with the request of mobilising public opinion in order to target discrimination against women. In the Universal Periodic Review, this principle was often obeyed without invoking a human rights treaty provision. This may imply that such a duty has some roots in customary law.

Based on the analysis of public opinion and racial discrimination and discrimination against women, the present study continues to ask whether States have a general duty to influence public opinion with regard to core human rights standards. The bases of the arguments are that education, as directed by international law, embodies an aim and content of moulding public attitudes in favour of human rights. This statement exists in the Constitution of UNESCO and the right to education clause of the Universal Declaration of Human Rights. But it has not received much attention. Later human rights instruments interpret the aim and content of education as to raise awareness of human rights principles, international humanitarian law and human rights violations, and to change attitudes toward discrimination, cultural diversity and a sense of belonging and a willingness to take positive actions. Human rights education, a recently developed concept designed to mobilise public opinion with regard to human rights, is recognised as an inherent part of the right to education. It is also increasingly regarded as an independent human right *per se*.

From another perspective, international law provides that to protect and promote a wide range of basic human rights, States ought to take educational measures. These include the prohibition of torture, slavery, violence, abuse and exploitation and the protection of children's rights, the rights of persons with disabilities, cultural rights, equality in employment and occupation as well as human rights in general through teaching, education and publication. Notably, recipients of States' educational measures, as designated by the preamble to the Universal Declaration of Human Rights, include not just their citizens but also those of territories under their jurisdiction. At the national level, many jurisdictions have established national human rights institutions with a mandate to directly inform public opinion or to recommend their governments to do so. A large number of States have taken educational measures and awareness-raising programmes to influence public opinion on human rights. These can be seen as their rhetoric and actual willingness to carry out their educational duties.

Last, but certainly not least, the present work tests the boundaries of States' duty to inform and educate public opinion by reflecting whether similar principles apply or will inevitably apply to the death penalty issue. The reason for choosing the death penalty case is that many States name public opinion as the justification or explanation to maintain the death penalty, noting the fact that public opinion is rarely cited to defend the existence of racial and gender discrimination. Currently the abolition of the death penalty is gradually moving toward a core human rights standard, as part of the requirement of the right to life and the prohibition of inhuman and degrading treatment. In this context, this book challenges the public opinion argument and questions whether the death penalty issue will follow the pattern of protecting other fundamental rights and whether States' educational duties would apply in this specific case.

Public opinion argument has many inherent flaws. For instance, opinion polls do not actually reveal what the public really wants. Even the term 'public opinion' has distinct interpretations. There are a number of myths around public opinion and capital punishment that need to be clarified. There are also hypotheses and empirical research that are worth considering. For example, the Marshall Hypothesis asserts that if the public is fully informed about capital punishment, opinion will turn against it. It was also argued that public support for the death penalty will drop naturally after the abolition of the death penalty. These hypotheses are supported by empirical studies. In many States, the government won the support of the public even after the 'unpopular' decision of abolishing the death penalty had been taken. One typical case is France. A comparative study of death penalty policies in Chinese societies (China, Macao, Hong Kong and Taiwan) further proves the marginal significance of public opinion in the decision of whether to retain the death penalty. In respect of international law, a remarkable number of legal documents urge States to mobilise public support against the death penalty, especially since the start of the new millennium. States' educational duties to promote and protect human rights can also serve to reinforce States' actions in leading public opinion against capital punishment.

This book has thoroughly examined the State duty to inform public opinion with regard to racial discrimination, discrimination against women and the death penalty. It has pointed out the application of the same principles in issues concerning the rights of children, persons with disabilities, migrant workers, indigenous and tribal peoples and issues with respect to political and religious rights. This study is, however, not able to provide detailed analysis. Further studies can complete it. For future research, it may be asked whether the State duty to inform and educate public opinion can be applied in other contemporary issues, such as the rights of gays, lesbians, bisexuals and transsexuals and the rights of asylum seekers.

At the operational level, how States should apply their educational duties is worth consistent discussion and practice. The current research only notes States' reported actions of initiating or supporting public awareness-raising activities and media campaigns, and mobilising formal and non-formal education, aimed at moulding public opinion in favour of human rights and freedoms. Some States have tasked governmental organs to lead the work of mobilising public opinion concerning basic human rights. They have even established permanent organisations such as national human rights institutions with the mandate to inform public opinion. States have reported their actions to human rights treaty bodies (e.g., the Human Rights Committee) as a means to comply with their human rights duties provided by international treaties. They have also submitted their actions to the newly established mechanism of the Universal Periodic Review when they are not bound by relevant treaties. This willingness may be explained through the State perception of the duty to inform public opinion on core human rights standards as being customary in nature.

In conclusion, when elements of public opinion are inconsistent with human rights standards, international law encourages States to take positive actions, with due regard to other rights such as the right to freedom of expression, opinion and association. This may involve legal and educational measures to lead public opinion. Degrees for such encouragement may vary, depending on several factors. The first factor can be the necessity to enlighten public opinion for the purpose of protecting and promoting human rights. For some rights, changing public opinion is much more urgent, for instance the right to equality. This is because public opinion is often held responsible for various violations of equality. But to progress some other rights such as the right to nationality or the right to own property, public opinion may not appear such an obstacle as it does for the right to equality. The right to nationality and the right to own property are both listed as fundamental human rights in the Universal Declaration of Human Rights.

The second factor can be the consensus achieved among States at the international level, which is recorded in international legal documents. For instance, to protect and promote women's rights, States agreed that they need to positively mould public opinion by ensuring certain elements been included in family education. That is article 5 of the Convention on the Elimination of All Forms of Discrimination against Women in which States shall make sure that 'family education includes a proper understanding of maternity as a social function and the recognition of the common responsibility of men and women in the upbringing and development of their children'. The significance of this development should be highlighted. Traditionally, family is considered as a private sphere. States' regulations are more on its structure (marriage, divorce and what the 'legal relationships' are, etc.) and less on its content (what should be included in family education).

This study has collected a variety of provisions that contain similar wording. One interesting example is the Convention on the Rights of the Child. In the Convention, the State duty to educate the public was not specified. Maybe States did not foresee that when they negotiated the terms of the Convention. But the supervisory body of the treaty, the Committee on the Rights of the Child, developed such a duty in the implementation of the treaty. In regard to the issue of corporal punishment against children, the Committee urges States to forbid the practice of physical punishment and to change the mindset of the public about the issue. This development similarly 'invades' the privacy of family life to some degree. It articulates States' positive duty when elements of public opinion are inconsistent with the protection of children's rights.

The third factor is States' compliance with provisions of international law and recommendations made by UN bodies. Practice shows that States have taken various measures to target public opinion in order to improve their human rights situations. These actions were recorded in the periodic reports that States submitted to UN bodies and in the meeting records of the Universal Periodic Review in which States interact with other UN member States. Practically speaking, these self-reported actions may be either exaggerated or ineffective. Whether they constitute States' compliance at the national level can be challenged. Nevertheless, they do serve well, particularly in the sense of revealing States' inconsistent positions on human rights.

In the written records, States agreed on different levels that, to protect and promote human rights, they need to take actions in order to influence public opinion. But they seem to forget that position when it comes to specific questions such as the death penalty and female genital mutilation. As to the question of whether to abolish the death penalty, some States even label public opinion as the reason to maintain the penalty, noting that this punishment has been increasingly recognised as inhuman and degrading. It would be hard to find States doing similar things when they were dealing with racial discrimination or discrimination against women. Concerning the practice of female genital mutilation, some States acted as if they could remain neutral, balanced between public opinion and international human rights standards. Under these circumstances, the collection of States' reports on how to inform public opinion in order to progress core human rights standards can be a strong signal, urging States to reconsider their inconsistent standpoints on human rights issues. It sends out a clear message to States that public opinion should not be used as an easy excuse to delay or hold back the realisation of human rights. States should not act as if they can do nothing about it.

As stated in the introduction of the book, this study has a potential impact on the rights of asylum seekers as well as the rights of gays, lesbians, bisexuals and transsexuals. On these issues, States need to reconsider whether they have affirmative education duties in order to improve their human rights records. On a practical level, how to effectively mould public opinion in favour of fundamental human rights principles is a complex mission facing all States. It requires the determination of a State to handle the dedicated issue of public opinion. In practice, it may be true that States that have taken or are willing to take actions to enlighten public opinion are not exactly those that we hope can do so to progress human rights. But this is not always true. More frequently, the situation is that States choose topics on which to take actions when they find that public opinion is inconsistent with core human rights standards. From this perspective, this work prescribes a new dimension from which States should reconsider their positions. To make it clear, this study urges States that:

1 they cannot blindly follow public opinion on every issue;
2 they need to stop using public opinion as a justification or excuse to avoid their human rights duties;
3 they should take substantial action on public opinion when it comes to core human rights standards.

Bibliography

Monographs

Acker J.R., Bohm R.M. and Lanier C.S. (eds), *America's Experiment with Capital Punishment* (2nd edn, Carolina Academic Press 2003).

Allport F.H., *Social Psychology* (Houghton Mifflin 1924).

Alvarez R.M. and Brehm J., *Hard Choices, Easy Answers: Values, Information, and American Public Opinion* (Princeton University Press 2002).

Anckar C., *Determinants of the Death Penalty: A Comparative Study of the World* (Routledge 2004).

An-Na'im A.A. (ed.), *Human Rights in Cross-Cultural Perspectives: A Quest for Consensus* (University of Pennsylvania Press 1992).

Badinter R., *L' Abolition* (Fayard 2000).

Badinter R., *Abolition: One Man's Battle against the Death Penalty* (Northeastern University Press 2008).

Bae S., *When the State No Longer Kills: International Human Rights Norms and Abolition of Capital Punishment* (State University of New York Press 2007).

Banton M., *International Action against Racial Discrimination* (Oxford University Press 1996).

Barak G. (ed.), *Media, Process, and the Social Construction of Crime: Studies in Newsmaking Criminology* (Garland 1995).

Bentham J., *The Book of Fallacies*, in vol. 2 of *The Works of Jeremy Bentham* (first published 1838, John Bowring ed., Russell & Russell 1962).

Bohm R.M., *Death Quest: An Introduction to the Theory and Practice of Capital Punishment in the United States* (4th edn, Anderson 2012).

Bryce J., *The American Commonwealth* (first published 1888, Cosimo 2007).

Byerly C.M. and Ross K., *Women and Media: A Critical Introduction* (Blackwell Publishing 2006).

Childs H., *Public Opinion* (Van Nostrand 1965).

Corrigan P.W. (ed.), *On the Stigma of Mental Illness: Practical Strategies for Research and Social Change* (American Psychological Association 2005).

Crespi I., *The Public Opinion Process: How the People Speak* (Psychology Press 1997).

Davies P. (ed.), *Human Rights* (Routledge 1988).

邓小平, *邓小平文选：第一卷* (人民出版社 1993).

Denbow J. and Thebe P.C., *Culture and Customs of Botswana* (Greenwood Press 2006).

Dewey J., *The Public and Its Problems* (Holt, Allen & Unwin 1927).

Dienel P.C., *Die Planungszelle: Ein Alternative zur Establishment-Demokratie. Der Bürger plant seine Umwelt* (Westdeutscher Verlag 1978).

Donnelly J., *Universal Human Rights in Theory and Practice* (Cornell University Press 2013).

Donsbach W. and Traugott M.W. (eds), *The SAGE Handbook of Public Opinion Research* (SAGE Publications 2008).

Evans R.J., *Rituals of Retribution: Capital Punishment in Germany 1600–1987* (Oxford University Press 1966).

Fishkin J.S., *The Voice of the People: Public Opinion and Democracy* (Yale University Press 1997).

Flanagan T.J. and Longmire D.R. (eds), *Americans View Crime and Justice: A National Public Opinion Survey* (SAGE Publications 1996).

Fleck D. (ed.), *Hand Book of Humanitarian Law in Armed Conflicts* (Oxford University Press 1995).

Forst M., 'The Abolition of the Death Penalty in France', Council of Europe (ed.), *The Death Penalty Abolition in Europe* (Council of Europe Publishing 1999).

Freeman M., *Human Rights: An Interdisciplinary Approach* (2nd edn, University of Michigan Press 2011).

Fujen University International Conference on Abolition of the Death Penalty, *Taiwan Opposes the Death Penalty: Proceedings of the Fujen University International Conference on Abolition of the Death Penalty 24–26 June 2001* (Fujen Catholic University 2001).

Hao Z., *Macau History and Society* (Hong Kong University Press 2011).

Hastrup K. (ed.), *Human Rights on Common Grounds: The Quest for Universality* (Kluwer 2001).

Hennis W., *Meinungsforschung und representative Demokratie [Opinion polls and representative democracy]* (Mohr 1957).

Herbst S., *Reading Public Opinion: How Political Actors View the Democratic Process* (University of Chicago Press 1998).

Herbst S., Glynn C.J. and O'Keefe G.J., *Public Opinion* (Westview Press 2004).

Herbst S., O'Keefe G.J., Shapiro R.Y., Lindeman M. and Glynn C.J., *Public Opinion* (2nd edn, Westview Press 2004).

Hodgkinson P. and Schabas W. (eds), *Capital Punishment: Strategies for Abolition* (Cambridge University Press 2004).

Hood R. and Deva S. (eds), *Confronting Capital Punishment in Asia: Human Rights, Politics and Public Opinion* (Oxford University Press 2013).

Hood R. and Hoyle C., *The Death Penalty: A Worldwide Perspective* (4th edn, Oxford University Press 2008).

Hood R. and Robert B., *The Death Penalty: Beyond Abolition* (Council of Europe Publishing 2004).

Hovland C.I., Lumsdaine A.A. and Sheffield F.D., *Experiments on Mass Communication: Studies in Social Psychology in World War II: Volume III* (Princeton University Press 1949).

Johnson D.T. and Zimring F.E., *The Next Frontier, National Development, Political Change, and the Death Penalty in Asia* (Oxford University Press 2009).

Kay A.F., Henderson H., Steeper F. and Lake C., *Interviews with the Public Guide U.S.: On the Road to Consensus* (Americans Talk Issues Foundation 1994).

Kay A.F., Henderson H., Steeper F., Lake C., Greenberg S.B. and Blunt C., *Steps for Democracy: The Many Versus the Few* (Americans Talk Issues Foundation 1994).

Kikuta K., *Q&A: Shikei Mondai no Kiso Chishiki* (Akashi Shoten 2004).

Lau S.K., *Society and Politics in Hong Kong* (Chinese University Press 1993).

Lazarsfeld P.F., Berelson B. and Gaudet H., *The People's Choice: How the Voter Makes Up His Mind in a Presidential Campaign* (Duell, Sloan & Pearce 1944).

Lee A.M. (ed.), *New Outline of the Principles of Sociology* (Barnes & Noble, 1946).

Lee A.M. (ed.), *Principles of Sociology* (Vol. 26, Barnes & Noble 1953).

Lee T., *Mobilizing Public Opinion: Black Insurgency and Racial Attitudes in the Civil Rights Era* (University of Chicago Press 2002).

Lérner N., *The UN Convention on the Elimination of All Forms of Racial Discrimination* (Sijthoff & Noordhoff 1980).

Lérner N., *Group Rights and Discrimination in International Law* (Vol. 77, Martinus Nijhoff Publishers 2003).

Lewis J., *Constructing Public Opinion: How Political Elites Do What They Like and Why We Seem to Go Along with It* (Columbia University Press 2001).

Lippmann W., *Public Opinion* (first published 1922, Createspace Independent Publishing Platform 2016).

Locke J., *Two Treatises of Government* (first published 1690, Peter Laslett ed., 3rd edn, Cambridge University Press 1964).

Lowell A.L., *Public Opinion and Popular Government* (first published 1913, Nabu Press 2012).

McDougall W., *The Group Mind* (Cambridge University Press 1920).

Mitterrand F., *Politique 2, 1977–1981* (Fayard 1981).

Morsink J., *The Universal Declaration of Human Rights: Origins, Drafting, and Intent* (University of Pennsylvania Press 1999).

Murano K., *Nihon no Shikei* (Soshoku Shobo 1992).

Neuman W.R., *The Paradox of Mass Politics: Knowledge and Opinion in the American Electorate* (Harvard University Press 1986).

Noelle-Neumann E., *The Spiral of Silence: Public Opinion, Our Social Skin* (University of Chicago Press 1984).

Nowak M., *UN Covenant on Civil and Political Rights: CCPR Commentary* (NP Engel 1993).

Oberwittler D. and Shenghui Qi, *Public Opinion on the Death Penalty in China* (Max-Plank Institute for Foreign and International Criminal Law 2009).

Petersen, R.D., *Understanding Ethnic Violence: Fear, Hatred, and Resentment in Twentieth-century Eastern Europe* (Cambridge University Press 2002).

Prémont D. (ed.), *Essais sur le concept de 'droit de vivre' en mémoire de Yougindra Khushalani* (Bruylant 1988).

Price V., *Public Opinion* (SAGE Publications 1992).

Ramcharan B.G. (ed.), *The Right to Life in International Law* (Martinus Nijhoff Publishers 1985).

Rehof L.A., *Guide to the Travaux Préparatoires of the United Nations Convention on the Elimination of All Forms of Discrimination against Women* (Martinus Nijhoff Publishers 1993).

Roberts J.V. and Hough M. (eds), *Changing Attitudes to Punishment: Public Opinion, Crime and Justice* (Willian Publishing 2002).

Rousseau J.-J., *The Social Contract* (first published 1762, Maurice Cranston tr, Penguin Books 1968).

Sarat A. and Kearns T.R. (eds), *Human Rights: Concepts, Contests, Contingencies* (University of Michigan Press 2001).

Saris W.E., Neijens P.C., and De Ridder J.A., *Kernenergie: Ja of Nee?* (SSO 1984).

Saris W.E. and Sniderman P.M. (eds) *Studies in Public Opinion: Attitudes, Nonattitudes, Measurement Error, and Change* (Princeton University Press 2004).

Schabas W., *The Abolition of the Death Penalty in International Law* (3rd edn, Cambridge University Press 2002).

Schumpeter J., *History of Economic Analysis* (Oxford University Press 1996).

Sills D.L. (ed), *International Encyclopedia of the Social Sciences* (Vol. 13, Free Press and Macmillan 1968).

司马迁, *史记* (中华书局 2012).

Sniderman P.M. and Carmines E.G., *Reaching Beyond Race* (Harvard University Press 1997).

Stahn C. and Sluiter G. (eds), *The Emerging Practice of the International Criminal Court* (Brill 2009).

Stimson J.A., *Public Opinion in America: Moods, Cycles, and Swings* (Westview Press 1999).

Tarde G., *The Laws of Imitation* (first published 1890, Henry Holt & Company 1903).

Tonry M., *Thinking about Crime: Sense and Sensibility in American Penal Culture* (Oxford University Press 2004).

Vlek C. and Cvetkovich G. (eds), *Social Decision Methodology for Technological Projects* (Kluwer Academic Publishers 1989).

Weitzer R. and Tuch S.A., *Race and Policing in America: Conflict and Reform* (Cambridge University Press 2006).

Wilson R., *Human Rights, Culture and Context: Anthropological Perspectives* (Pluto Press 1997).

Wood J.L. and Gannon T.A. (eds), *Public Opinion and Criminal Justice* (Willian Publishing 2009).

武汉大学刑事法研究中心，德国马普外国刑法与国际刑法研究所，*中国死刑态度调研报告* (元照出版社 2010).

吴志良 (编), *澳门华人政治文化* (澳门基金会出版社 1993).

Zaller J. (ed.), *The Nature and Origins of Mass Opinion* (Cambridge University Press 1992).

张晋藩 (编), *中国法制通史：战国秦汉* (法律出版社 1999).

Zirmring F., *The Contradictions of American Capital Punishment* (Oxford University Press 2003).

左丘明, 左传 (中华书局 2012).

Articles

Addo M.K., 'Practice of United Nations Human Rights Treaty Bodies in the Reconciliation of Cultural Diversity with Universal Respect for Human Rights' (2010) 32 *Human Rights Quarterly* 601.

Alwin D.F. and Scott J., 'Attitude Change: Its Measurement and Interpretation Using Longitudinal Surveys' (1996) *Understanding Change in Social Attitudes* 75.

Angermeyer M.C. and Matschinger H., 'The Stereotype of Schizophrenia and its Impact on Discrimination against People with Schizophrenia: Results from a Representative Survey in Germany' (2004) 30 (4) *Schizophrenia Bulletin* 1049.

Bae S., 'South Korea's De Facto Abolition of the Death Penalty' (2009) 82 (3) *Pacific Affairs* 407.

Baker D.N., Lambert E.G. and Jenkins M., 'Racial Differences in Death Penalty Support and Opposition: A Preliminary Study of White and Black College Students' (2005) 35 (4) *Journal of Black Studies* 201.

Bardis P.D., 'Abortion and Public Opinion: A Research Note' (1972) 34 (1) *Journal of Marriage and Family* 111.

Beck S.H., Mijeski K.J. and Stark M.M., '¿Qué Es Racismo?: Awareness of Racism and Discrimination in Ecuador' (2011) 46 (1) *Latin American Research Review* 102.

Bishop G.F., Oldendick R.W., Tuchfarber A.J. and Bennett S.E., 'Pseudo-Opinions on Public Affairs' (1980) 44 (2) *Public Opinion Quarterly* 198.

Blake J., 'Abortion and Public Opinion: The 1960–1970 Decade' (1971) 171 (3971) *Science* 540.

Blumer H., 'Public Opinion and Public Opinion Polling' (1948) 13 *American Sociological Review* 542.

Bohm R.M., 'The Effects of Classroom Instruction and Discussion on Death Penalty Opinions: A Teaching Note' (1989) 17 *Journal of Criminal Justice* 123.

Bohm R.M., 'Death Penalty Opinions: Effects of a Classroom Experience and Public Commitment' (1990) 60 *Sociological Inquiry* 285.

Bohm R.M., Clark L.J. and Aveni A.F., 'The Influence of Knowledge on Death Penalty Opinions: An Experimental Text' (1990) 7 *Justice Quarterly* 175.

Bohm R.M., Clark L.J. and Aveni A.F., 'Knowledge and Death Penalty Opinion: A Test of the Marshall Hypotheses' (1991) 28 *Journal of Research in Crime and Delinquency* 360.

Bohm R.M. and Vogel R.E., 'A Comparison of Factors Associated with Uninformed and Informed Death Penalty Opinions' (1994) 22 (2) *Journal of Criminal Justice* 125.

Bohm R.M., Vogel R.E. and Maisto A.A., 'Knowledge and Death Penalty Opinions: A Panel Study' (1993) 21 *Journal of Criminal Justice* 29.

Bowers W., 'Capital Punishment and Contemporary Values: People's Misgivings and the Court's Misperceptions' (1993) 27 (1) *Law & Society Review* 157.

Brewer P.R., 'The Shifting Foundations of Public Opinion about Gay Rights' (2003) 65 (4) *Journal of Politics* 1208.

Brewer P.R., 'Values, Political Knowledge, and Public Opinion about Gay Rights: A Framing-Based Account' (2003) 67 (2) *Public Opinion Quarterly* 173.

Burns P. and Gimpel J.G., 'Economic Insecurity, Prejudicial Stereotypes, and Public Opinion on Immigration Policy' (2013) 115 (2) *Political Science Quarterly* 201.

Cho B.-S., 'South Korea's Changing Capital Punishment Policy: The Road from De Facto to Formal Abolition' (2008) 10 (2) *Punishment & Society* 171.

Clark B., 'The Vienna Convention Reservations Regime and the Convention on Discrimination against Women' (1991) 85 (2) *American Journal of International Law* 281.

Clarke A.W., Lambert E. and Whitt L.A., 'Executing the Innocent: The Next Step in the Marshall Hypotheses' (2001) 26 (3) *Review of Law and Social Change* 309.

Coccia M., 'Reservations to Multilateral Treaties on Human Rights' (1985) 15 *California Western International Law Journal* 1.

Cochran J.K. and Chamlin M.B., 'Can Information Change Public Opinion? Another Test of the Marshall Hypotheses' (2005) 33 *Journal of Criminal Justice* 573.

Cohen J., Marcoux, I., Bilsen, J., Deboosere, P., van der Wal, G. and Deliens, L., 'Trends in Acceptance of Euthanasia among the General Public in 12 European Countries (1981–1999)' (2006) 16 (6) *European Journal of Public Health* 663.

Cook R.J., 'Reservations to the Convention on the Elimination of All Forms of Discrimination against Women' (1990) 30 *Virginia Journal of International Law* 643.

Coulehan J., 'The Man with Stars Inside' (1997) 126 (10) *Annals of Internal Medicine* 799.

Crawford E., 'The Modern Relevance of the Martens Clause' (2006) 6 *ISIL Yearbook of International Humanitarian and Refugee Law* 1.

Crenshaw K., 'Demarginalizing the Intersection of Race and Sex: A Black Feminist Critique of Antidiscrimination Doctrine, Feminist Theory and Antiracist Politics' (1989) 1 *University of Chicago Legal Forum* 139.

Crisp A.H., 'Stigmatization of and Discrimination against People with Eating Disorders including a Report of Two Nationwide Surveys' (2005) 13 (3) *European Eating Disorders Review* 147.

Crisp A.H., Gelder M.G., Rix S., Meltzer H.I. and Rowlands O.J., 'Stigmatisation of People with Mental Illnesses' (2000) 177 *British Journal of Psychiatry* 4.

Cullen F.T., Fisher B.S. and Applegate B.K., 'Public Opinion about Punishment and Corrections' (2000) 27 *Crime and Justice* 1.

Davis K., 'Intersectionality as Buzzword: A Sociology of Science Perspective on What Makes a Feminist Theory Successful' (2008) 9 *Feminist Theory* 67.

Domke D., McCoy K. and Torres M., 'News Media, Racial Perceptions, and Political Cognition' (1999) 26 (5) *Communication Research* 570.

Donders Y., 'Do Cultural Diversity and Human Rights Make a Good Match?' (2010) 6 (199) *International Social Science Journal* 15.

Donnelly J., 'Cultural Relativism and Universal Human Rights' (1984) 6 *Human Rights Quarterly* 400.

Duncan O.D. and Parmelee L.F., 'Trends in Public Approval of Euthanasia and Suicide in the US, 1947–2003' (2006) 32 (5) *Journal of Medical Ethics* 266.

Ebaugh H.R.F. and Haney C.A., 'Shifts in Abortion Attitudes: 1972–1978' (1980) 42 (3) *Journal of Marriage & Family* 491.

Ellsworth P. and Gross S., 'Hardening of the Attitudes: Americans' Views on the Death Penalty' (1994) 50 *Journal of Social Issues* 19.

Ellsworth P. and Ross L., 'Public Opinion and Capital Punishment: A Close Examination of the Views of Abolitionists and Retentionists' (1983) 29 (1) *Crime & Delinquency* 116.

Erskine H.G., 'The Polls: The Informed Public' (1962) 26 (4) *Public Opinion Quarterly* 669.

Erskine H.G., 'The Polls: Exposure to International Information' (1963) 27 (4) *Public Opinion Quarterly* 658.

Farrior S., 'The Neglected Pillar: The "Teaching Tolerance" Provision of the International Convention on the Elimination of All Forms of Racial Discrimination' (1998–1999) 5 *ILSA Journal of International & Comparative Law* 291.

Fattah E.A., 'Canada's Successful Experience with the Abolition of the Death Penalty' (1987) 25 *Canadian Journal of Criminology* 421.

Fineman M.A., 'Feminist Legal Theory' (2005) 13 (1) *Journal of Gender, Social Policy & the Law* 13.

Goreczny A.J., Bender E.E., Caruso G. and Feinstein C.S., 'Attitudes toward Individuals with Disabilities: Results of a Recent Survey and Implications of Those Results' (2011) 32 (5) *Research in Developmental Disabilities* 1596.

Gostin L., 'The HIV-Infected Health Care Professional: Public Policy, Discrimination, and Patient Safety' (2007) 18 (4) *Journal of Law, Medicine & Ethics* 303.

Graber D.A., 'The Impact of Media Research on Public Opinion Studies', (1982) 3 *Mass Communication Review Yearbook* 555.

Green D.A., 'Public Opinion Versus Public Judgment: Correcting the "Comedy of Errors"' (2006) 46 *British Journal of Criminology* 131.

Gross S.R., 'Update: American Public Opinion on the Death Penalty—It's Getting Personal' (1998) 83 *Cornell Law Review* 1448.

Gupta A. and Ferguson J., 'Beyond "Culture": Space, Identity, and the Politics of Difference' (1992) 7 (1) *Cultural Anthropology* 6.

Herek G.M., 'AIDS and Stigma' (1999) 42 (7) *American Behavioral Scientist* 1106.

Herek G.M., 'Gender Gaps in Public Opinion about Lesbians and Gay Men' (2002) 66 (1) *Public Opinion Quarterly* 40.

Herek G.M., Capitanio J.P. and Widaman K.F., 'Stigma, Social Risk, and Health Policy: Public Attitudes toward HIV Surveillance Policies and the Social Construction of Illness' (2003) 22 (5) *Health Psychology* 533.

Herek G.M. and Glunt E.K., 'An Epidemic of Stigma: Public Reactions to AIDS' (1988) 43 (11) *American Psychologist* 886.

Ho R., 'Assessing Attitudes toward Euthanasia: An Analysis of the Subcategorical Approach to Right to Die Issues' (1998) 25 (4) *Personality and Individual Differences* 719.

Hollekim R., Slaatten H. and Anderssen N., 'A Nationwide Study of Norwegian Beliefs About Same-sex Marriage and Lesbian and Gay Parenthood' (2012) 9 (1) *Sexuality Research and Social Policy* 15.

Hood R., 'Capital Punishment: A Global Perspective' (2001) 3 *Punishment & Society* 331.

Hurwitz J. and Peffley M., 'Public Perceptions of Race and Crime: The Role of Racial Stereotypes' (1997) 41 (2) *American Journal of Political Science* 375.

Jenks C.W., 'The Application of International Labour Conventions by Means of Collective Agreements' (1958) 19 *Zeitschrift für ausländisches öffentliches Recht und Völkerrecht* 197.

Jessee P.O., Nagy M.C. and Gresham C., 'Public Opinion concerning Group Involvement for Children with Aids' (2001) 166 (1) *Early Child Development and Care* 29.

Jiang S.H. and Lambert E.G., 'Capital Punishment Views in China and the United States' (2007) 51 (1) *International Journal of Offender Therapy and Comparative Criminology* 84.

Johnson D.H.N., 'Effect of Resolutions of the General Assembly of the United Nations' (1955) 32 *British Yearbook of International Law* 97.

Johnson D.T., 'The Death Penalty in Asia: Introduction to a Special Issue of Punishment & Society' (2008) 10 (2) *Punishment & Society* 99.

Korengold M.A.G., 'Lessons in Confronting Racist Speech: Good Intentions, Bad Results, and Article 4 (a) of the Convention on the Elimination of All Forms of Racial Discrimination' (1993) 77 *Minnesota Law Review* 719.

Krysan M., 'Prejudice, Politics, and Public Opinion: Understanding the Sources of Racial Policy Attitudes' (2000) 26 *Annual Review of Sociology* 135.

Lambert E. and Clarke A., 'The Impact of Information on an Individual's Support of the Death Penalty: A Partial Test of the Marshall Hypothesis among College Students' (2001) 12 *Criminal Justice Policy Review* 215.

Lax J.R. and Phillips J.H., 'Gay Right in the States: Public Opinion and Policy Responsiveness' (2009) 103 (3) *American Political Science Review* 367.

Lord C.G., Ross L. and Lepper M.R., 'Biased Assimilation and Attitude Polarization: The Effects of Prior Theories on Subsequently Considered Evidence' (1979) 37 *Journal of Personality and Social Psychology* 2098.

Lynch M., 'Capital Punishment as Moral Imperative: Pro-death-penalty Discourse on the Internet' (2002) 4 (2) *Punishment & Society* 213.

McMurtrie S.M. García S.G., Wilson K.S., Diaz-Olavarrieta C., Fawcett G.M., 'Public Opinion about Abortion-Related Stigma among Mexican Catholics and Implications for Unsafe Abortion' (2012) 118 *International Journal of Gynecology & Obstetrics* 160.

Meron T., 'The Meaning and Reach of the International Convention on the Elimination of All Forms of Racial Discrimination' (1985) 79 *American Journal of International Law* 283.

Meron T., 'The Martens Clause, Principles of Humanity, and Dictates of Public Conscience' (2000) 94 (1) *American Journal of International Law* 78.

Messner S.F., Eric P.B. and Richard R., 'Distrust of Government, the Vigilante Tradition, and Support for Capital Punishment' (2006) 40 (3) *Law & Society Review* 559.

Minar D.W., 'Public Opinion in the Perspective of Political Theory' (1960) 13 (1) *Western Political Quarterly* 31.

Mohrenschlager M., 'The Abolition of Capital Punishment in the Federal Republic of Germany: The German Experience' (1987) 58 *Revue Internationale de Droit Pénal* 509.

Monteith M.J., 'Contents and Correlates of Whites' and Blacks' Racial Attitudes' (2000) 36 (2) *Journal of Experimental Social Psychology* 125.

Mullender R., 'Human Rights: Universalism and Cultural Relativism' (2003) 6 (3) *Critical Review of International Social and Political Philosophy* 5.

Noelle-Neumann E., 'Public Opinion and the Classical Tradition: A Re-evaluation' (1979) 43 (2) *Public Opinion Quarterly* 143.

Ogland C.P. and Verona A.P., 'Religion and Attitudes toward Abortion and Abortion Policy in Brazil' (2011) 50 (4) *Journal for the Scientific Study of Religion* 812.

Parker R. and Aggleton P., 'HIV and AIDS-related Stigma and Discrimination: A Conceptual Framework and Implications for Action' (2003) 57 (1) *Social Science & Medicine* 13.

Patenaude A.L., 'May God Have Mercy on Your Soul! Exploring and Teaching a Course on the Death Penalty' (2001) 12 *Journal of Criminal Justice Education* 405.

Picca G., 'La peine de mort: Un problème politique et social' (1987) 68 *Revue Internationale de Droit Pénal* 435.

Preis A.-B.S., 'Human Rights as Cultural Practice: An Anthropological Critique' (1996) 18 *Human Rights Quarterly* 286.

Price V. and Neijens P., 'Deliberative Polls: Toward Improved Measures of "Informed" Public Opinion?' (1998) 10 (2) *International Journal of Public Opinion Research* 145.

Puhl R.M. and Heuer C.A., 'Public Opinion about Laws to Prohibit Weight Discrimination in the United States', (2011) 19 (1) *Obesity* 77.

Quillian L., 'New Approaches to Understanding Racial Prejudice and Discrimination' (2006) 32 *Annual Review of Sociology* 299.

Roberts J.V., 'Public Opinion, Crime, and Criminal Justice' (1992) 16 *Crime and Justice* 99.

Rodriguez J.V., Wilson K.S., Díaz C., Garcia S.G. and Sanchez Fuentes ML, 'Public Opinion on Abortion in Eight Mexican States amid Opposition to Legalization' (2011) 42 (3) *Studies in Family Planning* 191.

Sandys M., 'Attitudinal Change among Students in a Capital Punishment Class: It May Be Possible' (1995) 20 *American Journal of Criminal Justice* 37.

Sarat A. and Vidmar N., 'Public Opinion, the Death Penalty, and the Eighth Amendment: Testing the Marshall Hypothesis' (1976) 17 *Wisconsin Law Review* 171.

Scales A., 'Toward a Feminist Jurisprudence' (1978) 56 (2) *Indiana Law Journal* 375.

Schwelb E., 'The International Convention on the Elimination of All Forms of Racial Discrimination' (1966) 15 *International and Comparative Law Quarterly* 996.

Sigelman L., Welch S., Bledsoe T. and Combs M., 'Police Brutality and Public Perceptions of Racial Discrimination: A Tale of Two Beatings' (1997) 50 (4) *Political Research Quarterly* 777.

Sloan F.B., 'The Binding Force of a "Recommendation" of the General Assembly of the United Nations' (1948) 25 (1) *British Yearbook of International Law* 1.

Speier H., 'Historical Development of Public Opinion' (1950) 55 (4) *American Journal of Sociology* 376.

Stack S., 'Public Opinion on the Death Penalty: Analysis of Individual-level Data from 17 Nations' (2004) 14 *International Criminal Justice Review* 69.

Steiker C., 'Capital Punishment and American Exceptionalism' (2001) 97 *Oregon Law Review* 81.

Terkildsen N. and Schnell F., 'How Media Frames Move Public Opinion: An Analysis of the Women's Movement' (1997) 50 (4) *Political Research Quarterly* 879.

Tesón F.R., 'International Human Rights and Cultural Relativism' (1985) 25 *Virginia Journal of International Law* 869.

Ticehurst R., 'The Martens Clause and the Laws of Armed Conflict' (1997) 37 (317) *International Review – Red Cross* 125.

Tynes B., Giang M., Williams D. and Thompson G., 'Online Racial Discrimination and Psychological Adjustment among Adolescents' (2008) 43 *Journal of Adolescent Health* 565.

Tynes B. and Markoe S., 'The Role of Color-Blind Racial Attitude in Reactions to Racial Discrimination on Social Network Sites' (2010) 3 (1) *Journal of Diversity in Higher Education* 1.

Unnever J.D. and Cullen F.T., 'White Perceptions of Whether African Americans and Hispanics Are Prone to Violence and Support for the Death Penalty' (2012) 49 (4) *Journal of Research in Crime and Delinquency* 519.

Unnever J.D. and Francis T.C., 'Executing the Innocent and Support for Capital Punishment: Implications for Public Policy' (2005) 4 (1) *Criminology & Public Policy* 3.

Van Boekel L.C., Brouwers E.P.M., Van Weeghel J. and Garretsen H.F.L., 'Public Opinion on Imposing Restrictions to People with an Alcohol or Drug Addiction: A Cross-Sectional Survey' (2013) 48 (12) *Social Psychiatry and Psychiatric Epidemiology* 2007.

Van Holsteyn J. and Trappenburg M., 'Citizens' Opinions on New Forms of Euthanasia. A Report from the Netherlands' (1998) 35 (1) *Patient Education and Counseling* 63.

Vidmar N. and Dittenhoffer T., 'Informed Public Opinion and Death Penalty Attitudes' (1981) 23 *Canadian Journal of Criminology* 43.

Vidmar N. and Ellsworth P., 'Public Opinion and the Death Penalty' (1974) 26 (6) *Stanford Law Review* 1245.

Williams N., Dunford C., Knowles A. and Warner J., 'Public Attitudes to Life-Sustaining Treatments and Euthanasia in Dementia' (2007) 22 (12) *International Journal of Geriatric Psychiatry* 1229.

Wright H.O., Bohm R.M. and Jamieson K.M., 'A Comparison of Uninformed and Informed Death Penalty Opinions: A Replication and Expansion' (1995) 20 *American Journal of Criminal Justice* 57.

Yang A.S., 'Trends: Attitudes toward Homosexuality' (1997) 61 (3) *Public Opinion Quarterly* 477.

Index

For Product Safety Concerns and Information please contact our
EU representative GPSR@taylorandfrancis.com Taylor & Francis
Verlag GmbH, Kaufingerstraße 24, 80331 München, Germany